# THE MILITARY LENS

A volume in the series

**CORNELL STUDIES IN SECURITY AFFAIRS**
edited by Robert J. Art, Robert Jervis, and Stephen M. Walt

*A list of titles in this series is available at www.cornellpress.cornell.edu.*

# THE MILITARY LENS

## DOCTRINAL DIFFERENCE
## AND DETERRENCE FAILURE IN
## SINO-AMERICAN RELATIONS

### CHRISTOPHER P. TWOMEY

Cornell University Press
Ithaca and London

Cornell University Press gratefully acknowledges a subvention from Pacific Dynamics, which aided in the publication of this book.

First published 2010 by Cornell University Press

Printed in the United States of America

Library of Congress Cataloging-in-Publication Data

Twomey, Christopher P.
    The military lens : doctrinal difference and deterrence failure in Sino-American relations / Christopher P. Twomey.
        p. cm. — (Cornell studies in security affairs)
    Includes bibliographical references and index.
    ISBN 978-0-8014-4914-7 (cloth : alk. paper)
    1. Military doctrine—China.   2. Military doctrine—United States.   3. Deterrence (Strategy)—China.   4. Deterrence (Strategy)—United States.   5. China—Foreign relations— United States.   6. United States—Foreign relations—China. I. Title.   II. Series.
    UA835.T89   2010
    355'.03351—dc22        2010017137

Cornell University Press strives to use environmentally responsible suppliers and materials to the fullest extent possible in the publishing of its books. Such materials include vegetable-based, low-VOC inks and acid-free papers that are recycled, totally chlorine-free, or partly composed of nonwood fibers. For further information, visit our website at www.cornellpress.cornell.edu.

Cloth printing        10  9  8  7  6  5  4  3  2  1

To my father, who taught me how to seek out knowledge,
and my mother, who taught me the questions to ask

# CONTENTS

# PREFACE

THIS BOOK GROWS out of a broader desire to grapple with the tension between the dangers of deterrence failure and spirals in international affairs. This dichotomy of sources of inadvertent escalation cries out for policy-relevant scholarship. Understanding when each of these two—often opposed—dangers is more prevalent would be highly valuable to national leaders. Conflict has many sources, but even these most preventable causes are not well understood.

The argument laid out in this book focuses on *one* mechanism by which *one* of these dangers is worsened: doctrinal differences can complicate signaling and assessments, leading to deterrence failure. Rather than offering a novel explanation of all international relations, it is an exercise in midlevel theory building. It addresses one area amenable to detailed empirical research and manipulable by policymakers. It does not claim to explain all cases or guide all states at all times. Instead, it offers a discrete explanation for a given set of (important) problems.

The book argues that doctrinal differences can lead to misperceptions between countries engaged in strategic coercion. States look at the world through the lens of their own military doctrine. At times, the lens blurs the view, complicating statecraft, signaling, interpreting the adversary's signals, and assessing the balance of power. The book examines five cases: three from Sino-American competition in the early Cold War and two shorter cases from the Middle East. It concludes with an application to contemporary Sino-American military competition in the Taiwan Strait. The main cases draw upon primary research in both English and Chinese. Such in-depth empirical work is necessary for developing an accurate understanding of the sources of misperception, which is clearly important for the conduct of foreign relations. Doctrinal differences are easily observed, and the problems they create across potentially competitive dyads are amenable to mitigation.

Beyond the formative debts noted in the dedication, an unusually large number of friends and colleagues have been invaluable as I have worked on this project. Stephen Van Evera, Barry Posen, Thomas Christensen, and Carl Kaysen patiently read numerous early versions of the manuscript and provided an enormous quantity of careful and constructive criticism that vastly improved the project. Their help in developing strategies to hone a bundle of diverse ideas into a workable manuscript was irreplaceable. David Burbach, Michael Glosny, and most especially Eric Heginbotham were unrelenting in their constructive criticism and extremely generous with both their ideas and their time over a period of years. The help of those seven individuals was integral to my ability to complete the book, and I am deeply grateful to one and all.

Many others contributed substantially in numerous ways, and I deeply appreciate their insights: Stephen Brooks, Jason Castillo, Anne Clunan, Timothy Crawford, David Edelstein, Taylor Fravel, Andrea Gabbitas, Gao Fei, John Garofano, Eugene Gholz, George Gilboy, P. R. Goldstone, He Yinan, Kerry Kartchner, Jane Kellett Cramer, Robert Jervis, Jeff Knopf, Alan Kuperman, Peter Lavoy, Jennifer Lind, Sean Lynn-Jones, Rose McDermott, John Mearsheimer, Evan Medeiros, Stephen Miller, John Mueller, Ken Oye, Daryl Press, Jeremy Pressman, Robert Ross, Richard Samuels, Phil Saunders, Andrew Scobell, Jeremy Shapiro, Tao Wenzhao, Tara Twomey, Wang Yuankang, and J. B. Zimmerman. Audiences at the International Security Program weekly seminars at the Belfer Center for Science and International Security, Kennedy School of Government, Harvard, at the Boston College Department of Political Science, and at the annual meetings of the International Studies Association and the American Political Science Association (both in 2003) all provided great questions and feedback. The unique Lone Star National Security Forum provided me with high-quality feedback on the bulk of the manuscript from faculty of the University of Texas–Austin, Texas A&M, and Southern Methodist University. Research staffs at the National Archive's College Park facility, the Military History Institute at Carlisle Barracks, and the Chinese Academy of Social Sciences all guided me toward very useful materials. Teresa Lawson's editorial assistance greatly improved both the substance and style of the manuscript. The reviewers for Cornell University Press made many helpful suggestions for revision and have substantially improved the substance of the book. It will come as no surprise to anyone who has worked with him to know that Roger Haydon guided me through the publication process with skill and professionalism, continually improving the book. All translations from the Chinese are my own. All romanizations are done in the Pinyin system except those in common use in Taiwan such as Kuomintang (KMT) and Taipei. Chinese names are rendered family name first.

I would like to recognize Harvard's Belfer Center for Science and International Affairs, the National Security Education Program, and especially two institutions at MIT—the Security Studies Program and the Center for International Studies—for their financial support. The Institute of American Studies at the Chinese Academy of Social Science facilitated my research while in China. The Naval Postgraduate School has also provided me with a supportive environment as I completed the manuscript as well as providing an engagement with policy-oriented consumers of academic work to emphasize the potential importance of the endeavor. The traditional absolution of the all of the above from any responsibility for the remaining limitations of the book applies to my employer as well. This book presents the arguments of the author alone and does not represent the views of any office of the U.S. government.

Finally, I thank my family members for their patience and support.

# PART I

# THE DANGERS OF DOCTRINAL DIFFERENCE

# I

# THE MILITARY LANGUAGE OF DIPLOMACY

THE DEATHS OF MILLIONS in the Korean War might have been avoided if China and the United States had read each other's military signals correctly. Similarly, the Arab-Israeli War of 1973 might have been averted if the antagonists had evaluated threats and the overall balance more accurately; if so, the Middle East might look very different now. Overoptimism in France, Germany, and the United States during World War II all stemmed from the same misunderstanding of the military balance. Today, across the Taiwan Strait the same dangers are growing. Practitioners and scholars alike emphasize that misperception pervasively affects international relations. The sources of perception have been studied extensively, yet the potential of military doctrine to distort perception has not been systematically examined. As this book will show, doctrinal differences can lead to severe misperceptions and tragic miscommunications, both of which can impose a huge human cost.

Doctrinal differences complicate the ability of leaders to accurately perceive the actions of other nations and the international system. Scholars have long known of the dangers stemming from "the inability of foreign-policy makers to view events from the perspective of their adversaries."[1] When nations have different doctrines and hold different beliefs about the nature

---

[1] Alexander L. George, *Presidential Decisionmaking in Foreign Policy: The Effective Use of Information and Advice* (Boulder, Colo.: Westview Press, 1980), 66–67. See also Keith B. Payne, *The Fallacies of Cold War Deterrence and a New Direction* (Lexington: University Press of Kentucky, 2001).

of effective military strategies and capabilities—in other words, different "theories of victory"—diplomacy and signaling will be more difficult. For international communication to be effective, both sides must understand the language of diplomacy being used. When that language depends on military threats, different theories of victory can lead to problems in "translation" or understanding and thus to unnecessary conflict. In order to send an effective signal to an adversary, nations must understand how that adversary will interpret the signal. Furthermore, doctrinal differences complicate assessments of the balance of power, leading policymakers to false optimism.[2] This also further complicates crisis diplomacy. In short, this book examines the causal claim that *doctrinal differences worsen misperceptions, which can lead to escalation.* Such troubles might be avoided if signals are better tailored to the adversary's perceptual framework with regard to military doctrine and effectiveness, that is, to its theory of victory. This is rarely done.

This book draws on theoretic work on the sources of military doctrine, the causes and dangers of misperception, false optimism, conventional deterrence, and the measurement of power, as well as approaches used in the study of crisis diplomacy. It contributes to understanding how information asymmetries can result in bargaining failure that leads to war, by examining a source of asymmetry that has not been studied, and whose correction requires specifically targeted policies.

The arguments of "doctrinal-difference theory" have important implications for international relations theorists in the areas of rationalist views of war, the roles of military doctrine in shaping international outcomes, the importance of substate variables in shaping international systemic outcomes, the understanding of the sources of deterrence failure, and the importance of crisis diplomacy and statecraft.

This book examines the implications of doctrinal differences with a particular focus on interactions between the United States and China during the 1950s. Beijing repeatedly disregarded both implicit and explicit American threats of nuclear attack and strategic air attacks, because it regarded nuclear weapons as mere "paper tigers." From the other side, the United States

---

[2] The term "false optimism" refers to unwarranted confidence about a situation or the near future. Several prominent scholars emphasize it is an important phenomenon in international politics. Geoffrey Blainey, *The Causes of War*, 3rd ed. (Basingstoke, U.K.: Macmillan, 1988), chapter 3, "Dreams and Delusions of a Coming War"; Stephen Van Evera, *Causes of War: Power and the Roots of Conflict* (Ithaca: Cornell University Press, 1999), chapter 2, "False Optimism: Illusions of the Coming War"; John G. Stoessinger, *Why Nations Go to War*, 8th ed. (New York: Wadsworth, 2001).

gave little credence to China's threats of intervention based on its strategy of "People's War." Each side, in other words, viewed the other's key military doctrine with disdain. This led each to miscalculate the overall balance of power between their two countries. It complicated the process of signaling, and so they had great difficulty influencing each other. As chapters 3–5 show, this contributed significantly to the outbreak of the Korean War and to its escalation. By contrast, in a similar political framework but in a different geographic context—naval confrontation in the Taiwan Strait in the same era—the same two adversaries' pertinent theories of victory were more alike. In that case, examined in chapter 6, there were neither misperceptions nor miscommunications, and there was no war. Examination of events in the Middle East in the 1960s and in 1973, taken up in chapter 7, reveals a similar pair of stories.

Doctrinal differences highlight a very specific subset of dangers that can be avoided, potentially averting war if policymakers recognize that an adversary's assessment of the balance will be different than their own and adjust policy accordingly. Most important, they must recognize that successful coercive diplomacy is an extremely demanding challenge. This problem is acute again in Sino-American relations today, given the great disparity in military doctrines between the two (both of which have evolved substantially in the past half century). As chapter 8 explains, the dangers posed by doctrinal differences loom large in contemporary Taiwan Strait contingencies. Attention to the issues raised in this book could reduce those risks.

This chapter next turns to a brief explanation of the theory. It continues with a brief discussion of some of the literature that this book builds upon and to which it contributes, dealing with deterrence and compellence, credibility, the measurement of power, strategic culture, and the dangers of false optimism. It concludes by explaining how the cases were selected and outlining the organization of the book.

## RATIONAL STATES RESORTING TO WAR: THE ROLE OF MISPERCEPTION

Assuming that states want to minimize costs while maximizing benefits, why would a rational state ever resort to war? Why would states, even entrenched adversaries, ever be unable to strike an agreement in accordance with their relative power in order to avoid a costly military test? The fact that wars take place despite this "inefficiency" suggests that—except for a few cases of

irrationally driven aggrandizement—many result from bargaining failures.[3]
How do we explain such bargaining failures? One useful approach focuses
on information asymmetries, that is, on the absence of a shared understanding of each side's capabilities and interests.[4]

Nations often use or threaten to use military force—explicitly or implicitly—to send signals about those capabilities and interests; however, evaluating
an adversary's military signals can be difficult.[5] Attempts at strategic coercion,
responses to such attempts by others, and decisions to cross the threshold to
the use of force or to escalate a limited conflict all depend on a state's expectation of gaining a relatively positive return from such steps. That assessment
depends on an evaluation of the military balance, whether through a formal
military net assessment, a campaign analysis process, or through less formal
methods. However, different actors may analyze the same military situation
and come to different conclusions. The resulting misperception, miscalculation, and miscommunication may raise the risk of the outbreak of conflict.[6]

Doctrinal-difference theory also highlights the difficulty of accurately
measuring power. Assessing an adversary's relative power is a critical task
for nations. At a broad level, it helps to determine the level of threat faced
by one's nation, and thus the costs and benefits of various courses of action
in the foreign sphere. Understanding the cost-benefit calculations an adversary is making is important since such calculations play a role in shaping
the adversary's behavior. In some crises, understanding an adversary's intent
requires interpretation of its signals. Since these signals often rely on threats
to use force, the actual deployment of military assets, or the limited use of
force, understanding these signals requires understanding the degree of
power that the adversary believes them to represent. When miscommunication occurs, attempts at strategic coercion—whether they are compellent or
deterrent in nature—are more likely to fail. In all these ways, then, different
theories of victory impede the conduct of diplomacy between potential adversaries, shaping the signaling and blurring the interpretation of those signals and of the overall assessment of the balance of power, and exacerbating

[3] James D. Fearon, "Rationalist Explanations for War," *International Organization* 49, no. 3
(1995); David A. Lake and Robert Powell, *Strategic Choice and International Relations* (Princeton:
Princeton University Press, 1999).
[4] See, for instance, Fearon, "Rationalist Explanations," 381.
[5] Robert Jervis, *The Logic of Images in International Relations* (Princeton: Princeton University
Press, 1970).
[6] These questions lie at the center of important debates in political science. See, for example,
Fearon, "Rationalist Explanations"; Jonathan D. Kirshner, "Rationalist Explanations for War?"
*Security Studies* 10, no. 1 (2000).

the problem of false optimism.[7] To the extent that doctrines and theories of victory provide the language of diplomacy, when the two sides in cases of strategic coercion are speaking different languages, important signals are likely to get lost in translation.

Chapter 2 begins by defining the universe of inquiry—attempts at strategic coercion including both deterrence and compellence—and the concept used as the independent variable, theories of victory. Then, it offers two specific hypotheses to develop the causal chain, drawing on scholarship about psychological and organizational dynamics. They are illustrated by a number of brief examples. The chapter then derives specific empirical predictions from the theoretical hypotheses which can be used to evaluate them: What should we find in the cases if the proposed hypotheses are true? What kind of evidence might disconfirm them? Chapter 2 ends by explaining the methodologies used and the criteria for case selection.

Five chapters then focus on several specific attempts at strategic coercion. The first three cases took place between the United States and China in 1950.[8] Two reflect attempts at deterrence that failed, resulting in the U.S. decision to cross the 38th parallel (discussed in chapter 4) and the Chinese decision to cross the Yalu River later in that same year (discussed in chapter 5). As chapter 6 explains, a third attempt at strategic coercion in 1950 was successful, when the United States deterred China, causing it to postpone a planned invasion of Taiwan. In chapter 7, a final pair of cases from the Middle East exhibits the same phenomenon as Egyptian and Israeli doctrines diverge in the early 1970s.

Chapter 3 provides context for the first two cases, describing the theories of victory held by Washington and by Beijing. U.S. doctrine focused on using airpower and nuclear weapons to win general wars; it considered mobile, integrated formations of armor, infantry, and artillery to be dominant on land. In contrast, China discounted the threat posed by atomic weapons or strategic bombing, and relied instead on a "People's War" doctrine, emphasizing infantry, quantity over quality, and guerrilla tactics to defeat what it considered the main threat, invasion of China itself. Thus, as chapter 3 explains, the two sides understood the language of military affairs quite

---

[7] On the prevalence of misperception in international affairs, see Robert Jervis, *Perception and Misperception in International Politics* (Princeton: Princeton University Press, 1976).

[8] These chapters and the conclusion draw on newly available Chinese-language sources. All translations are my own. All romanizations are done in the Pinyin system except those in common use in Taiwan such as the ruling Kuomingtang (KMT) and Taipei. Chinese names are rendered family name first.

differently: they viewed the world through very different military lenses. Neither understood the other's doctrine with any degree of sophistication.

Chapters 4 and 5 explore how these two theories of victory affected the dependent variable, the success of strategic coercion. The United States crossed the 38th parallel, provoking war, only after disregarding and discounting a series of Chinese signals attempting to deter the United States, described in chapter 4. These signals were seen to U.S. analysts, but their implications were ignored by a wide range of military leaders (not just General Douglas MacArthur, a traditional scapegoat here). Many of China's signals can be seen, in retrospect, to have been based on China's own views regarding military effectiveness. The United States did not recognize the threats inherent in those signals and therefore it disregarded them. The Chinese threats to the United States got lost in translation and lacked credibility; deterrence failed.

Chapter 5 looks at a reciprocal situation in which the United States subsequently sought to deter China. It examines how the two sides' differing views on military affairs influenced statecraft before China's decision to attack U.S. forces in October 1950. Given the very acute security dilemma present, there was little chance to avoid war. Nevertheless, the dynamics at the center of this book continued to be present and to shape perceptions and important decisions in this case. American signals were strongly influenced by U.S. doctrinal views. Available data on the Chinese interpretation of the American signals suggests that Beijing underestimated American intent and capability in ways that were consistent with China's theory of victory. China was surprised, once the battle was joined, by its own forces' substantial losses in battle, which forced China to reappraise its strategy.

Chapter 6 examines a case with a different context and a different outcome: U.S. efforts to deter China's planned invasion of Taiwan, involving U.S. deployment of the 7th Fleet to the Taiwan Strait in 1950, resulted in a Chinese decision to put off its planned invasion indefinitely. The primary military theater was naval; successful amphibious operations were the critical goal. The evidence suggests that the two sides had broadly similar views of amphibious warfare. This shared understanding, due in part to lessons learned by China in the latter stages of its civil war, meant that, even though the signal that the United States sent in this case was militarily weak—only a small part of the Seventh Fleet deployed in the short term—China understood the seriousness of American intent and capabilities and adjusted its behavior accordingly.

Chapter 7 turns to a different geographic region. In the pre-1973 period, the history of the Arab-Israeli conflict presents much more nuanced implications for the theory. The basic causal processes that underlie doctrinal-difference theory indeed do hold: from 1956 through the early 1970s, both Egypt and Israel approached warfare with rather similar doctrines, and this led to a clarity in understanding the overall balance of power and the military signals each side sent. The major outbreak of conflict in this period—the Six Days' War—occurred despite acute pessimism on the Arab side and was the direct result of Soviet manipulation of Egyptian threat perceptions. By 1973, the situation had changed dramatically. Egypt had engaged in substantial doctrinal innovation. As predicted by doctrinal-difference theory, however, Israeli assessments of Egypt did not keep pace. Israel's own doctrine—and its distance from that of Egypt—heavily biased the Israeli assessment of the balance of power prior to the war. The doctrinal differences account for the central intelligence construct that the consensus historiography puts at the core of the failure to anticipate the Egyptian attack. The Israeli hard-line diplomatic strategy depended on that same assessment of the military balance, leading to a much firmer position by Tel Aviv's diplomats than would have been the case had a less biased assessment been available.

Chapter 8 concludes the book by summarizing the results of the study and reviewing how the cases support the hypotheses; it applies the theory to future Sino-American relations, and suggests directions for additional research. The Taiwan Strait today is very prone to the dangers described by doctrinal-difference theory. Policymakers can use the insights from this book, as chapter 8 outlines, to reduce the risk of misperceptions of other nations and to advance national interests more effectively without needless wars.

## DOCTRINAL DIFFERENCES AND WAR AVOIDANCE

The approach taken in this book is important for two main reasons. First, it fills in an important lacuna in our understanding of how to achieve deterrence success. Second, a key causal mechanism—false optimism—is a particular danger, as identified in international relations scholarship.

### ACHIEVING DETERRENCE SUCCESS

Three elements that are key to strategic coercion—to deterrence or compellence—are credibility, capability, and communication.[9] Political science has

---

[9] For a good review of the demands of strategic coercion, see Jack S. Levy, "When Do Deterrent Threats Work?" *British Journal of Political Science* 18 (1989).

long emphasized the challenges of assessing an adversary's credibility when it attempts strategic coercion, but the other two have been relatively neglected.[10] Doctrinal-difference theory suggests that differences between the two sides' theories of military doctrine will make it more difficult for each to interpret the other's signals and to assess the overall balance correctly. The differing perceptions of states about the nature of military capabilities can impede international diplomacy and statecraft by making communication—the third and least studied element of strategic coercion—more difficult. It can also lead to an inappropriately robust policy in the face of an unfavorable military balance.

A state's policies toward other states are based, in part, on its perceptions of the balance of their relative capabilities. Studies that use large-N methods have identified capability—particularly locally deployed capability—as a primary factor in whether deterrence is successful.[11] However, measuring relative capabilities is difficult to do.[12] While military establishments often rely on simplified "dominant indicators," such as numbers of divisions or ships of the line,[13] accurate assessment of military capability requires not simply data collection but a complex process of interpretation that can be shaped by many factors. General opacity in the international system impedes assessment, as do incentives to misrepresent.[14] The ambiguity and uncertainties of feedback, the lack of conclusive tests, and the dynamic nature of the balance add to the problems.[15] Andrew Marshall, later the long-time head of the

---

[10] On credibility and reputation, in addition to ibid., see Daryl G. Press, *Calculating Credibility: How Leaders Assess Threats during Crises* (Ithaca: Cornell University Press, 2005). The best works on assessing capabilities are William C. Wohlforth, *The Elusive Balance: Power and Perceptions during the Cold War* (Ithaca: Cornell University Press, 1993), and John Prados, *The Soviet Estimate: U.S. Intelligence Analysis and Soviet Strategic Forces* (Princeton: Princeton University Press, 1986).

[11] See Christopher H. Achen and Duncan Snidal, "Rational Deterrence Theory and Comparative Case Studies," *World Politics* 41, no. 2 (1989); Paul K. Huth, "Reputations and Deterrence: A Theoretical and Empirical Assessment," *Security Studies* 7, no. 1 (1997); Richard Ned Lebow, "Deterrence: A Political and Psychological Critique," in *Perspectives on Deterrence*, ed. Paul C. Stern et al. (New York: Oxford University Press, 1989).

[12] Wohlforth, *Elusive Balance;* Prados, *Soviet Estimate;* John Arquilla, *Dubious Battles: Aggression, Defeat, and the International System* (Washington, D.C.: Crane Russak, 1992). Noting the even more challenging problem of linking any assessment of the military balance to predictions about coercive success is Richard K. Betts, "Conventional Deterrence: Predictive Uncertainty and Policy Confidence," *World Politics* 37, no. 2 (1985).

[13] Scott Sigmund Gartner, *Strategic Assessment in War* (New Haven: Yale University Press, 1997).

[14] Blainey, *Causes of War;* Van Evera, *Causes of War,* 47, 83, 137. Indeed, opacity is the core of the critique of Fearon made by Kirshner, "Rationalist Explanations for War?"

[15] Wohlforth, *Elusive Balance,* 296–300.

Office of Net Assessment in the Office of the Secretary of Defense, described these problems during the Cold War:

> The fact that estimating procedures [for the military balance] are so vague and impressionistic at one level, and so mechanical at another level, is not altogether surprising.... The conceptual problems in constructing an adequate or useful measure of military power have not yet been faced. Defining an adequate measure looks hard, and making estimates in real situations looks even harder.[16]

Adding the effects of strategy into the mix makes analysis even more complex.

Doctrinal differences compound these well-studied impediments: actors also bring to their assessments of power their own biases and predilections based on their own theories of victory, history, and military variations in doctrine and force structure. Certainly doctrines—in particular, blitzkrieg and doctrines depending on surprise—are already understood to be problematic for achieving conventional deterrence.[17] The problems highlighted in this book are more far reaching and extend those results to more cases.

Communication is the least studied of the elements of successful deterrence, a point little changed since Jervis noted in 1970 that

> military and economic resources, the main instrumentalities of power, have been widely studied [, but] less has been written about the role of diplomatic skill, and the authors of this literature have rarely focused on the full range of techniques by which a state can influence the inferences others are making about it and have not explored in any detail the ways desired images, which may be accurate or inaccurate, not only supplement the more usual forms of power, but are indispensable for reaching certain goals.[18]

Communication is often complicated by states' reliance on tacit signaling rather than explicit communication, even to communicate messages of great

---

[16] Andrew M. Marshall, *Problems of Estimating Military Power*, P-3417 (Santa Monica, Calif.: RAND, August 1966), 9.

[17] John J. Mearsheimer, *Conventional Deterrence* (Ithaca: Cornell University Press, 1983). See also chapter 7's discussion of the Egyptian doctrine.

[18] Jervis, *Logic of Images*, 3.

importance.[19] (Worse yet, cases in which surprise is intended to play a major role preclude some signaling.) Neither of the two classics in the field of coercive diplomacy, written by Alexander L. George and William E. Simons and by Thomas Schelling, focuses on impediments to communication.[20] Both generate a set of abstract prescriptions for successful deterrence and compellence that focus on credibility, capability, and some assurances that the threats are contingent. Beyond calling for "clarity" in the threat, however, they do not examine the difficulties associated with communication.

Jervis also notes the interconnections between perception and difficulties in communication:

> The signaling actor may try to compensate for the fact that ambiguous signals sent in an environment of noise are especially susceptible to distortion. *This would be relatively easy if all actors had the same perceptual predispositions.* Introspection would then permit the actor to understand the influences present when the signals were received and allow him to correct for them. But these predispositions vary and are determined by complex factors, some of which are beyond the knowledge of even the most careful and intelligent observer.[21]

The impediments to communication caused by this sort of perceptual difference are the focus of this book. As the cases show, a nation's theory of victory shapes its perception about the meaning of signals it receives, and guides the signals it chooses to send, complicating communication in cases where doctrinal differences are large. In international politics, miscommunication can lead to war.

## FALSE OPTIMISM

Misestimation of an adversary—whether by overestimation or by underestimation—causes severe problems in international politics.[22] A great many

---

[19] On the importance of tacit signaling, see ibid., 18–26; Thomas C. Schelling, *The Strategy of Conflict* (Cambridge: Harvard University Press, 1960); George W. Downs and David M. Rocke, *Tacit Bargaining, Arms Races, and Arms Control* (Ann Arbor: University of Michigan Press, 1990); Robert M. Axelrod, *The Evolution of Cooperation* (New York: Basic Books, 1984).

[20] Alexander L. George and William E. Simons, *The Limits of Coercive Diplomacy,* 2nd ed. (Boulder, Colo.: Westview Press, 1994); Thomas C. Schelling, *Arms and Influence* (New Haven: Yale University Press, 1966).

[21] Jervis, *Logic of Images,* 134.

[22] Works that have shaped the modern debate on these distinct dangers include Jervis, *Perception and Misperception,* chapter 3; Charles L. Glaser, "Political Consequences of Military Strategy: Expanding and Refining the Spiral and Deterrence Models," *World Politics* 44 (1992).

scholars have studied the sources[23] and the dangers[24] of overestimating one's opponent. This is undoubtedly an important problem in international affairs, but it is not the only source of inadvertent conflict. This book focuses instead on how differences in theories of victory can lead to *underestimation* of an adversary, with negative consequences.

The dangers of underestimating an adversary—of false or unwarranted optimism—can be substantial.[25] As Stephen Van Evera notes: "The historical record suggests that false optimism is a potent and pervasive cause of war. False expectations of victory widely coincide with the outbreak of war. This suggests that false optimism is a strong and common cause of war."[26]

Deterrence is more likely to fail when an aggressor perceives, or misperceives, its adversary as being relatively weak. The implications of false optimism for deterrence are clear: it will make states more likely to fail at deterrence and compellence. Thus, the causes of false optimism merit study. Doctrinal-difference theory explains one source of false optimism.

## HOW THE CASES WERE SELECTED

In chapters 3–7, three Sino-American cases from the early Cold War and two Arab-Israeli cases from the middle of that period test the hypotheses of doctrinal-difference theory and its associated predictions as spelled out in chapter 2. They examine particular stages within crises during which critical decisions were made, with particular focus on the outcome of attempts at strategic coercion. This focus on crisis periods is appropriate, since the theory centers on the difficulties in signaling and interpretation, and crises are often periods of intense communication between the two sides.

The set of three Sino-American cases evaluated in this book all took place in 1950. The first two are the core decisions in the escalation of the Korean

[23] For instance, Samuel P. Huntington, *The Soldier and the State: The Theory and Politics of Civil-Military Relations* (Cambridge: Harvard University Press, 1957), 66; A. Trevor Thrall and Jane K. Cramer, eds., *American Foreign Policy and the Politics of Fear: Threat Inflation since 9/11* (New York: Routledge, 2009).

[24] John Herz, "Idealist Internationalism and the Security Dilemma," *World Politics* 2, no 2 (1950); Robert Jervis, "Cooperation under the Security Dilemma," *World Politics* 30, no. 2 (1978); Richard Ned Lebow and Janice Gross Stein, *We All Lost the Cold War* (Princeton: Princeton University Press, 1993).

[25] See footnote 2, above.

[26] Van Evera, *Causes of War,* 34.

War.[27] In the third—the Chinese decision to postpone the invasion of Taiwan in the face of the American deployment of the Seventh Fleet to the Taiwan Strait—U.S. strategic coercion was successful, and the great powers avoided expansion of their conflict to another theater.

(During the same period, one other coercive attempt had no chance of success and, thus, it is not treated as a case. The U.S. decision to intervene in the war in late June 1950 could not have been deterred by the Chinese: nothing the Chinese could have threatened would have changed the American calculus.[28] Such a case would not teach us very much about strategic coercion.)

The U.S. attempt to deter Chinese intervention after U.S. troops had crossed the 38th parallel, the case addressed in chapter 5, was a particularly challenging deterrence attempt. The Chinese viewed any American presence in that part of the Korean Peninsula as inimical to their interests.[29] When China entered the war, it seemed to have expected large-scale war with the United States to ensue.[30] Thus, deterrence failure stemming from doctrinal differences was not the sole cause of the eventual entry of Chinese forces. Other factors also played important roles.

The Arab-Israeli conflicts of 1967 and 1973 make up another formal test of this theory. Across the time period of that case, there were substantial doctrinal shifts in Egypt; this allows for the isolation of variables such as culture, strategic geography, and some elements of the balance of power, so that the single variable of doctrinal difference can be examined. In 1973,

[27] If, as Robert Jervis and others have argued, the Korean War was a central cause of the militarized competition between the United States and the Soviet Union that came to be known as the Cold War, then understanding the Korean War correctly is even more important than understanding most other wars. Robert Jervis, "The Impact of the Korean War on the Cold War," *Journal of Conflict Resolution* 24, no. 4 (1980).

[28] Primary sources show that America expected, during the early days, that China and the Soviets would get involved in war: "Memorandum of National Security Council Consultants' Meeting, Thursday, June 29, 1950," in U.S. Department of State, *Foreign Relations of the United States* (hereafter FRUS), *1950*, vol. I: *National Security Affairs; Foreign Economic Policy* (Washington, D.C.: U.S. Government Printing Office, 1977), 327–28; "Memorandum of Conversation, by Mr. Frederick E. Nolting, Special Assistant to the Deputy Under Secretary of State (Mathews)," June 30, 1950, in FRUS *1950*, vol. VII: *Korea* (Washington, D.C.: U.S. GPO, 1976), 258.

[29] The key piece of evidence here comes from a telegram Mao drafted to send to Stalin. 毛泽东、"关于决定派军队人朝作战给四斯大林的电报"、1950 年十月二日、《建国以来毛泽东文稿》、第一册:9/1949–12/1950 (北京:中央文献出版社、1987) [Mao Zedong, "Telegram to Stalin Regarding the Decision to Send Troops to Korea for Combat," October 2, 1950, *Mao Zedong's Manuscripts since the Founding of the State* (Beijing: Central Party Documents Publishers, 1987), 539].

[30] For additional discussion, see chapter 5.

the Egyptian doctrine was substantially different from Israel's, so this case provides an extreme value for studying the independent variable.[31]

In both the Middle East and Korean War cases, other causes help to explain the conflicts. This book is not designed to determine which of the many possible approaches best explains these specific wars. This book tests two different theories against each other to probe their general validity for other, similar situations.

There are several reasons why these cases are particularly attractive for study. The different crises within an individual conflict can each be considered a "set of crises"; the scholar can obtain a deeper understanding of the history and culture of the countries involved, thus "reduc[ing] the 'property space'" and creating "comparable cases," in Arend Lijphart's terms.[32]

Both sets of cases are useful as plausibility probes since, in some of the cases, the two sides had such vastly dissimilar perspectives on military power. In the Sino-American cases, China's faith in the concept of People's War was at its height in this period, in contrast to the heavy U.S. dependence on airpower, capital-intensive ground forces, and nuclear weapons. In the 1973 Middle East case, Egypt's doctrine was developed explicitly to compensate for its inability to compete using a doctrine similar to Israel's. Both sets of cases therefore present examples of extreme values in the independent variable.[33] Thus, these cases provide a relatively easy test: if the theory does not provide explanatory value here, it should not be expected to do so elsewhere. There is also variation across cases in the value of the independent variable: in one case from each set (the Taiwan Strait in 1950 and Egypt-Israel before 1967), there is little difference between the theories of victory of the two adversaries. Thus, together, these cases allow both empirical thoroughness and methodological rigor.

Beyond these methodological advantages, the cases are valuable for other reasons. If, as some have argued, the Korean War was a central cause of the militarized competition between the United States and the Soviet Union that

---

[31] Study of this case is facilitated, too, by the existence of an extensive secondary literature, including one study that reflects an approach similar to that of doctrinal-difference theory: Jonathan Shimshoni, *Israel and Conventional Deterrence: Border Warfare from 1953 to 1970* (Ithaca: Cornell University Press, 1988).

[32] On the importance of such immersion, see Gary King, Robert O. Keohane, and Sidney Verba, *Designing Social Inquiry: Scientific Inference in Qualitative Research* (Princeton: Princeton University Press, 1994), 37–41; Arend Lijphart, "Comparative Politics and the Comparative Method," *American Political Science Review* 65, no. 3 (1971): 687.

[33] Stephen Van Evera, *Guide to Methods for Students of Political Science* (Ithaca: Cornell University Press, 1997), 43.

came to be known as the Cold War, then understanding this case is even more important.[34] In the Middle East, the 1967 and 1973 wars played a similarly foundational role in shaping contemporary affairs.

The Sino-American cases are especially pertinent to current American foreign policy for two reasons. First, China was substantially behind the United States technologically. The United States is still vastly ahead of any potential adversary,[35] and therefore lessons drawn from the earlier period could shed useful light on current U.S. foreign policy. Second, U.S. relations with China are likely to continue to be tense and to include attempts at strategic coercion. Many scholars argue that culture and ideology play especially important roles in shaping Chinese foreign policy in general.[36] Learning more about the ways in which miscommunications and misperceptions affected the two nations in the past can help policymakers avert trouble in the future, perhaps decreasing the risk of nuclear or large-scale conventional war.

The phenomena discussed in this book are timeless. In 432 BC, Pericles exhorted his fellow Athenians, a naval power, to take on the Spartans, a land power:

> As to war and the resources of either party, a detailed comparison will not show you the inferiority of Athens...for our naval skill is of more use to us for service on land, than their military skill for service at sea. Familiarity with the sea they will not find an easy acquisition. If you who have been practicing at it ever since the Persian invasion have not yet brought it to perfection, is there any chance of anything considerable being effected by an agricultural, unseafaring population, who will besides be prevented from practicing by the constant presence of strong squadrons of observation from Athens?[37]

---

[34] Jervis, "Impact of the Korean War."

[35] For a convincing discussion of just how far ahead the United States is, see Stephen G. Brooks and William C. Wohlforth, *World out of Balance: International Relations and the Challenge of American Primacy* (Princeton: Princeton University Press, 2008).

[36] John W. Garver, *Foreign Relations of the People's Republic of China* (Englewood Cliffs, N.J.: Prentice Hall, 1992); Michael H. Hunt, *The Genesis of Chinese Communist Foreign Policy* (New York: Columbia University Press, 1995); Ross Terrill, *The New Chinese Empire, and What It Means for the United States* (New York: Basic Books, 2003).

[37] Thucydides, *The Landmark Thucydides: A Comprehensive Guide to the Peloponnesian War [History of the Peloponnesian War. English]* (New York: Free Press, 1996), 81–82.

Two years later, however, as Thucydides wrote, this optimism had been revealed as baseless and false through great bloodshed:

> After the second invasion of the Peloponnesians a change came over the spirit of the Athenians. Their land had now been twice laid waste; and war and pestilence at once pressed heavy on them. They began to find fault with Pericles, as the author of the war and the cause of all their misfortunes, and became eager to come to terms with Sparta.[38]

Centuries later, the error is often repeated: leaders who view security competition only through their own doctrinal lens sometimes impose heavy costs that could have been avoided.

---

[38] Ibid., 123.

# 2

# DOCTRINAL DIFFERENCES AND MISPERCEPTION

DOCTRINAL-DIFFERENCE THEORY states that when nations have different doctrines and hold different beliefs about what kinds of military strategies and capabilities may be effective, diplomacy and signaling will be more difficult, and this can cause escalation or conflict. In this chapter, the two stages of this process are expressed as a pair of hypotheses: first, the doctrinal-difference misperception (DDM) hypothesis, suggests how the differences in beliefs lead to misperception; the second, doctrinal-difference escalation (DDE) hypothesis, explains how this may, in turn, cause miscommunication and crisis outcomes such as escalation or even violent conflict. Their logic is sketched out in the next section of this chapter. An alternative explanation for failed coercion is also laid out, one emphasized in the existing literature: the weakness hypothesis, which focuses on a failure to send strong signals in a crisis. Then, the predictions that follow from these hypotheses are specified: that is, what should we expect to find in the cases studied in chapters 3 through 7? The chapter concludes with an explanation of the methodology of the inquiry reflected in the rest of this book.

## STRATEGIC COERCION AND THEORIES OF VICTORY: DEFINITIONS AND THE UNIVERSE OF CASES

Two terms important to this study are *strategic coercion*, which is part of the definition of the universe of cases studied here, and *theories of victory*.

## THE PROJECT'S UNIVERSE OF CASES:
## ATTEMPTS AT STRATEGIC COERCION

Strategic coercion encompasses a large universe of cases, since "the use of intimidation of one kind or another in order to get others to comply with one's wishes is an everyday occurrence in human affairs."[1] For my purposes, strategic coercion is the process by which one nation tries to convince another nation to do something it would not otherwise have done, through implicit or explicit threats and limited uses of violence, either to thwart the adversary's action or to punish it.

Three distinctions that are commonly made in the field are not pertinent here: compellence versus deterrence, general versus immediate deterrence, and peacetime crisis diplomacy versus signaling in a limited war. In each case, the reasons for differentiation are not important for my purposes, and so all will be conflated under the term coercive diplomacy. (However, rare instances of total—rather than limited—war are excluded.) This usage is consistent with that of other scholars in the field. Lawrence Freedman defined "strategic coercion" as "the deliberate and purposive use of overt threats to influence another's strategic choices."[2] For him, both deterrence and compellence are both part of a "threat based bargaining process."[3] As he notes, the historical origins of each term have somewhat exaggerated the difference between deterrence and compellence:

> [Although] deterrence and coercive diplomacy...are two sides of the same coercive coin, the difference between them came to be exaggerated through the research that they stimulated. The study of deterrence was largely concerned with the United States' essentially symmetrical relationship with the Soviet Union, while [compellence] was bound up with its asymmetrical relationship with smaller powers.[4]

---

[1] Alexander L. George, "Introduction: The Limits of Coercive Diplomacy," in *The Limits of Coercive Diplomacy,* ed. Alexander L. George and William E. Simons (Boulder, Colo.: Westview Press, 1994), 2. Indeed the limitation of "human affairs" may be too narrow; see Christopher Boehm, "Egalitarian Behavior and the Evolution of Political Intelligence," in *Machiavellian Intelligence II: Extensions and Evaluations,* ed. Andrew Whiten and Richard W. Byrne (New York: Cambridge University Press, 1997), 342.

[2] Lawrence Freedman, "Strategic Coercion," in *Strategic Coercion: Concepts and Cases,* ed. Lawrence Freedman (New York: Oxford University Press, 1998), 15.

[3] Freedman, introduction to in *Strategic Coercion,* 3.

[4] Freedman, "Strategic Coercion," 32.

In practice, the lines separating the various forms of compellence, deterrence, and coercion are not so clear, as nearly all scholars working in the field have noted.[5]

Similarly, although there may be circumstances when it is useful to separate general from immediate deterrence,[6] these two concepts are better viewed as part of a continuum. General deterrence can fail for the same reasons that immediate deterrence does: because of questions about capability and intent.[7] Doctrinal-difference theory has implications for both kinds of questions.

The approach I adopt includes both threats and the use of force if it has some communicative element and is not simply part of a total-war strategy. Violence can play a communicative role in all conflicts except those that have escalated to Carl von Clausewitz's theoretical extreme, all-out war (since there is little left to threaten).[8] Diplomatic crises, militarized crises, limited wars, and total wars are best viewed as lying along a continuum of conflict. Any study of bargaining along this continuum could examine several different sorts of interaction.[9] Furthermore, although much attention in the field focuses on explicit signals and threats, it is important not to neglect tacit signals. They are ubiquitous: John Arquilla finds "tacit signals" used by military forces in 60 percent of the cases he studied, and they can convey a message with considerable clarity.[10] Indeed, the entire

[5] Making this point forcefully is Peter Viggo Jakobsen, *Western Use of Coercive Diplomacy after the Cold War: A Challenge for Theory and Practice* (New York: St. Martin's Press, 1998), 13. See also Robert J. Art and Patrick M. Cronin, *The United States and Coercive Diplomacy* (Washington, D.C.: United States Institute of Peace Press, 2003); Daniel Byman, Matthew C. Waxman, and Eric V. Larson, *Air Power as a Coercive Instrument*, MR-1061-AF (Santa Monica, Calif.: RAND, 1999), 12, figure, "Deterrence and Compellence Blur in Practice." Even those whose research design is centered on the difference admit difficulties in operationalizing it. James W. Davis Jr., *Threats and Promises: The Pursuit of International Influence* (Baltimore: Johns Hopkins University Press, 2000), 415 and 421.

[6] Arguing that general deterrence will be increasingly important in the post–Cold War world is Patrick M. Morgan, *Deterrence Now* (New York: Cambridge University Press, 2003).

[7] Ibid.

[8] Carl von Clausewitz, *On War* (Princeton: Princeton University Press, 1989), 76, 78–80, and 87.

[9] As indeed the classics in the field do: Thomas C. Schelling, *Arms and Influence* (New Haven: Yale University Press, 1966), 2–3 (in chapter 1, "Diplomacy and Violence"); Robert Pape, *Bombing to Win: Air Power and Coercion in War* (Ithaca: Cornell University Press, 1996); Freedman, "Strategic Coercion," 20–23; Jakobsen, *Western Use of Coercive Diplomacy*, 14–15; George, "Introduction: The Limits of Coercive Diplomacy," 2.

[10] John Arquilla, "Louder Than Words: Tacit Communication in International Crises," *Political Communication* 9 (1992): 163; George W. Downs and David M. Rocke, *Tacit Bargaining, Arms Races, and Arms Control* (Ann Arbor: University of Michigan Press, 1990).

"tit-for-tat" literature sparked by Robert Axelrod's work centers on tacit signaling.[11]

In contrast to the broader literature on strategic coercion, this book does not examine incentives or "carrots"; it examines only threats—sticks, not carrots—as tools of policy.[12] The causal dynamic of misperceptions caused by different theories of victory focuses primarily on impediments to the communication of threats, not on incentives.

## THEORIES OF VICTORY: DOCTRINE AND MORE

The degree of difference between the "theories of victory" of two nations is the independent variable in this study: "Every military organization, explicitly or implicitly, has a theory of victory, a notion of the combination of human and material resources and tactics that it believes is most likely to produce success on the battlefield. The theory of victory is the organization's military doctrine."[13]

Military strategies link force structures to political or military goals. Military doctrine reflects an understanding of how elements of military power can be used to achieve victory. Doctrine, the central component to a theory of victory, refers to a concept more specific than a grand strategy, but more general than operational or tactical military strategy. Doctrines can be based on organizational frameworks (such as, for example, levée en masse), specific technologies (ballistic missile or tanks), or more conceptual elements (blitzkrieg).

Recent American security policy offers illustrations. The term "military doctrine" does not refer to U.S. strategies of maintaining and ensuring global predominance or the preemption of threats, which are more appropriately called grand strategy. Nor does it refer to something like the "left hook" approach used by the United States to win the first Gulf War; this is operational or tactical strategy.[14] In the context of recent U.S. policy, military doctrine

---

[11] Robert M. Axelrod, *The Evolution of Cooperation* (New York: Basic Books, 1984); Robert M. Axelrod, *The Complexity of Cooperation: Agent-Based Models of Competition and Collaboration* (Princeton: Princeton University Press, 1997).

[12] David Cortright, *The Price of Peace: Incentives and International Conflict Prevention* (Lanham, Md.: Rowman and Littlefield, 1997).

[13] Barry R. Posen, "Measuring the European Conventional Balance: Coping with Complexity in Threat Assessment," *International Security* 9, no. 3 (1984–85): 51. For similar usage, see Stephen Peter Rosen, *Winning the Next War: Innovation and the Modern Military* (Ithaca: Cornell University Press, 1991), 20.

[14] Robert H. Scales, *Certain Victory: The U.S. Army in the Gulf War* (Washington, D.C.: Brassey's, 1994).

in high intensity conventional wars is a theory of victory that is based on the heavy use of airpower and precision-guided munitions aimed to decapitate an adversary, followed up if needed by heavy mechanized forces and very mobile infantry forces.[15] This is how the United States plans to win wars in general.

Building on the usage of Barry Posen and others, this book defines a "theory of victory" as a belief or set of beliefs about what constitutes effective military power and how it should be used operationally and tactically. It is centered on doctrine, but also comprises the makeup of military forces as well as some elements of grand strategy. The theory of victory describes the general understanding of how to win wars. It is a mental construct that may be informed by past empirical experience. It has visible effects on policy: it guides the procurement of forces, shapes the doctrine of how those forces are used, and prioritizes grand-strategic goals for the nation.[16]

## HOW DOCTRINAL DIFFERENCES CAN CAUSE AND ESCALATE CONFLICT

After a brief summary of the sources of doctrinal beliefs, I will discuss the two stages of the proposed causal chain: first, the hypothesis that differences in theories of victory can lead to an overestimation of one's own power relative to that of one's adversary (doctrinal-difference misperception or DDM hypothesis); second, the hypothesis that such an overestimation can increase the risk of failure of strategic coercive policies, and thus the risk of unnecessary conflict (doctrinal difference escalation or DDE hypothesis).

---

[15] A representative statement is *FM 3–0: Operations* (Washington, D.C.: Headquarters, Department of the Army, June 14, 2001). An earlier U.S. military strategy is found in the 1982 edition of FM 100–5 that introduced AirLand Battle. The more recent emphasis on counterinsurgency doctrine has been encapsulated in the 2006 edition of FM-3-24.

[16] The term used here is similar to concepts used by others as well. Builder, for example, describes different "concepts of war" of the various service branches of the U.S. military. Carl H. Builder, *The Masks of War: American Military Styles in Strategy and Analysis* (Baltimore: Johns Hopkins University Press, 1989), chapter 12, "The Service Concepts of War." The term "concept of operations" (or CONOPS) is also similar, although less precise, as it can refer to a wide range of scales. Also similar is the term "organizational culture" of the People's Liberation Army used in Scobell's discussion of cultural influences on China's propensity to use military force. Andrew Scobell, *China's Use of Military Force: Beyond the Great Wall and the Long March* (New York: Cambridge University Press, 2003), 7–8. Weigley's term "the way of war" comes very close to the meaning used here. Russell F. Weigley, *The American Way of War: A History of United States Military Strategy and Policy* (Bloomington: Indiana University Press, 1977).

## THE SOURCES AND EFFECTS OF DOCTRINAL BELIEFS

My goal is to explain the effects, not the sources, of different theories of victory. Nevertheless, doctrine is shaped by many factors, not just material constraints or strategic cultures. Scholarship on this topic is easily divided into four approaches.

First, systemic and geographic imperatives can have a powerful effect by forcing doctrinal innovation.[17] Military defeat punishes laggards, and the international system presents powerful incentives to find effective military solutions to strategic dilemmas.[18] Financial and other resource constraints can also play a role in shaping a nation's choice of strategy; states may choose a strategy because it is the only one they can afford.

Second, closely related to this argument is the role of technological advancement in leading to military innovation, which makes new options in weapons and tactics available to states.[19] For instance, the proliferation of a variety of technologies—the railroad, artillery, improvements in personal arms—may have driven the adoption of general staffs, an organizational change.[20] The rise of general staffs, in turn, created strategic and operational opportunities.

A third important source of leaders' perceptions of optimal strategies is past historic practice. One manifestation of this is the well-known adage that "states often prepare to fight the last war."[21] When states have found strategies that worked, they are reluctant to change them.

Fourth, organizational structures and practices can shape doctrine by reifying the lessons of history, setting standard operating practices, and

---

[17] The most prominent such argument is Barry R. Posen, *The Sources of Military Doctrine: France, Britain, and Germany between the World Wars* (Ithaca: Cornell University Press, 1984). Also see John J. Mearsheimer, *Conventional Deterrence* (Ithaca: Cornell University Press, 1983); Sten Rynning, "Shaping Military Doctrine in France: Decisionmakers between International Power and Domestic Interests," *Security Studies* 11, no. 2 (2001–02).

[18] Some scholars argue that other states in the international system will sometimes emulate effective military strategies without the spur of defeat. Colin Elman, "The Logic of Emulation: The Diffusion of Military Practices in the International System," PhD diss., Columbia University, 1999; João Resende-Santos, "Anarchy and the Emulation of Military Systems: Military Organization and Technology in South America, 1870–1930," *Security Studies* 5, no. 3 (1996).

[19] On the role of technology in fostering innovation, see Martin L. Van Creveld, *Technology and War: From 2000 B.C. to the Present*, rev. and expanded ed. (New York: Free Press, 1991). For a counterargument, see Keir A. Lieber, "Grasping the Technological Peace: The Offense-Defense Balance and International Security," *International Security* 25, no. 1 (2000).

[20] Dallas D. Irvine, "The Origin of Capital Staffs," *Journal of Modern History* 10, no. 2 (1938).

[21] Eliot Cohen and John Gooch, *Military Misfortunes: The Anatomy of Failure in War* (New York: Free Press, 1990).

defining actors' interests. Many organizational sources of innovation exist: the intervention of civilian leaders, the nature of the institutions of civilian oversight, interservice and interbranch rivalry, continuity in the officer corps, and a historically derived organizational culture.[22] Organizations may also shape doctrine more directly: for example, a professionalized force has options that a conscript military does not, due to the skill levels of its officers and noncommissioned officers.[23]

Thus, there is a flourishing scholarly debate on the sources of doctrine. Since states vary in their natural resources, workforce education, capital, and other factor endowments, in their recent histories in security affairs, and in their national and organizational cultures, there are significant variations in theories of victory across space and time. Consider the variation within the Napoleonic wars, various dyads in World War II such as U.S.-Germany or France-Germany,[24] and the wars of Louis XIV.[25] Material differences alone are insufficient to explain this wide range of choices. Indeed, even with material disparity, nations sometimes have similar theories of victory.[26] There are significant differences in military cultures even among European and North Atlantic nations that have similar levels of development.[27] Although

[22] Posen, *Sources of Military Doctrine;* Elman, "The Logic of Emulation"; Deborah D. Avant, *Political Institutions and Military Change: Lessons from Peripheral Wars* (Ithaca: Cornell University Press, 1994); Owen R. Cote Jr., "The Politics of Innovative Military Doctrine: The United States Navy and Fleet Ballistic Missiles," PhD diss., Massachusetts Institute of Technology, 1996; Rosen, *Winning the Next War;* Harvey M. Sapolsky, *The Polaris System Development: Bureaucratic and Programmatic Success in Government* (Cambridge: Harvard University Press, 1972); Elizabeth Kier, "Culture and French Military Doctrine before World War II," in *The Culture of National Security: Norms and Identity in World Politics,* ed. Peter J. Katzenstein (New York: Columbia University Press, 1996); Scobell, *China's Use of Military Force.*

[23] See, for instance, the discussions on French strategy in Jack L. Snyder, *The Ideology of the Offensive: Military Decision Making and the Disasters of 1914* (Ithaca: Cornell University Press, 1984). Arguing that professionalism was critical at all levels of the German Wehrmacht is R. Ernest Dupuy and Trevor N. Dupuy, *A Genius for War: The German Army and General Staff, 1807–1945* (New York: Nova Publications, 1995).

[24] The traditional view on this issue is expressed in Marc Bloch, *Strange Defeat: A Statement of Evidence Written in 1940* (New York: Octagon Books, 1968), 36–68; Williamson Murray and Allan R. Millett, *A War to Be Won: Fighting the Second World War* (Cambridge: Belknap Press of Harvard University Press, 2000), chapter 2. In contrast, May emphasizes the similarities between the militaries: Ernest R. May, *Strange Victory: Hitler's Conquest of France* (New York: Hill and Wang, 2000).

[25] John Arquilla, *Dubious Battles: Aggression, Defeat, and the International System* (Washington, D.C.: Crane Russak, 1992), 103–29.

[26] The cases provide examples of this. See chapter 6, "China Postpones the Invasion of Taiwan."

[27] Joseph L. Soeters, "Value Orientations in Military Academies: A Thirteen Country Study," *Armed Forces and Society* 24, no. 1 (1997): 24.

differences in factor endowments contributed to the Sino-American doctrinal differences discussed in the next chapters, clearly other factors were influential.

Rather than join this debate, however, in this book I look at the wide-ranging effects of a particular doctrinal choice. It will shape future force procurement decisions. Training will be geared to implementing the doctrine, even at senior levels of the military. Political leaders will be educated in the doctrine by the military leadership. Once incorporated into a nation's doctrine, specific beliefs will, through the creation and use of standard operating procedures (SOPs), be applied to unexpected and perhaps inappropriate situations:[28] "In the short-response-time, come-as-you-are nature of most international crisis situations, the employment of the armed forces places critical importance on existing forces and their existing organizational routines (SOPs, doctrine, etc.). The structure and doctrine of armed forces establishes how they operate."[29]

Although military doctrine is necessary in order to rehearse and plan, once accepted it reinforces beliefs in its efficacy.[30] Even sharp external shocks may not be enough to lead to change: "The enemy's sudden attack [at Pearl Harbor] produced no quick reorientation of American ideas about the use of air power. The first impulse was to resurrect schemes concocted under different circumstances. As in many other matters, so too in the use of air power. Pearl Harbor was not the watershed it came to seem."[31]

This inherent inflexibility of adopted doctrine, coupled with its application to a wide range of policies and issues, emphasizes its importance as an independent variable: a cause with wide-ranging consequences. A number of other scholars have proven its influences in related areas.[32]

---

[28] The classic 1971 statement on the role of standard operating procedures in foreign policy was updated in 1999: Graham Allison and Philip Zelikow, *Essence of Decision: Explaining the Cuban Missile Crisis*, 2nd ed. (New York: Addison-Wesley Longman, 1999); Graham T. Allison, "Conceptual Models and the Cuban Missile Crisis," *American Political Science Review* 63, no 3 (1969).

[29] Colonel Richard A. Lacquement Jr., "Preaching after the Devil's Death: Shaping American Military Capabilities in the Post–Cold War Era," PhD diss., Princeton University, 2000, 13.

[30] For one example of this, see Tami Davis Biddle, *Rhetoric and Reality in Air Warfare: The Evolution of British and American Ideas about Strategic Bombing, 1914–1945* (Princeton: Princeton University Press, 2002).

[31] Michael S. Sherry, *The Rise of American Air Power: The Creation of Armageddon* (New Haven: Yale University Press, 1987), 117.

[32] Lynn Eden, *Whole World on Fire: Organizations, Knowledge, and Nuclear Weapons Devastation* (Ithaca: Cornell University Press, 2006); Isabel V. Hull, *Absolute Destruction: Military Culture and the Practices of War in Imperial Germany* (Ithaca: Cornell University Press, 2006); Jeffrey Legro,

Thus doctrinal-difference theory treats doctrine—and more broadly, theories of victory—as an independent variable to argue that differences in theories of victory can lead to misperceptions. In turn, such misperceptions can lead to miscommunications, escalation, and conflict—due to deterrence failure, and coercive failure more generally. Everything is caused by something. No theory can explain the entire chain of causality in international politics. This book starts with doctrine—itself dependent on many causes but observable and influential in its own right—and examines its effects.

These effects are examined as two separate hypotheses: the doctrinal-difference misperception (DDM) hypothesis and then the doctrinal-difference escalation (DDE) hypothesis.

## DOCTRINAL-DIFFERENCE MISPERCEPTION (DDM) HYPOTHESIS

*DDM Hypothesis:* When two nations have different theories of victory, they will be more likely to misperceive each other's relative capabilities, and these misperceptions will raise the risk of underestimation of the adversary.

As a result of differing theories of victory, this hypothesis predicts *opacity* in general, which primarily manifests as *underestimation.* The central logic is that it is hard to understand unfamiliar doctrines, particularly when they seem flawed. Where two nations have different theories of victory, seven more specific causal chains explain how they will be more likely to underestimate each other. Three of the logics arise from organizational politics and the effects of culture on perception. The other four logics trace their roots to perceptual arguments, primarily from the psychology literature.

First, the military innovation literature suggests that organizations in general, and militaries in particular, are reluctant to innovate.[33] Organizations are reluctant to change, have trouble thinking outside of established ideas, and resist changing standard operating procedures. Militaries are particularly prone to this since change not only threatens the organization but involves putting soldiers' lives at risk. Because members of a military organization tend to devalue and avoid innovation in their own organization, they can also be expected to discount its value to others, thus leading to an

---

*Cooperation under Fire: Anglo-German Restraint during World War II* (Ithaca: Cornell University Press, 1995); Biddle, *Rhetoric and Reality in Air Warfare.*

[33] For the problems and potential mitigation, see Rosen, *Winning the Next War,* esp. 8–52.

underestimation of the others' capabilities.[34] This can be the case even when other countries have innovated successfully and all that the country in question must do is to emulate others, a less risky step.

This is illustrated by the well-known example of the horse cavalry between the world wars in the U.S. Army. Even after the carnage on the front lines of the European battlefields at the Somme and Verdun, and the success of tanks at the end of the war, a dominant group of horse cavalry officers in the interwar period continued to insist that superior maneuverability and flexibility meant that horses were still superior to tanks as weapons platforms.[35] Thus, at the outbreak of World War II in Europe, the United States had a mere twenty-eight tanks in service that were not obsolete.[36] Even as late as 1944, the desires of military leaders to continue to emphasize high mobility kept them from deploying heavy armor and antitank weapons.[37] Such a doctrine, consistent with the prevailing understanding of cavalry doctrine, seems quite irrational in the face of German Tiger tanks.

Second, establishing a strategy is a costly, risky endeavor. Getting a strategy implemented is difficult and may push military and political leaders to oversell its merits and depreciate alternatives, again leading to an underestimation of adversaries with different doctrines.[38] For instance, "The U.S. lacked a competitive tank engine in the period before World War II, but in the absence of hard data to the contrary, the chief of the [American] Ordnance Department was able to assert in 1938 that U.S. tank engines were among the best in the world."[39] There are many other cases of unjustified best-case assumptions in the absence of good information about

[34] For a related argument afflicting the intelligence communities, see Thomas G. Mahnken, *Uncovering Ways of War: U.S. Intelligence and Foreign Military Innovation, 1918–1941* (Ithaca: Cornell University Press, 2002).

[35] See Elman, "Logic of Emulation," 169; Edward L. Katzenbach Jr., "The Horse Cavalry in the Twentieth Century," in *The Use of Force: Military Power and International Politics*, ed. Robert Art and Kenneth Waltz (Lanham, Md.: University Press of America, 1993).

[36] Elman, "Logic of Emulation," 177. Note that even these were all light and medium tanks. Budgetary pressures alone cannot account for this as the War Department's budget nearly tripled between 1935 and 1940 (Elman, "Logic of Emulation," 176).

[37] Rosen, *Winning the Next War,* 188. See also David E. Johnson, *Fast Tanks and Heavy Bombers: Innovation in the U.S. Army, 1917–1945* (Ithaca: Cornell University Press, 1998).

[38] For examples of denigration of alternative doctrines, see Perry M. Smith, "The Role of Doctrine," in *American Defense Policy*, ed. John E. Endicott and Roy W. Stafford Jr. (Baltimore: Johns Hopkins University Press, 1977). On overselling at the political level and, to some extent, the grand-strategic level, see Jane Kellett Cramer, "Militarized Patriotism: Why the US Marketplace of Ideas Failed before the Iraq War," *Security Studies* 16, no. 3 (2007).

[39] Rosen, *Winning the Next War,* 188.

an adversary.[40] One U.S. Army general, a military historian, writes that "on every occasion, modern nations involved in recent small wars have overestimated the destructive power of their own forces. Inevitably, this overestimate has led to optimism and expectations greater than either men or machines could deliver."[41] Similar phenomena pervade the literature: "Air Corps leaders had reached a doctrinal decision by 1935 as to the efficacy of unescorted long-range strategic bombardment and were unwilling either to question that decision or even to observe technological advances that might cause them to modify this doctrine."[42] Such trends would lead to an overestimation of one's own capabilities relative to those of the adversary.

Third, military organization culture, like strategic or indeed any culture, can shape perceptions in critical ways. By creating norms and expectations about patterns of behavior, culture profoundly shapes people's understanding of reality; it "refers both to a set of evaluative standards, such as norms or values, and to cognitive standards, such as rules or models defining what entities and actors exist in a system and how they operate and interrelate."[43] Military cultures affect grand-strategic preferences.[44] They can even shape basic issues such as the way data is collected and evaluated in conflict.[45]

Theories of victory are a type of military strategic and doctrinal culture, and thus similarly affect perceptions of power and signals. Differences in such cultures will lead to differences in perceptions about power and signals across countries, as this hypothesis predicts, and thus the chance of misperception in such situations increases.

Fourth, leaders understand best what they have had experience with. If they lack experience with a military weapon or strategy, then it is hard for them to understand it. If they also lack advisers with experience with the weapon or strategy, this problem is exacerbated. One example of this is noted in a chapter by John Arquilla called "Why 'Losers' Start Wars."[46]

---

[40] Ibid., 194. Also see Smith, "Role of Doctrine."

[41] Robert H. Scales, *Firepower in Limited War* (Washington, D.C.: National Defense University Press, 1990), 289.

[42] Smith, "Role of Doctrine," 40.

[43] Ronald L. Jepperson, Alexander Wendt, and Peter J. Katzenstein, "Norms, Identities, and Culture in National Security," in *The Culture of National Security: Norms and Identity in World Politics,* ed. Peter J. Katzenstein (New York: Columbia University Press, 1996), 56.

[44] Peter Feaver and Christopher Gelpi, *Choosing Your Battles: American Civil-Military Relations and the Use of Force* (Princeton: Princeton University Press, 2004).

[45] Scott Sigmund Gartner, *Strategic Assessment in War* (New Haven: Yale University Press, 1997), 3.

[46] Arquilla, *Dubious Battles.* The passage quoted is the title of chapter 5 in his book, and that question underlies his entire project.

Another is the "imperfect understanding of sea power and its role in land-sea war" by leaders of continental powers.[47] The same phenomenon can occur more generally whenever leaders lack an understanding of their adversary's theory of victory.

Fifth, differences in military forces of a qualitative nature are harder to assess than those of a quantitative nature. Andrew Marshall describes one manifestation of this difficulty, "the symmetry syndrome of...classical military planning":

> This is the typical reaction pattern: If an opponent buys bombers, we tend more to increase our bomber forces, *rather than to increase our air defense;* when an opponent deploys an ABM system, we deploy an ABM system.... If the enemy has so many divisions, the planners say we ought to have so many divisions; if he has so many naval ships of various classes, we should have the same proportional number.[48]

Even when qualitatively different forces might be more suitable, as in the case of air defenses in Marshall's quote, "symmetry" in planning calls for a quantitative response. Jonathan Shimshoni's conclusions from a study of the Arab-Israeli conflict from 1953 to 1970 also emphasize the difficulty of assessing the advantage presented by qualitative differences across different military forces.[49]

This argument in support of the DDM hypothesis emphasizes not only that diplomacy is impeded because nations have incentives to be secretive about the sources of their power when they depend on qualitative differences, as Shimshoni points out, but also that the evaluation of qualitative differences is more challenging than those based on quantitative differences.[50] It is relatively easy to think about how an opponent's extra division or warship would affect a particular military balance. However, predicting outcomes affected by a new type of tank or submarine is more challenging, and

[47] Ibid., 121. The findings reflected in this book are almost the opposite of Arquilla's: as chapters 4, 5, and 6 show, when a land power faced off against a sea power (over Taiwan), there were few mistakes, and deterrence and peace prevailed. However, when a sea power faced a land power on land (in Korea), mistakes and escalation were pervasive. This suggests that something deeper is at play, at least in these cases.

[48] Andrew M. Marshall, *Problems of Estimating Military Power*, P-3417 (Santa Monica, Calif.: RAND, August 1966), 10. Emphasis added.

[49] Jonathan Shimshoni, *Israel and Conventional Deterrence: Border Warfare from 1953 to 1970* (Ithaca: Cornell University Press, 1988), 226–28.

[50] This point is consistent with, although not made explicitly by, Shimshoni, ibid.

conducting net assessments or campaign analysis with fundamentally different sorts of forces even more so.

Sixth, leaders tend to believe that their own views are correct because they chose them. That is, a psychological defense mechanism of self-justification exists. The so-called fundamental attribution error—a concept grounded in psychological experimental research—is closely related to this point. The fundamental attribution error emphasizes that contextual justifications for choices have less effect on those choices than they would objectively merit. For instance, even if subjects are told that a lecturer has been ordered to defend a particular position, they nevertheless perceive that the lecturer believes the content of his speech.[51] A particular theory of victory might be chosen for any number of reasons other than functional optimality, but once it is chosen the context or situation that led to its selection will fade into the background, and people will tend to ignore the particular contingent reasons why a militarily suboptimal strategy might have been chosen and thus fail to recognize when the context that justifies it has altered.

Elizabeth Kier, a scholar of doctrine, notes precisely this phenomenon:

> Social psychologists have shown that stating an idea often leads to changes in personal convictions....Getting people to commit themselves publicly to a particular belief can lead them to internalize that belief....If "saying is believing," many aspects of the military's culture [and thus doctrine, in Kier's analyses] may have originated as politically expedient strategies.[52]

Thus, again, one might ignore the shortcomings of one's own theory of victory. The phenomenon of self-justification might also lead to underestimation of an adversary's different views.

Seventh, psychologically, humans are predisposed to have an exaggerated sense of themselves, which psychologists refer to as a "positive illusion." The key research into this phenomenon suggests that "most people exhibit positive illusions in three important domains: (a) They view themselves in unrealistically positive terms; (b) they believe they have greater control over

---

[51] Erica Goode, "How Culture Molds Habits of Thought," *New York Times*, August 8, 2000, F 1. An example of political science research that utilizes this concept is Jonathan Mercer, *Reputation and International Politics* (Ithaca: Cornell University Press, 1996).

[52] Elizabeth Kier, *Imagining War: French and British Military Doctrine between the Wars* (Princeton: Princeton University Press, 1997), 156.

environmental events than is actually the case; and (c) they hold views of the future that are more rosy than base-rate data can justify."[53]

This finding is widely accepted in the field of social psychology.[54] There is evidence that this phenomenon exists in some way in many cultures,[55] including, of particular interest to this book, that of China.[56] This psychological phenomenon has been studied in the context of international conflict.[57]

From the perspective of this study, such positive illusions are likely to be particularly pronounced in cases of different theories of victory because, in such circumstances, cognitive errors may be more difficult to overcome. If doctrines are similar in nature, exaggerations would be harder to sustain;[58] differences in the nature of capabilities (or strategies), by contrast, leaves more room for errors. "It is often hard to distinguish reality from illusion...especially...when one is dealing with people's interpretations or subjective perceptions of stimuli and events that do not have a [quantifiable] physical basis."[59] When both sides are operating under similar theories of victory, assessments of the opponent's forces and plans will be less subject to "interpretations or subjective perceptions" than if the two sides have very different theories of victory.

Any one of the above seven causal chains could lead a state to perceive an adversary's capabilities as being relatively weaker than the adversary itself views them to be. If more of the causal chains are present, this increases the likelihood of miscommunications and differences in perception. It is also important to emphasize that most of the seven reasons for discounting an adversary's doctrine hold even in cases when nations are forced to

[53] Shelley E. Taylor and Jonathon D. Brown, "Positive Illusions and Well-Being Revisited: Separating Fact from Fiction," *Psychological Bulletin* 116, no. 1 (1994): 22.

[54] Ibid., 25.

[55] See Chihiro Kobayashi, "Relationships among Self- and Other-Positive Illusions and Social Adaptation," *Japanese Journal of Interpersonal and Social Psychology*, no. 2 (2002).

[56] V. S. Y. Kwan, M. H. Bond, and T. M. Singelis, "Pancultural Explanations for Life Satisfaction: Adding Relationship Harmony to Self-Esteem," *Journal of Personality and Social Psychology* 73 (1997).

[57] Dominic D. P. Johnson, *Overconfidence and War: The Havoc and Glory of Positive Illusions* (Cambridge: Harvard University Press, 2004); Dominic D. P. Johnson, Richard W. Wrangham, and Stephen Peter Rosen, "Is Military Incompetence Adaptive? An Empirical Test with Risk-Taking Behaviour in Modern Warfare," *Evolution and Human Behavior* 23 (2002)

[58] On the ability of decisionmakers to overcome such biases, see Jane Kellett Cramer, "9/11, Exaggerating Threats and the Poverty of Psychological Theories for Explaining National Misperceptions" (paper presented at the International Studies Association Annual Meeting, Portland, Oregon, February 2003), 12.

[59] Taylor and Brown, "Positive Illusions," 22.

choose doctrines for budgetary reasons or factors particular to a local strategic geography.[60]

In short, unfamiliar doctrines are hard to understand and easy to denigrate as inferior. Of course, strategic coercion or coercive diplomacy can fail for many reasons other than miscommunication. (A prime example is where both sides care deeply and irreconcilably about a particular issue.) However, as shown in the rest of the book, misperception as a source of failure has been historically important.

*Opacity, Inflation, and Underestimation*

Each of those seven factors suggests how differences in theories of victory could lead to misperceptions regarding an adversary's military power, and most specifically further support the underestimation component of the DDM hypothesis. Of course, no variable explains all outcomes, and thus underestimation will not always occur in the context of doctrinal differences; sometimes other outcomes may result from other causes. For instance, the effects of "motivated bias" may dominate.[61] Thus, in the 1970s and 1980s, opacity between the United States and the Soviet Union permitted elements of the U.S. military to inflate the Soviet threat.[62] Although opacity might make such threat inflation easier, when organizations are strongly motivated to exaggerate a threat they will often find a way to do so, regardless of the clarity with which analysts might see the world.[63]

Similarly, some argue that there is a systemic pressure in international relations toward reliance on worst-case analyses.[64] Worst-case analyses might be

---

[60] The first two rationales are less likely to play a role in such cases; first, states are not likely to discount innovation in others if their own failure to innovate is due primarily to their own budgetary constraints. Second, the organization might feel less of a need to oversell its own innovation if it was forced to innovate by material constraints. The other five rationales for doctrinal difference leading to overconfidence will still hold in these cases.

[61] "Motivated biases refer to individuals' psychological needs to maintain their own emotional well-being and to avoid fear, shame, guilt, and stress… [they] generate perceptions based on needs, desires, or interests." Jack S. Levy, "Political Psychology and Foreign Policy," in *Oxford Handbook of Political Psychology*, ed. David O. Sears, Leonie Huddy, and Robert Jervis (New York: Oxford University Press, 2003), 268.

[62] Posen, "Measuring the European Conventional Balance."

[63] Chaim Kaufman, "Threat Inflation and the Failure of the Marketplace of Ideas: The Selling of the Iraq War," *International Security* 29, no. 1 (2004); Jane Kellett Cramer, "National Security Panics: Overestimating Threats to National Security," PhD diss., Massachusetts Institute of Technology, 2002; Stephen Van Evera, *Causes of War: Power and the Roots of Conflict* (Ithaca: Cornell University Press, 1999), chapter 6.

[64] John J. Mearsheimer, *The Tragedy of Great Power Politics* (New York: W. W. Norton and Company, 2001).

prudent in an uncertain and anarchic world, leading toward overestimation of an adversary. This too can be thought of as a form of "motivated bias."

This study has not been designed to assess the relative impacts of motivated bias toward threat inflation, nor of the organizational and cognitive-based hypothesis leading to underestimation, nor of scores of other variables. Threat inflation is clearly an important problem, but it is not the sole source of inadvertent international conflict. Thus, this book merely aims to sketch out a plausibility probe of one of the less studied of these factors: the way in which differences in theories of victory may lead to persistent underestimations of the adversary.

*Historical Examples of DDM*

An example of the phenomenon described by the DDM hypothesis occurred in the early part of World War II, as the United States considered how to face Germany on the plains of Europe. Its beliefs led to a set of policy decisions that, when it came to battle, would prove disastrous:

> The belief that tank vs. tank combat could be avoided, combined with a continuing stress on mobility, led to an almost complete reliance on medium tanks.... Light tanks were of little use on the modern battlefield.... American doctrine had no place for slow, heavy tanks that could take on German Panthers and Tigers. Although it was recognized that Sherman medium tanks would be unequal to German heavy tanks in a fight, official policy held that such combat was a matter of choice not necessity.... The fact was that [in actual battle] tanks *did* fight tanks, and the U.S. tanks were not very good at it.[65]

Even though the United States had engaged Tigers (Panzer Mark VI) as early as 1943 in Tunisia, only after defeat at the Battle of the Bulge in 1945 did it begin experimenting with heavier tanks on the battlefield.[66]

The United States had doctrinal problems in this period as well. The U.S. Army had been slow to accept a role for an independent armor force. As late as 1939, official doctrine stated, "As a rule, tanks are employed to assist the advance of infantry foot troops, either preceding or accompanying the

---

[65] Elman, "Logic of Emulation," 102–3.
[66] Jonathan M. House, *Combined Arms Warfare in the Twentieth Century* (Lawrence: University Press of Kansas, 2001), chapter 5, "The Complexity of Total War, 1942–45." For a discussion of the costs of a doctrine emphasizing maneuver and lighter tanks late in the war, see Johnson, *Fast Tanks and Heavy Bombers*, part 4: "Dying for Change, 1942–1945."

infantry assault echelon."[67] Before the 1941 Louisiana Maneuvers (a training exercise regarded as a seminal point in U.S. doctrinal innovation), armor was an integral part of cavalry or infantry units.[68] Even some officers who would later be identified with armor breakthrough battles still firmly supported horse cavalry in 1940.[69]

The sad result was, simply put, "the Germans destroyed a lot of American tanks."[70] In this case, the American theory of victory, manifested in weapons purchases and doctrine, led to an underestimation of the enemy that resulted in substantial losses and casualties.

As Napoleon weighed his strategy against the British at the dawn of the nineteenth century, he too made a number of underestimations that can be attributed to the vast differences between British and French approaches to warfare. Sea power had many advantages at the time: "six times as many guns of much heavier caliber could be transported daily by Nelson's fleet as by Napoleon's army, at one-fifth of the logistic cost and at five times the speed."[71] Napoleon's inability to grasp British prowess at naval warfare repeatedly caused him to overestimate his own capabilities relative to the British. In 1805 his "grandiose plan"[72] to invade England had many problems that stemmed from his limited understanding of naval affairs:

> Although Napoleon could impose a ruthlessly enforced timetable for the grand army's marches from Boulogne to Austerlitz, he could not so order the movements of wind driven ships. The ocean was not the "drill-ground" he assumed it to be and his plan took little account of the difficulties of evading the blockading British.[73]

---

[67] Quoted in George S. Patton and Martin Blumenson, *The Patton Papers, 1885–1940* (Boston: Houghton Mifflin, 1972), 1048.

[68] For discussion of this period, see Jonathan M. House, *Toward Combined Arms Warfare: A Survey of 20th-Century Tactics, Doctrine, and Organization* (Fort Leavenworth, Kan.: U.S. Army Command and General Staff College, 1985); Johnson, *Fast Tanks and Heavy Bombers.*

[69] Patton was one of these. See Patton and Blumenson, *Patton Papers, 1885–1940,* especially 1034.

[70] Elman, "Logic of Emulation," 103.

[71] John Keegan, *The Price of Admiralty: The Evolution of Naval Warfare* (New York: Viking, 1989), 48.

[72] David Gates, *The Napoleonic Wars, 1803–1815* (New York: Arnold Publishing, 1997), 103.

[73] Richard Woodman, *The Sea Warriors: Fighting Captains and Frigate Warfare in the Age of Nelson* (New York: Carroll and Graf, 2001), 173–74. Similarly, Keegan writes: "Napoleon the general might have found ways of defying winter on land....Napoleon the admiral could not command the waters." Keegan, *Price of Admiralty,* 20.

The scope of Napoleon's resulting defeat became legendary: "Trafalgar was, in short, a massacre."[74]

## DOCTRINAL-DIFFERENCE ESCALATION (DDE) HYPOTHESIS

The examples just stated highlight the influence of doctrinal and strategic thinking on power assessments; they illustrate the first hypothesis (DDM), linking doctrinal differences to misperception. The doctrinal-difference escalation (DDE) hypothesis suggests the importance of this effect on international security:

> *DDE Hypothesis:* An underestimation of an adversary's capabilities (described by the DDM hypothesis) can lead to failure of deterrence and efforts at coercion, to escalation, and to conflict, because it complicates both assessments of the balance of power and interpretation of the adversary's signals.

The DDE hypothesis explains the ways in which unwarranted optimism leads to war by highlighting two distinct but interacting causal chains. One pertains to capability, the other to intent.

First, underestimation of an adversary's capabilities leads to a misunderstanding of the overall military balance (the first element of the DDE hypothesis). As Jervis notes, "Since the interpretation of indices depends on theories, perceivers are likely to go astray when these are incorrect."[75] This can lead the underestimating nation to think that it is stronger than it really is. As a result, that nation may pursue more assertive policies than it would have if it had correctly estimated its adversary's capabilities. This false optimism could lead to failures of strategic coercion and unnecessary conflict, as shown by a large body of work on the causes of war.[76]

Second, when a nation underestimates an adversary's capabilities, the signals that the adversary sends that emphasize its own capabilities will seem weak: this is the second component of the DDE hypothesis. An adversary's warship steaming into one's own harbor may send a clear signal to a state with a background in naval warfare, but to states with no such

---

[74] Keegan, *Price of Admiralty*, 100. See also Tom Pocock, *The Terror before Trafalgar: Nelson, Napoleon, and the Secret War* (New York: W.W. Norton and Company, 2003), 90 and 95.

[75] Robert Jervis, "Signaling and Perception: Drawing Inferences and Projecting Images," in *Political Psychology*, ed. Kristen R. Monroe (Mahwah, N.J.: Lawrence Erlbaum Associates, 2002), 304.

[76] See the second footnote in the previous chapter.

background, the meaning is less clear. Nations often use such military signals to communicate the depth of their interests, hoping or expecting that they convey a message with powerful clarity.[77] This clarity may often be overestimated.[78] When a nation has an inaccurate view about the efficacy of the adversary's forces and strategies, military signals indicating depth of interest will be harder to interpret.

Both causal chains—misperceptions of the overall military balance and miscommunications of the depth of one side's interest—can result in the failure of coercive diplomacy. Moreover, they may interact: states expect their adversaries to make decisions based on cost-benefit analyses, and this expectation will affect a state's understanding of the other state's intent. Intentions always must be informed by the costs and benefits of pursuing specific goals, but each side makes such cost-benefit calculations using its own theory of victory. If state A thinks, based on its own doctrinally laden view of their relative capability, that state B must believe that a particular conflict will lead to B's own destruction, then state A may expect restraint by B; this is a judgment about B's intent. However, B will actually use its own theory of victory, which might be different, to make that determination of their relative capabilities.

When strategic coercion fails, violence may result, as states follow through on their deterrent or compellent threats. Thus, the DDE hypothesis predicts the potential militarization of a crisis or escalation of an existing conflict.[79]

### Historical Examples of DDE

Examples of this second hypothesis leap from the annals of military history. French and British leaders made no effort to understand how or why German thinking might differ from theirs prior to the outbreak of World War II.[80] Similarly, Gen. Heinz Guderian provides an example of inferring the intent of the adversary through the lens of one's own doctrine:

---

[77] Arquilla, "Louder Than Words," 157 and 163. See also Downs and Rocke, *Tacit Bargaining*.
[78] See for instance the various misperceptions surround Nixon's bomber alert as described in William Burr and Jeffrey Kimball, "Nixon's Secret Nuclear Alert: Vietnam War Diplomacy and the Joint Chiefs of Staff Readiness Test, October 1969," *Cold War History* 3, no. 2 (2003): 113–56.
[79] For examples of the link between failures of coercive diplomacy and war, see Alexander L. George and Richard Smoke, *Deterrence in American Foreign Policy: Theory and Practice* (New York: Columbia University Press, 1974); Alexander L. George and William E. Simons, *The Limits of Coercive Diplomacy*, 2nd ed. (Boulder, Colo.: Westview Press, 1994); Paul W. Schroeder, "Failed Bargain Crises, Deterrence, and the International System," in *Perspectives on Deterrence*, ed. Paul C. Stern et al. (New York: Oxford University Press, 1989).
[80] May, *Strange Victory*, 480.

So far as the French leaders were concerned, we were amazed that they had not taken advantage of their favorable situation during the autumn of 1939 to attack, while the bulk of the German forces, including the entire armored force, was engaged in Poland. Their reasons for such restraint were at the time hard to see. We could only guess. Be that as it may, the caution shown by the French leaders led us to believe that our adversaries hoped somehow to avoid a serious clash of arms.[81]

Guderian thus inferred French intent or motivation from French action, but the French inaction actually seems to have been based on the French theory of victory, which neglected the offensive potential of blitzkrieg warfare. A policy taken primarily because of a particular doctrine (France's failure to assess the potential danger of blitzkrieg and its faith in the Maginot Line) communicated a mistaken view to Germany that France intended to avoid conflict.

## PARALLEL AND RELATED ARGUMENTS

There is some existing work that is related to the approach taken in this book. Closest to the approach taken here, John Mearsheimer has examined how one specific novel doctrine—the blitzkrieg—caused unwarranted optimism and deterrence failure.[82] By extending this beyond a single particular doctrine, this book builds on those insights to provide a more comprehensive approach to the relationship between any two doctrines and perception.

A number of political scientists have suggested arguments that reinforce those I am making in this book, but none make it their focus theoretically or empirically. For instance, Richard Betts's critique of rationality in international security notes the tension of "culture versus coercion": "coercive strategies aimed at an adversary's will depend on communication. Cultural blinders prevent the common frames of reference necessary to ensure that the receiver hears the message that the signaler intends to send."[83] At a more general level, Jervis notes that "perception is laden with interpretation and theory. Almost no inferences—perhaps none at all—are self-evident in the sense that all people under all circumstances looking at the information

---

[81] General Heinz Guderian, *Panzer Leader* (Cambridge, Mass.: DaCapo Press, 1996), 97.
[82] Mearsheimer, *Conventional Deterrence*.
[83] Richard K. Betts, "Is Strategy an Illusion?" *International Security* 25, no. 2 (2000): 28–29.

would draw the same conclusion. Thus knowing how theorists read a signal does not tell us how the perceiver does."[84]

Eliot Cohen argues that different concepts of operation and strategies led American analysts to underestimate the dangers posed by the Soviet Red Army.[85] More generally, Thomas Mahnken notes that intelligence bureaucracies tend to focus on existing doctrine and weapons and thereby miss the implications of innovation and change in potential adversaries.[86] John Arquilla notes that continental powers engaging in land-sea wars have often misperceived significant aspects of their conflict with one another.[87] Mark Haas highlights the difficulties posed by broader ideological differences between great powers.[88] Jonathan Shimshoni points out that states that rely on qualitative advantages and surprise will have a particularly difficult time deterring their adversaries; they cannot enhance the credibility of their threats by pointing out their own military advantages, because doing so would erode their prospects for surprise.[89]

Lastly, the argument in this book builds on elements of some strategic cultural work. This broad literature incorporates arguments regarding the role of strategic culture, civil-military culture, and organizational culture in international security issues.[90] (The study of Chinese foreign policy has yielded some of the best insights of this work.[91]) Seeking to build the level of positivist rigor that characterizes the best scholarship on strategic culture and constructivism,[92] this book focuses on one particular ideational

---

[84] Jervis, "Signaling and Perception," 298.

[85] Eliot A. Cohen, "Toward Better Net Assessment: Rethinking the European Conventional Balance," *International Security* 13, no. 1 (1988). See also vigorous rebuttals and Cohen's reply in John J. Mearsheimer, Barry R. Posen, and Eliot A. Cohen, "Reassessing Net Assessment," *International Security* 13, no. 4 (1989).

[86] Mahnken, *Uncovering Ways of War.*

[87] Arquilla, *Dubious Battles.*

[88] Mark L. Haas, *The Ideological Origins of Great Power Politics, 1789–1989* (Ithaca: Cornell University Press, 2005).

[89] Shimshoni, *Israel and Conventional Deterrence.*

[90] Scobell suggests these three components of cultural studies (and also includes political culture). Scobell, *China's Use of Military Force,* 4–8. For useful reviews of the entire literature on strategic culture, see Theo Farrell, "Culture and Military Power," *Review of International Studies* 24, no. 3 (1998); Jeffrey S. Lantis, "Strategic Culture and National Security Policy," *International Studies Review* 4, no. 3 (2002).

[91] See, for instance, Alastair Iain Johnston, *Cultural Realism: Strategic Culture and Grand Strategy in Chinese History* (Princeton: Princeton University Press, 1995); Zhang Shuguang, *Deterrence and Strategic Culture: Chinese-American Confrontations, 1949–1958* (Ithaca: Cornell University Press, 1992); Scobell, *China's Use of Military Force.*

[92] For a forceful argument, see Alastair Iain Johnston, "Thinking about Strategic Culture," *International Security* 19, no. 4 (1995). But also see Colin S. Gray, "Strategic Culture as

construct—doctrine—and examines how it plays a role in shaping perceptions and outcomes. As I have argued elsewhere, this "organizational culture" variant within the full range of strategic cultural work is likely to prove
most valuable to scholars and practitioners alike.[93]

Doctrinal-difference theory advances all these strains of the scholarly literature. It examines a source of false optimism and explains how to reduce
it. It fleshes out the understudied aspect of "communication" in strategic
coercion. It takes a rigorous approach to the role of (one specific form of)
culture in shaping foreign policy perceptions. Finally, it essentially implement's Jervis' recommendation for scholars and policy makers to

> look at the image an actor is trying to project, the behaviors that it
> adopts to do so, and then, shifting attention to the perceiver, examine
> what influences the perceiver and what inferences it draws. At the next
> stage we can see what the perceiver thinks it must do in order to send
> the desired message in response, what it does to reach this goal, and
> how the actor in turn both judges the other's behavior and determines
> how the other perceived its behavior. I suspect it is rare for actors, espe-
> cially adversaries, to understand the situation the same way, to be able
> to discern how the other sees them and their behavior, or even to know
> what signals are taken to be most important.[94]

## RESEARCH METHODOLOGY

The argument of doctrinal-difference theory is that, if there is a difference
in theories of victory then both sides are likely to make mistakes in their perceptions of each other's military power. This can lead each side to underestimate its adversary's overall power, and to underestimate the signals that the
other sends using its capabilities. Figure 2.1 illustrates this causal chain. This

Context: The First Generation of Theory Strikes Back," *Review of International Studies* 25,
no. 1 (1999). More generally, see Ted Hopf, *Social Construction of International Politics: Identities
and Foreign Policies, Moscow, 1955 and 1999* (Ithaca: Cornell University Press, 2002); Peter J.
Katzenstein, ed., *The Culture of National Security: Norms and Identity in World Politics* (New York:
Columbia University Press, 1996).

[93] Christopher P. Twomey, "Lacunae in the Study of Culture in International Security,"
*Contemporary Security Policy* 29, no. 2 (2008). On "organizational culture," see Scobell, *China's
Use of Military Force*, 7–8.

[94] Jervis, "Signaling and Perception," 310. Jervis notes the empirical challenges and the relatively few empirical examples of work that have pursued such a time-consuming research
strategy.

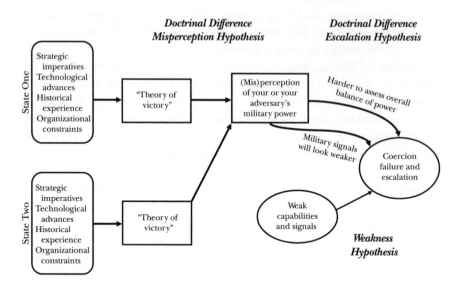

**Figure 2.1.** Doctrinal differences, misperception, and escalation.

book tests the doctrinal-difference misperception (DDM) hypothesis and the doctrinal-difference escalation (DDE) hypothesis, using several cases. It also tests an alternative, the Weakness Hypothesis.

This section outlines several aspects of the research methodology, discusses specific empirical predictions of the general theoretical hypotheses, and considers alternate explanations, the manner in which each case is approached, and criteria for coding the independent variable in each case.

## PREDICTIONS

The two hypotheses lead to eleven specific predictions of what evidence we could expect to see in the empirical record as indicators of the validity of the theory. They are grouped here into predictions about four categories: perceptions of the balance of power and the nature of war; signaling and intent; surprise; and extreme values and outcomes.

### Perceptions of the Balance of Power and the Nature of War

We should expect to see that perceptions about war and the balance of power exhibit underestimation of the enemy and overconfidence regarding a state's own capability; this is reflected in four specific predictions.

*Misperception Prediction:* If there are differences in theories of victory, then we should expect to see more evidence of states underestimating an adversary's capabilities, while if there are similarities in beliefs, we should more often see states making more accurate assessments of each other's military capabilities.

*Discounting Prediction:* If states have different theories of victory, then we might see evidence that their leaders discount the other side's theory of victory before conflict.

*Superficial Views Prediction:* If states have different theories of victory, then we should not expect to see a state's leaders having many nuanced discussions of the merits of their adversary's strategies, nor acknowledging that their adversary's financial and strategic situations mandate a choice of strategy different from the state's own.

*Doctrinal Confidence Prediction:* We may find evidence that a state believes that battles will be dominated by factors emphasized by its own theory of victory.

### Signaling and Intent Issues

We should expect to see that signaling and judgments about intent are viewed through the lens of a state's own theory of victory.

*Nature of Signaling Prediction:* If a state signals to the other side by use or threat of force, we should expect evidence that each side uses force in ways that accord with its own theory of victory.

*Assessing Intent Prediction:* If opposing states have different theories of victory, then we may find that the first state's assessment of its adversary's intent depends, in part, on its understanding of the adversary's cost-benefit analysis, but that this understanding is likely to be incorrect, because the two states assess costs and benefits differently.

*Downplaying Prediction:* If leaders of states with different theories of victory face off, we may see evidence that each minimizes the likelihood that the other side will get involved in, or will escalate, the conflict.

### When Perceptions Meet Reality: Surprise!

We should expect to see that actors are surprised when reality contradicts their perceptions.

*Startling Battlefield Outcomes Prediction:* If nations have different theories of victory guiding their forces, we may see that actual battle outcomes deviate substantially from leaders' expectations. This might be revealed in several different ways:

a) If one side forced the battle on the other, we may see that the side taking the initiative gets a surprise in the form of difficulties on the battlefield.

b) In cases where both sides pursued battle, we may see evidence that both sides get an unwelcome surprise in the form of battlefield difficulties.

c) More generally, if leaders believe they have a viable strategy in the context of the current conflict, in the event of a battle we should expect to see evidence that they are surprised at the shortcomings of their strategy.

d) Since leaders often have incentives to conceal their surprise, the evidence of surprise might manifest itself as such steps as hasty reinforcing or last-minute changes in strategy.

*Surprise Regarding Intentions Prediction:* We may find evidence that, when an adversary's signaling over an issue has relied on military forces (or military threats) in ways that are different than a state's own strategy, its leaders are surprised about the degree of adversary interest in an issue and may even ascribe aggressive motives to the adversary because of this.

Such surprise is congruent with rational choice literature's understanding battles as a process by which private information is shared between adversaries.[95]

*Extreme Values of Independent Variable Lead to Extreme Indicators*
We may see that extreme values on the independent variable (at either an individual or national level) lead to extreme outcomes.

*Extreme Differences Prediction:* If the differences between the two states' theories of victory are more extreme, we should see evidence of larger or more frequent underestimation of the adversary's capability.

---

[95] Alastair Smith and Allan C. Stam, "Bargaining and the Nature of War," *Journal of Conflict Resolution* 48, no. 6 (2004).

*Depth of Immersion Prediction:* The more a state's political and military leaders are immersed in its own theory of victory, the more likely we are to find evidence that they misperceive and miscalculate.

Investigation of the empirical record in the cases is centered on these predictions; they focus on relatively operationalized factors stemming from the hypotheses, and thus ease the task of assessing the theory's validity. They are summarized in table 2.1. To the extent the evidence in the cases does align with these predictions, doctrinal-difference theory is supported.

TABLE 2.1. THEORY SUMMARY

**Hypotheses**

*Doctrinal Difference Misperception (DDM) Hypothesis*
When two nations have different theories of victory, they will be more likely to misperceive each other's relative capabilities, and these misperceptions will raise the risk of underestimation of the adversary.

*Doctrinal Difference Escalation (DDE) Hypothesis*
An underestimation of an adversary's capabilities (described by the DDM hypothesis) can lead to failure of deterrence and efforts at coercion, to escalation, and to conflict, because it complicates both assessments of the balance of power and interpretation of the adversary's signals.

*Weakness Hypothesis*
Weak capabilities and signals are more likely to lead to failure of coercion attempts and thus to conflict escalation, while strong signals are more likely to lead to success.

**Predictions**

*Perceiving the Balance of Power and the Nature of War*
   1. *Misperception Prediction:* If there are differences in theories of victory, then we should expect to see more evidence of states underestimating an adversary's capabilities, while if there are similarities in beliefs, we should more often see states making more accurate assessments of each other's military capabilities.
   2. *Discounting Prediction:* If states have different theories of victory, then we might see evidence that their leaders discount the other side's theory of victory before conflict.
   3. *Superficial Views Prediction:* If states have different theories of victory, then we should not expect to see a state's leaders having many nuanced discussions of the merits of their adversary's strategies, nor acknowledging that their adversary's financial and strategic situations mandate a choice of strategy different from the state's own.
   4. *Doctrinal Confidence Prediction:* We may find evidence that a state believes that battles will be dominated by factors emphasized by its own theory of victory.

*Signaling and Intent Issues*
   5. *Nature of Signaling Prediction:* If a state signals to the other side by use or threat of force, we should expect evidence that each side uses force in ways that accord with its own theory of victory.

6. *Assessing Intent Prediction:* If opposing states have different theories of victory, then we may find that the first state's assessment of its adversary's intent depends, in part, on its understanding of the adversary's cost-benefit analysis, but that this understanding is likely to be incorrect, because the two states assess costs and benefits differently.

7. *Downplaying Prediction:* If leaders of states with different theories of victory face off, we may see evidence that each minimizes the likelihood that the other side will get involved in, or will escalate, the conflict.

*When Perceptions Meet Reality: Surprise!*

8. *Startling Battlefield Outcomes Prediction:* If nations have different theories of victory guiding their forces, we may see that actual battle outcomes deviate substantially from leaders' expectations. This might be revealed in several different ways:
    a) If one side forced the battle on the other, we may see that the side taking the initiative gets a surprise in the form of difficulties on the battlefield.
    b) In cases where both sides pursued battle, we may see evidence that both sides get an unwelcome surprise in the form of battlefield difficulties.
    c) More generally, if leaders believe they have a viable strategy in the context of the current conflict, in the event of a battle we should expect to see evidence that they are surprised at the shortcomings of their strategy.
    d) Since leaders often have incentives to conceal their surprise, the evidence of surprise might manifest itself as such steps as hasty reinforcing or last-minute changes in strategy.

9. *Surprise Regarding Intentions Prediction:* We may find evidence that, when an adversary's signaling over an issue has relied on military forces (or military threats) in ways that are different than a state's own strategy, its leaders are surprised about the degree of adversary interest in an issue and may even ascribe aggressive motives to the adversary because of this.

*Extreme Values of Independent Variable Lead to Extreme Indicators*

10. *Extreme Differences Prediction:* If the differences between the two states' theories of victory are more extreme, we should see evidence of larger or more frequent underestimation of the adversary's capability.

11. *Depth of Immersion Prediction:* The more a state's political and military leaders are immersed in its own theory of victory, the more likely we are to find evidence that they misperceive and miscalculate.

## ALTERNATIVE EXPLANATIONS: THE WEAKNESS HYPOTHESIS

Existing explanations for failures of strategic coercive attempts can be used to create a baseline for comparison with the proposed theory. If the proposed theory does no better, then it is of no value and existing explanations garner further support. The overall balance of power, the existence of aggressive intent, and the "objective" quality of any signal all provide alternate explanations for bargaining failure leading to deterrence failure and conflict. These three elements represent the most important elements of conventional wisdom about assessing the prospects for success in strategic coercion, and are incorporated in the Weakness Hypothesis:

*Weakness Hypothesis:* Weak capabilities and signals are more likely to lead to failure of coercion attempts and thus to conflict escalation, while strong signals are more likely to lead to successful coercion.

This representation of the basic logic of deterrence encompasses arguments about strength or weakness of the would-be coercer's capabilities (both local and global) as well as the clarity of the signal.

The Weakness Hypothesis is used in this book to evaluate the proposed theory as part of a Lakatosian three-cornered test.[96] Does doctrinal-difference theory allow us to predict coercive failure better than focusing on the "objective" size and quality of the signal alone? (Although it is evaluated as an alternate hypothesis, the proposed theory of doctrinal differences should be thought of as additive rather than strictly alternative. Since common sense suggests that the Weakness Hypothesis has some validity, the question is whether accuracy of explanation and prediction is significantly improved by consideration of the hypotheses suggested here in addition to the Weakness Hypothesis.)

## METHODS AND PROCEDURES

This book uses congruence tests, process tracing within the cases, and the method of differences across the cases to evaluate the hypotheses from doctrinal-difference theory, the Weakness Hypothesis, and associated predictions. Predictions derived from the hypotheses allow for detailed process tracing to assess the causal force of the theory through examination of leaders' statements, policies implemented, and reactions to the adversary's behavior. The cases characterize macro-level outcomes, along with tracing the micro-level processes by which the outcomes occur, to judge whether these correspond with the theory's predictions. The data requirements for this methodology are thus substantial.

After a brief summary of the relevant history, each case study begins with an evaluation of the two nations' beliefs regarding doctrine and effective

---

[96] Imre Lakatos, "Falsification and the Methodology of Scientific Research Programmes," in *Criticism and the Growth of Knowledge,* ed. Imre Lakatos and Alan Musgrave (Cambridge: Cambridge University Press, 1970).

military strategies. Drawing on existing work on strategic beliefs and doctrine, the cases use contemporaneous writings on strategy, tactics, and doctrine, as well as the makeup of military forces, to code the independent variable. Also, attention is paid to the degree to which each side understood the adversary's doctrine.

Next, each case assesses the signaling involved in a particular period: What was the nature of the signaling? Did it depend on implicit or explicit threats of the use of force? Was the signal in question easily comprehensible to the other side? Then each case seeks to assess the interpretation of the signals. How well were the signals interpreted? Did the responder's theory of victory impede interpretation?

Finally, evidence is examined that is relevant to either side's postevent evaluation, after the attempt at strategic coercion fails or succeeds. Was either side surprised by the difficulties its forces faced or about the degree of opposition from its opponent? These questions, suggested by the predictions section above, help to ascertain the accuracy and usefulness of the theory in these cases.

## CODING DIFFERENCES IN THEORIES OF VICTORY (THE INDEPENDENT VARIABLE)

Theories of victory are likely to vary across nations and across time. The various sources of doctrine discussed above are one set of influences; additionally, of course, nations' goals or national interests differ. In order to describe the difference between any two theories of victory (that is, the independent variable for the doctrinal-difference misperception hypothesis), it is useful to be familiar with the range of possible beliefs at a general level.

For this purpose, many factors can be used to compare nations' theories of victory. One dimension is the makeup of the forces: Are the components of the two nations' forces similar? Do both have an air force, for instance? If so, do they have similar mixes of fighters and bombers? Several dimensions are useful in coding, such as manpower-based versus technology-based or machine-based (labor versus capital); maneuver versus firepower and fortifications; preferences for quantity over quality; emphasis on one service over another; or reliance on particular platforms within services.

A second dimension looks at the military doctrine and tactics planned for using a given set of forces. For example, a force made up of approximately eighty divisions with some 2,500 to 3,000 tanks might concentrate its tanks, or it might spread them out across its whole army.[97] A doctrine might emphasize flanking maneuvers or head-on attacks, mobility versus positional warfare. The preference of one side might be for offensive strategies or for defensive ones.[98] One force might be optimized to inflict attrition on an adversary across a front, while another might aim to secure and exploit a breakthrough.[99] Another dimension would look to the political goals that military force is aimed to advance: Will victory be secured by reducing the relative power of the adversary's military, or is it the intention to punish the adversary's society and economy?[100]

Answers to questions such as these then characterize the differences in theories of victory in each case. Other elements may also sometimes play a role. The potential variation is very large. At different periods and in different theaters, some distinctions are more important than others. Furthermore, doctrines central in peacetime, and therefore in signaling in the lead up to war, may be thrown out once conflict breaks out. Still, it is the doctrine in existence during the signaling and interpretation periods that is most important to the success or failure of strategic coercion.

Writings on strategy, tactics, and doctrine, as well as the makeup of both sides' military forces, are used to evaluate and characterize the differences between two nations' theories. Even in authoritarian countries, a significant amount of material on such doctrinal and strategic debates is available.[101] Those sources, as well as some declassified (or leaked) documents, are used.[102]

---

[97] This was the case for the two sides in the opening days of World War II in Western Europe. On May 10, 1940, on the Western Front, the British and the French together deployed 3,074 tanks, while Germany deployed 2,439; the allies deployed 93 first-line divisions, the Germans 76. May, *Strange Victory*, 477–78.

[98] For arguments on this point, see Posen, *Sources of Military Doctrine*; Snyder, *Ideology of the Offensive*; Stephen Van Evera, "The Cult of the Offensive and the Origins of the First World War," in *Military Strategy and the Origins of the First World War*, ed. Steven E. Miller, Sean M. Lynn-Jones, and Stephen Van Evera (Princeton: Princeton University Press, 1991).

[99] See Mearsheimer, *Conventional Deterrence*, 67–133.

[100] This dimension is similar to the concept of a grand strategy. See Posen, *Sources of Military Doctrine*, 13.

[101] This was the case even for the Soviet Union during the peak of the Cold War. "Careful sifting of a very rich open Soviet military literature can contribute great[ly] to [the study of Soviet concepts of operations]. Senior Soviet officers, in far larger numbers than their Western counterparts, write reams of history and contemporary military analysis. Despite the stultifying and false character of their ideological framework, which makes these works tiresome to read and frequently hard to accept, they merit study." Cohen, "Toward Better Net Assessment," 12.

[102] For Chinese sources, the translations are my own unless otherwise noted.

Having described the main hypotheses of doctrinal-difference theory and the kinds of evidence that would support them, we turn to the first set of cases, those involving efforts at deterrence using military signaling by the United States and China during the Korean War. The next chapter addresses the independent variable, by outlining the two sides' differing theories of victory.

# PART II

# CHINESE AND
# AMERICAN PUZZLES

# 3

# COMPARING THEORIES OF VICTORY

## FACING OFF OVER KOREA

THE CENTRAL PAIR OF CASES in this book examines crucial turning points in the Korean War: the U.S. decision to cross the 38th parallel
into North Korea (chapter 4) and Mao Zedong's decision to cross the Yalu
River to meet the American forces (chapter 5). Both cases involve a similar
assessment of the two sides' military capabilities. For simplicity, therefore,
this chapter examines the independent variable that applies to both chapter
4 and chapter 5: the differences between the two sides' theories of victory on
land. (The third case, Mao's decision not to attack Taiwan in that same year,
involves a rather different military calculation, and so the independent variable is treated entirely separately in chapter 6.)

In this chapter I begin with an examination of American thinking about
military effectiveness, turn to China's views, and then contrast the two. I
conclude by examining how each side viewed the other's doctrine and sum-
marize the very large differences between the two countries' theories, thus
making explicit the coding or characterization of doctrinal differences for
this period to derive the independent variable for the cases discussed in
chapter 4 and 5.

## THE U.S. THEORY OF VICTORY ON LAND

The general American theory of victory in 1950 centered primarily on the
use of strategic bombing and atomic weapons in a general war context.

Additionally, American strategic thought emphasized the utility of tactical airpower, mechanized forces, and combined arms in the event of conventional war.

## STRATEGIC BOMBING IN GENERAL...

One of the key beliefs of American policymakers was the perceived effectiveness of strategic bombing in general. This view had its roots to the pre–World War II era and had changed little over time:

> An understanding of American air power and of the problem of aerial warfare can be achieved only in the context of cultural and intellectual history. The ways people have thought about air power proved so remarkably consistent, despite rapidly changing technology over a half-century, that a mere recital of a particular invention or an individual bombing raid sheds little light on the appeals and uses of air power. The bomber in imagination is the most compelling and revealing story.[1]

The lessons taken from World War II hardened this belief: "Immediately after the war, it appeared relatively certain that strategic bombing would be an integral part of any proper military effort."[2] This perception came out of the "formative common experience" held by senior military leaders from the previous world war.[3] The U.S. Strategic Bombing Survey, conducted at the behest of President Roosevelt, came to a simple, sweeping conclusion: "Allied air power was decisive in the war in Western Europe."[4] Indeed, even aside from atomic weapons, the Air Force continued to foresee an important role for *conventional* strategic bombing: "Many targets were not appropriate for scarce and expensive atomic weapons anyway, and a requirement would

---

[1] The consistency and causal importance of these beliefs is the story told in Michael S. Sherry, *The Rise of American Air Power: The Creation of Armageddon* (New Haven: Yale University Press, 1987), x. See also Robert Pape, *Bombing to Win: Air Power and Coercion in War* (Ithaca: Cornell University Press, 1996), chapters 4 and 8; Tami Davis Biddle, *Rhetoric and Reality in Air Warfare: The Evolution of British and American Ideas about Strategic Bombing, 1914–1945* (Princeton: Princeton University Press, 2002).

[2] Christopher M. Gacek, *The Logic of Force: The Dilemma of Limited War in American Foreign Policy* (New York: Columbia University Press, 1994), 31.

[3] Michael Howard, as quoted in ibid., 30–31.

[4] *United States Strategic Bombing Survey, Summary Report (European War)* (Washington, D.C.: United States Government Printing Office, September 30, 1945), 16. The report on the Pacific War was similarly positive. *United States Strategic Bombing Survey, Summary Report (Pacific War)* (Washington, D.C.: United States Government Printing Office, July 1, 1946).

continue for conventional bombing forces."[5] The utility of conventional strategic bombing in a campaign against China was thought to be high.[6]

### ...AND ATOMIC WEAPONS SPECIFICALLY

Integral to and intertwined with the beliefs regarding the efficacy of strategic bombing was a confidence in the utility of atomic weapons. The Hiroshima and Nagasaki bombs had important effects on American thinking about the usefulness of nuclear weapons: "The advent of atomic weapons and the image of the mushroom cloud surely strengthened the vague perception that strategic bombing would remain a deadly aspect of war."[7] This thoroughly permeated national security thinking at the time.[8]

> Strategic bombing with atomic weapons had been at the core of U.S. war plans ever since the military began thinking seriously about the prospects of armed conflict with the Soviet Union.... Comparatively, atomic weapons were cheap, and Truman accepted plans and approved budgets that made the United States dependent on their use should war erupt.[9]

The Joint Outline Emergency War Plan of October 1949 called for attacks on over a hundred Soviet cities, using multiple weapons on most, with a reserve of over seventy weapons.[10] Similarly, long-term planning in 1949 was based on the presumption that nuclear weapons would be at the center of warfare:

> At the close of 1949 the Joint Staff drew up Dropshot, a long-term procurement plan for a hypothetical war in 1957.... Dropshot proposed ending the war as soon as possible, and that meant a massive atomic campaign. It proposed up to 435 atomic bombs for use in the first

---

[5] Conrad C. Crane, *American Airpower Strategy in Korea, 1950–1953* (Lawrence: University Press of Kansas, 2000), 16–17.

[6] "Memorandum by Mr. John P. Davies, Jr., of the Policy Planning Staff," August 24, 1949, in *FRUS, 1949*, vol. IX: *The Far East: China* (Washington, DC: U.S. GPO, 1974), esp. 538.

[7] Gacek, *Logic of Force*, 31.

[8] McGeorge Bundy, *Danger and Survival: Choices about the Bomb in the First Fifty Years* (New York: Random House, 1988), 230; Biddle, *Rhetoric and Reality in Air Warfare*, 293–97.

[9] Melvyn P. Leffler, *A Preponderance of Power: National Security, the Truman Administration, and the Cold War* (Stanford: Stanford University Press, 1992), 323.

[10] David Alan Rosenberg, "The Origins of Overkill: Nuclear Weapons and American Strategy, 1945–1960," *International Security* 7, no. 4 (1983): 16.

month against industrial and military targets in the Soviet Union and its satellites.[11]

The Navy was trying to secure a role for itself in delivering nuclear weapons as a way to ensure its relevance for the defense of the country.[12] Even Army generals were insisting that retaliatory strategic bombing should be central to American plans at this time.[13] This emphasis on nuclear exchanges prevented consideration of other forms of warfare:

> Some kind of air-atomic war dominated strategic thinking, and all the more so with the continued slashing of nonatomic forces. The Joint Chiefs gave no attention to any strategic alternatives. For instance, they never took up a State Department view in 1948 and 1949 that the United States should have highly mobile divisions to fight limited wars of containment, not atomic wars of annihilation or conquest.[14]

A survey of American doctrine of the Korean War period concluded, "Americans, including the government, succeed[ed] in convincing themselves that the atomic bomb was a sovereign remedy for all military ailments."[15]

The American arsenal was large.[16] At its core were 369 atomic warheads, which could be loaded rapidly on long-range bombers.[17] Completion of the

---

[11] George W. Baer, *One Hundred Years of Sea Power: The U.S. Navy, 1890–1990* (Stanford: Stanford University Press, 1994), 313. The war game focused on 1957, not 1950, but it was conducted in 1949, and so it does illustrate the thinking about what constituted important weapons on the eve of the Korean War from the perspective of the American military leadership.

[12] Ibid., 296–97. However, contrary arguments were also being made within the Navy at the time. See Baer, *One Hundred Years of Sea Power*, 304.

[13] William Whitney Stueck Jr., *The Road to Confrontation: American Policy toward China and Korea, 1947–1950* (Chapel Hill: University of North Carolina Press, 1981), 155–56.

[14] Baer, *One Hundred Years of Sea Power*, 302–3.

[15] Russell F. Weigley, *The American Way of War: A History of United States Military Strategy and Policy* (Bloomington: Indiana University Press, 1977), 382 and more generally on this point, see chapter 15, "The Atomic Revolution."

[16] On the tendency of American military and strategic leaders to regard any size arsenal as too small, see Rosenberg, "Origins of Overkill." An arsenal of several hundred weapons has been regarded as more than adequate for a number of nuclear powers over the past several decades. See Avery Goldstein, *Deterrence and Security in the 21st Century: China, Britain, France, and the Enduring Legacy of the Nuclear Revolution* (Stanford: Stanford University Press, 2000).

[17] The Natural Resources Defense Council website, www.nrdc.org, has historical data on both American and Soviet nuclear arsenals. Although the precise month of this figure (369 warheads) is not apparent from the NRDC database, the previous year's figure (of 235 warheads) suggests that a significant arsenal existed throughout 1950. Similarly, Leffler suggests an arsenal of "a little under 300 in June 1950." Leffler, *A Preponderance of Power*, 324. The DOE

"Sandstone" research program had increased the efficiency of the atomic bombs, so the United States could produce 63 percent more warheads with the same stockpile of fissile material; this led to a surge in the quantity of bombs.[18] Further, "by January 1949 actual and foreseen shortages of bombers and bombs had begun to be alleviated."[19] Overall, the Strategic Air Command (SAC) was beginning to improve across the board on its late 1940s position in integration of capabilities: "By 1950, the command operated 225 atomic bomb carrying aircraft (including B-29s, B-50s, and 34 B-36s), flew 263 combat ready crews, and was training forty-nine more. Eighteen bomb assembly teams were fully qualified, and four would be added by June."[20]

Even pessimists were forced to conclude that by August 1949, "Strategic Air Command began to achieve a measure of deterrent capability."[21] Nevertheless, by January 31, 1950, President Truman had decided to move forward even further in this area by publicly beginning research on the thermonuclear bomb.[22]

Atomic strategy at this point focused on strategic bombing rather than tactical battlefield attacks. Although development of large artillery guns that could deliver atomic weapons had begun in late 1949, these and other tactical weapons were not available in significant numbers until mid-1952.[23] Nevertheless, the tactical use of nuclear weapons had also been considered and studied. Atomic weapons were in many cases expected to substitute for shortfalls in conventional armament.[24] For instance, one study "led the JCS to task the Strategic Air Command in the fall of 1949 with the 'retardation

---

provides similar, although slightly smaller, numbers. It lists 170 weapons available in 1949 and 299 in 1950, and also notes that there were 264 warheads built in 1950, and some 135 warheads retired (which includes weapons taken out of service to be modified into more efficient designs in subsequent years). The total megatonnage available in 1950 was just under 10 megatons. See "DOE Facts: Summary of Declassified Nuclear Stockpile Information," Department of Energy, Office of the Press Secretary, Washington, DC (1994) available online at http://www.osti.gov/html/osti/opennet/document/press/pc26.html.

[18] Richard Rhodes, *Dark Sun: The Making of the Hydrogen Bomb* (New York: Simon and Schuster, 1995), 320; Gacek, *Logic of Force*, 33.

[19] Ibid. Rosenberg contrasts the period from 1945 through 1948, when weapons and delivery systems were scarce, to the period after 1949 when those limitations relaxed significantly. Rosenberg, "Origins of Overkill."

[20] Harry R. Borowski, *A Hollow Threat: Strategic Air Power and Containment before Korea* (Westport, Conn.: Greenwood Press, 1982), 191.

[21] Ibid., 187.

[22] Bundy, *Danger and Survival*, 197.

[23] Mark A. Ryan, *Chinese Attitudes toward Nuclear Weapons: China and the United States during the Korean War* (Armonk, N.Y.: M. E. Sharpe, 1989), 141, 138.

[24] Steven L. Rearden, *The Formative Years, 1947–1950*, vol. 1 (Washington, D.C.: Historical Office Office of the Secretary of Defense, 1984), 445.

of Soviet advances in Western Europe.'"[25] Further, once the Korean War broke out, atomic use was repeatedly discussed.[26] When General of the Army Douglas MacArthur, the battlefield commander, proposed using nuclear weapons in December 1950, he sent to Washington "a list of retardation targets which he considered would require 26 bombs . . . [including] 4 bombs to be used on invasion forces and 4 bombs to be used on critical concentrations of enemy air power, both targets of opportunity."[27] (Provocatively, some of the other "retardation targets" apparently included locations within China.)

Thus, U.S. policymakers saw the utility of atomic weapons as ubiquitous.

## GENERAL WAR

Closely related to the emphasis on nuclear weapons at the time was a near-exclusive U.S. focus on general war rather than limited war.[28] Indeed, "a school of detailed writings about limited war did not appear until the 1950s," well into the Korean War.[29] This led American strategists to avoid worrying about how to win a local, limited war of containment (which would very likely have involved a heavy focus on enhancing conventional capabilities) and rather to focus on ensuring that apocalyptic general war would be devastating to the Soviets:

> Having prepared in the late 1940s for general war, the government and the services were caught off guard by the North Korean attack in June. Defense Secretary Louis Johnson admitted in the first top-level conference on the crisis that his department had no war plan for Korea and thus no recommendation. The Joint Chiefs as well did not attempt

[25] Rosenberg, "Origins of Overkill," 16. The arsenal the United States had at the time was far from ideal for this sort of targeting, but the weapons could have been used in a tactical setting, had the president so ordered.

[26] See Roger Dingman, "Atomic Diplomacy during the Korean War," in *Nuclear Diplomacy and Crisis Management,* ed. Stephen Van Evera (Cambridge: MIT Press, 1990), 119, 124 n. 48, and 130–31.

[27] Quoted from an Army archival source (a G-3, or operations, report) in Rosemary Foot, *The Wrong War: American Policy and the Dimensions of the Korean Conflict, 1950–1953* (Ithaca: Cornell University Press, 1985), 114–5. See also Gacek, *Logic of Force,* 58. Ryan, *Chinese Attitudes toward Nuclear Weapons,* 38. The Air Force also felt atomic weapons would have been valuable in an interdiction role during the retreat of the Eighth Army. John W. Dower, *War without Mercy* (New York: Pantheon Books, 1986), 701.

[28] Gacek, *Logic of Force,* chapter 2: "Patterns in America's Use of Force before the Korean War"; Bruce Cumings, *The Origins of the Korean War: The Roaring of the Cataract, 1947–1950,* vol. 2 (Princeton: Princeton University Press, 1981), 161.

[29] Gacek, *Logic of Force,* 37.

formal estimate of the military situation in Korea, and they were not sure what would be required to mount United States military operations in the area.[30]

NSC-68 began to address this by alluding to the prospect of limited wars, but it did not reflect any sophisticated analysis that considered such prospects:[31] "So ingrained was the American habit of thinking of war in terms of annihilative victories, that occasional warnings of limited war went more than unheeded, and people, government, and much of the military could scarcely conceive of a Communist military thrust of lesser dimensions than World War III."[32]

Thus, American strategic thought remained centered on general war.

## HEAVILY ARMED, MECHANIZED U.S. GROUND FORCES

In general U.S. ground-force doctrine, mechanized and combined arms were viewed as optimal for conventional forces. This section describes the *general doctrinal perspective* toward armor and combined arms held by the U.S. military, even though in some geographic areas, U.S. forces would not have had enough equipment to implement that doctrine fully. Nevertheless, the leadership nationwide would be still be indoctrinated by the theory of victory, so it is important to understand its characteristics.

Each of America's eight *infantry* divisions in 1950, according to the standard "table of organization and equipment" (TOE, the list of equipment allotments for generic military units and how they are organized) had 143 tanks.[33] This was only somewhat fewer than the number of tanks deployed in Soviet *armored* units of the same size at the end of World War II.[34] The U.S. Army also had a dedicated armor division, a cavalry division, four armored cavalry

---

[30] Richard K. Betts, *Soldiers, Statesmen, and Cold War Crises* (New York: Columbia University Press, 1991), 154, see also 17.

[31] See NSC-68, in *FRUS, 1950*, vol. I: *National Security Affairs; Foreign Economic Policy* (Washington, D.C.: U.S. GPO, 1977). See also Samuel F. Wells Jr., "Sounding the Tocsin: NSC 68 and the Soviet Threat," *International Security* 4, no. 2 (1979).

[32] Weigley, *American Way of War*, 382–83.

[33] Clay Blair, *The Forgotten War: America in Korea* (New York: Times Books, 1988), 48, note. The divisions in the Far East Command were substantially less well endowed in this regard, having only twenty-two tanks assigned to each infantry division and a small detachment of armor available to corps and Army level commands.

[34] Typically, Soviet armored corps were regarded as the equivalent of Western (or German) divisions during World War II. These were generally armed with 165–195 tanks; thus, the American infantry units at 143 tanks were less than 25 percent lighter than Soviet armored units. See Williamson Murray and Allan R. Millett, *A War to Be Won: Fighting the Second World*

regiments, and six independent regimental combat teams; each of these would have been substantially heavier in terms of allotment of armor.[35]

Army-wide, there were even more tanks available than the TOE would suggest: there were enough tanks for each division to be equipped with three hundred tanks, with a similar number available for replacement use and parts.[36] Additionally, "machine guns and towed artillery were in plentiful supply," although more modern heavy equipment was less abundant.[37] At the time of the Korean War, "the average American infantry division had a third more artillery than its World War II predecessor."[38] However, the U.S. Army viewed even these comparatively large endowments as insufficient at the time, due to the depth of its beliefs in the utility of mechanization and armor in general.

COMBINED ARMS AND CLOSE AIR SUPPORT

In addition to the quantity of equipment, the doctrine of combined arms emphasized the value of integrating multiple types of capabilities in military operations to take advantage of their synergies. The U.S. Army of World War II had increasingly integrated heavy weapons at every level of its force structure, swapping infantry elements for heavy weapons elements at the company and platoon levels.[39] Training emphasized flexibility, combined arms, and jointness, or cross-service cooperation. The primary organizational structure for the army at the outbreak of the Korean War, the regimental combat team (RCT), was a direct descendant of the late World War II innovation of the combined arms task forces that integrated armor, artillery, and infantry at the battalion and regimental levels.[40] These were emphasized in the

---

*War* (Cambridge: Belknap Press of Harvard University Press, 2000), 286; R. J. Overy, *Why the Allies Won* (New York: W.W. Norton, 1996), 211.

[35] James F. Schnabel, *United States Army in the Korean War,* vol. 3: *Policy and Direction: The First Year* (Washington, D.C.: Office of the Chief of Military History United States Army/GPO, 1972), 43–44.

[36] Author's calculations based on data from ibid., 43–46. Although these were mostly World War II vintage tanks, so was the T-34 used by the North Koreans. The forces available to MacArthur lacked the relatively large armor component that would imply, as discussed in chapter 5; however, the point here speaks to the culture of the military in general.

[37] Ibid., 46.

[38] Eliot Cohen and John Gooch, *Military Misfortunes: The Anatomy of Failure in War* (New York: Free Press, 1990), 182.

[39] Jonathan M. House, *Toward Combined Arms Warfare: A Survey of 20th-Century Tactics, Doctrine, and Organization* (Fort Leavenworth, Kan.: U.S. Army Command and General Staff College, 1985); John H. Bradley, *The Second World War: Asia and the Pacific,* vol. 2 (Wayne, N.J.: Avery Publishing Group, 1989), 24.

[40] Eric Heginbotham, "Military Learning," *Military Review* 80, no. 3 (2000).

Asian theater: "Divisions were directed to complete RCT field exercises and develop effective air ground combat procedures."[41] This focus on combined arms permeated the American ground forces at all levels.

The utility of close air support (CAS) to augment ground forces was another lesson from the World War II experience that remained relevant in 1950: "Close air support as practiced in Korea was rooted in Field Manual (FM) 31–35, Air-Ground Operations. First published in August 1946, this manual distilled the lessons and procedures learned by the Army's 12th Army Group and the Army Air Force's Ninth Air Force primarily in Europe during World War II."[42]

While the Air Force had focused its efforts on strategic bombing, the other services emphasized CAS; during the Korean War, "tactical support from Navy and Marine Corps aircraft was excellent."[43] Early discussions regarding the appropriate American response to the North Korean attack reflect this belief:

> [U.S. Navy officers] wanted an immediate "fly-over" of American airplanes for psychological effect while the aggressors pondered the terms of the Security Council resolution...The [U.S.] Air Force was considering the possibility of sending tactical air unit[s] to South Korean airfields, a move which would involve the commitment of ground forces to protect the bases, but the Navy believed that the situation was "made to order" for carrier based air power.[44]

American ground forces expected their air forces to defend them from the enemy's planes and CAS was integral to their views on joint operations.[45]

## OTHER DOCTRINAL INFLUENCES FOR PENINSULAR WARFARE

An additional strategic concept influenced American thinking during the Korean War: America's World War II strategy of isolating the battlefield in Italy as well as island-hopping in the Pacific shaped strategy for peninsular

[41] Schnabel, *United States Army in the Korean War,* 55.

[42] William T. Y'Blood, *Down in the Weeds: Close Air Support in Korea* (Washington, D.C.: Air Force History and Museums Program, 2002), 1.

[43] Weigley, *American Way of War,* 384. On the Air Force's abandonment of the tactical air role in this period, see Crane, *American Airpower Strategy in Korea, 1950–1953,* 21–22. Also commending the role of the Navy in providing CAS, see John R. Bruning, *Crimson Sky: The Air Battle for Korea* (Dulles, Va.: Brassey's, 1999), 83.

[44] Glenn D. Paige, *The Korean Decision, June 24–30, 1950* (New York: Free Press, 1968), 136, note 137.

[45] Y'Blood, *Down in the Weeds,* 6–7.

Korea.[46] In Italy, the U.S. campaign relied on a *sequence* of amphibious landings in places such as Sicily, Solarno, and Anzio.[47] This allowed the United States to take advantage of the strategic mobility that its dominant Navy provided. Both in Italy and in the Pacific, the U.S. focus on isolating the battlefield through the use of airpower and naval forces aimed to limit the adversary's ability to resupply and reinforce. Tactical and operational interdictions were key. The American leaders were confident these tactics would apply easily and decisively in Korea.

## SUMMARY OF THE U.S. THEORY OF VICTORY

The American theory of victory had several elements, all of which shared one essential element: the substitution of capital for manpower. Scholars have identified this as a consistent theme in American military policy over a wide span of time.[48] With these associated beliefs—strategic bombing, nuclear weapons, combined arms—the United States would face off against China in northeast Asia. The contrast between the two could hardly have been greater.

## CHINA'S THEORY OF VICTORY ON LAND

As the leaders of the Chinese Communist Party (CCP) shifted their focus from their own violent rise to power to the emerging international Cold War, they had just emerged victorious from two decades of civil war and a seven-year fight against Japan. In both conflicts, their adversary had been better equipped and often more numerous. These experiences left China with a robust set of strategic beliefs that it incorporated into its own theory of victory. The differences between the manpower-intensive People's Liberation Army (PLA) and the capital-intensive U.S. military were stark.

Much of the evidence in this section comes from doctrinal discussions within the PLA. It is heavily laced with Maoist propaganda, and thus it may be tempting to write it off on the presumption that military leaders would not actually follow such guidance. However, to neglect it would ignore the

---

[46] Weigley, *American Way of War,* 385.

[47] Thomas B. Buell et al., *The Second World War: Europe and the Mediterranean,* vol. 1 (Wayne, N.J.: Avery Publishing Group, 1989), 227–251.

[48] On the more general American tendency to substitute firepower for manpower, see Robert H. Scales, *Firepower in Limited War* (Washington, D.C.: National Defense University Press, 1990), 3–4, inter alia.

dominance of Maoist ideology in China, even at that early date.[49] As Zhang Shuguang argued persuasively in *Mao's Military Romanticism*, such ideas profoundly shaped policy.[50] Indeed, China's evolving military culture still retains elements of this Maoist thought and continues to shape Beijing's foreign and security policy today:[51]

> Western scholars tend to mock the notion of "man over weapons."...It is easy in retrospect to dismiss what was in actuality the enormously stifling effect of Maoist doctrine on innovative thinking in the Chinese officer corps. When Liu [Shaoqi] gave his lectures in the early 1950s, Mao's military thought had not yet ascended to the biblical proportions it would assume in the 1960s. Nonetheless, Liu had to struggle against an incipient Maoist orthodoxy in attempting to turn the attention of younger officers to problems about which Maoist thought offered little but dismissive (albeit morale boosting) aphorisms.[52]

Similarly, Ellis Joffe, while asserting that Maoist "doctrine is merely a rationalization" of choices made for other reasons, goes on to emphasize the substantial effects of such ideas on perceptions—particularly when they are grounded in a long history that supports them.[53] In a slightly different issue area, but one with many parallels, Lucian Pye writes that "political culture continues for many reasons to be singularly important in shaping Chinese politics," and speaks of "the special importance of political culture for understanding China."[54] In fact, the PLA put Maoist doctrine into practice in a number of tangible ways.

[49] Although there was some variation of beliefs between Mao and a few leaders who were less supportive of his views, on balance there was widespread acceptance of Mao's views within the senior leadership. The role of dissenting views is discussed later in this chapter and also in chapter 6.

[50] Zhang Shuguang, *Mao's Military Romanticism: China and the Korean War, 1950–53* (Lawrence: University Press of Kansas, 1995).

[51] Nan Li, *From Revolutionary Internationalism to Conservative Nationalism: The Chinese Military's Discourse on National Security and Identity in the Post-Mao Era*, Peaceworks No. 39 (Washington, DC: U.S. Institute of Peace, May 2001).

[52] Evan A. Feigenbaum, *China's Techno-Warriors: National Security and Strategic Competition from the Nuclear to the Information Age* (Stanford: Stanford University Press, 2003), 22.

[53] Ellis Joffe, *Party and Army: Professionalism and Political Control in the Chinese Officer Corps, 1949–1964* (Cambridge: Harvard University Press, 1965), 50–52.

[54] Lucian W. Pye, *The Spirit of Chinese Politics*, new ed. (Cambridge: Harvard University Press, 1992), ix.

Communist China's beliefs regarding the nature of warfare began with an assessment of the likely threat China would face—general invasion—and a view on the appropriate way to deal with such a threat—lure the enemy in deep. Mao downplayed the importance of nuclear weapons (and indeed was ignorant of their implications) and instead emphasized light infantry forces and "People's War." These are the doctrinal beliefs with which the Chinese People's Volunteers went to battle in Korea.[55]

## FEAR OF INVASION, BUT CONFIDENCE IN STRATEGIC VALUE OF HINTERLAND

The Chinese theory of victory in this period anticipated a land invasion of China fought off by trading land for time and embroiling the adversary in a war deep in China's interior.[56] In the wars of the twentieth century against the Kuomintang (KMT) and against the Japanese, the Communists faced existential threats from adversaries that aimed to occupy the entire area of the previous Chinese empire. Mao maintained this threat perception during the Korean War; one Chinese scholar wrote that Mao expressed fears that Japan might deploy troops to the Korean Peninsula.[57]

To address China's concern about being invaded, and because of its relative weakness, China's strategic thinking emphasized the policy of "trading space for time"[58] by "luring the enemy in deep."[59] Chinese doctrine reflected the fact that China had a vast hinterland into which its military could withdraw. The CCP had pursued such a strategy against the Japanese in World War II, with ultimate success.[60] The main point of Mao's famous May 1938 manifesto "On Protracted War" was to describe this strategy.[61] Indeed, he

---

[55] The PLA units that deployed to Korea were called the People's Volunteers, to provide a veneer of separation between them and Beijing. In fact Beijing exerted complete and direct control over these forces.

[56] Gerald Segal, *Defending China* (New York: Oxford University Press, 1985), 48–49.

[57] 宋连生、《抗美援朝在回首》（昆明:云南人民出版社、2002）[Song Liansheng, *Recollections on the Korean War* (Kunming: Yunnan People's Press, 2002), 170–71].

[58] See Mao Tsetung, "Strategy for the Second Year of the War of Liberation [September 1, 1947]," in *Selected Military Writings of Mao Tse-Tung* (Beijing: Foreign Languages Press, 1966), 329, see also 155 and 167; Mao Tsetung, "Problems of Strategy in China's Revolutionary War [December 1936]," in *Selected Military Writings of Mao Tse-Tung* (Beijing: Foreign Languages Press, 1966), 133.

[59] Mao, "Problems of Strategy in China's Revolutionary War [December 1936]," 113.

[60] Dick Wilson, *China's Revolutionary War* (New York: St. Martin's Press, 1991), chapter 5, "Invasion," and chapter 6, Battle Lines Drawn."

[61] Mao Tsetung, "On Protracted War [May 1938]," in *Selected Military Writings of Mao Tse-Tung* (Beijing: Foreign Languages Press, 1966), espec. at 215ff.

continued to advocate avoiding positional war in the civil war through late 1947, favoring instead mobile, guerrilla warfare that avoided preoccupation with controlling territory.[62] (Note that this was quite late in the war; the KMT would begin to crumble rapidly early in 1948.)

That history shaped views about the future. "Mao made it plain that in defeating an invader, geography was China's first ally.... The essential principle that China's vastness aids the defender and allows space to be traded for time, is an accurate one."[63] In late 1949, the Chinese took steps to implement the strategies called for by this aspect of their theory of victory:

> In order to respond to this, instead of maintaining a positional defense along the coast, the Chinese Communists also decided to build an in-depth defense—a defensive zone of several layers with forces deployed in such a way to maneuver and reinforce one another.... This was an essential element of traditional Chinese strategy: *houfazhiren*, to gain mastery by striking only after the enemy has struck.[64]

As a result, China did not need to attack any would-be aggressor pre-emptively, but rather could await attack in the confidence that such patience would not jeopardize China's overall security.[65] (Although this can be used on a defensive level, awaiting the adversary on your own home territory, it could also be used in a war of power projection, as was done in the fight to push the UN Command off the Korean Peninsula.) At a tactical level, the CCP had utilized this approach many times during the civil war. Once the Korean War broke out, they would turn to it again:

> Peng suggested to Mao that UN forces be lured into preset "traps" as far north as possible so that individual UN units would be extended with longer supply lines and thus be more easily isolated and destroyed. Mao quickly approved the plan. Peng instructed that each CPVF [Chinese People's Volunteer Force] army would withdraw its main force farther north but leave one division "to conduct mobile and guerrilla

---

[62] Mao Tsetung, "The Present Situation and Our Tasks [December 25, 1947]," in *Selected Military Writings of Mao Tse-Tung* (Beijing: Foreign Languages Press, 1966), 349.

[63] Segal, *Defending China*, 48–49, see also 14.

[64] Zhang, *Mao's Military Romanticism*, 47. For a similar view on early Chinese strategy, see Harlan W. Jencks, *From Muskets to Missiles: Politics and Professionalism in the Chinese Army, 1945–1981* (Boulder, Colo.: Westview Press, 1982), 259–60.

[65] Segal, *Defending China*, 14.

warfare... to wipe out small enemy units while engaging and luring larger enemy units to the trap."[66]

Thus, Mao and the other Chinese leaders felt that they had a solid approach to the main type of threat they perceived from the outside.

## CHINA'S VIEWS ON ATOMIC WEAPONS: "PAPER TIGERS"

The atom bomb is a paper tiger that the U.S. reactionaries use to scare people. It looks terrible, but in fact it isn't. Of course, the atom bomb is a weapon of mass slaughter, but the outcome of a war is decided by the people, not by one or two new types of weapon.[67]

So wrote Mao Zedong in 1947. Mao's statements may have had an element of bravado, but throughout the early part of the Cold War, Mao did view such weapons as relatively weak and Mao's views dominated the senior Chinese leadership.[68] In a well-regarded history of China's nuclear program, John Wilson Lewis and Xue Litai conclude: "For Mao in the late 1940s, the strategic calculus was clear. The struggle against imperialism could be intensified and need not be intimidated by the American nuclear threat."[69] As discussed below, the topic was not even studied carefully until well after the Korean War.

Mao and his colleagues expressed their disdain for atomic and nuclear weapons over a sustained period.[70] For instance, in an internal debate in July 1948, Mao and Zhou Enlai argued that nuclear weapons were weak and irrelevant to important global security affairs.[71] Similarly, during the Korean War China's acting chief of staff Nie Rongzhen averred: "After all,

[66] Yu Bin, "What China Learned from Its 'Forgotten War' in Korea," in *Mao's Generals Remember Korea*, ed. Li Xiaobing, Allan Reed Millett, and Yu Bin (Lawrence: University Press of Kansas, 2001), 15.
[67] Quoted in Sergei Goncharov, John Lewis, and Xue Litai, *Uncertain Partners: Stalin, Mao, and the Korean War* (Stanford: Stanford University Press, 1993), 23.
[68] Ibid.
[69] John Wilson Lewis and Xue Litai, *China Builds the Bomb* (Stanford: Stanford University Press, 1988), 7.
[70] The consistency of these expressions of belief is important as it suggests that confidence in the Soviet alliance and in any extended deterrence it might provide were not critical in shaping this view. Both before 1949 and after the late 1950s, the support provided by Soviet extended deterrence would have looked rather weak.
[71] Ryan, *Chinese Attitudes toward Nuclear Weapons,* 20.

China lives on the farms. What can atom bombs do there?"[72] As late as 1961, some members of the Chinese leadership were still downplaying the importance of nuclear weapons. One of the most senior military leaders, a member of the standing committee of the Military Affairs Committee (the most powerful decision-making body in the PLA and the PRC), stated that "although atomic bombs are very powerful they can only be used to destroy the centers and the economic reserves of the opponent during the strategic bombing phase."[73]

Other evidence of this view of the utility of atomic weapons comes from conversations that Chinese leaders had with the Soviets in a later period. In one such exchange, Zhou Enlai suggested that the Communist nations should not fear a nuclear war, and he went so far as to discourage Soviet retaliation in the event of the use of tactical nuclear weapons against China by the United States:[74] "The PRC has taken into consideration the possibility of the outbreak in this region [Jinmen and Mazu islands] of a local war between the United States and the PRC, and it is now ready to take all the hard blows, including atomic bombs and the destruction of cities."[75]

Nikita Khrushchev's memoirs also recall that in 1955–56 Mao declared that "war is war. The years will pass, and we'll get to work producing more babies than ever before."[76] In September 1958, Mao had advised Soviet foreign minister Andrei Gromyko on how to respond to a war between the United States and China. Chen Jian writes:

> The Chinese chairman, according to Gromyko, stated that if the Americans were to invade the Chinese mainland or to use nuclear weapons the Chinese forces would retreat, drawing American ground forces into China's interior. The chairman proposed that during the initial stage of the war, the Soviets should do nothing but watch. Only after the American forces had entered China's interior should Moscow

---

[72] Nie Rongzhen quoted in Segal, *Defending China*, 100. The original source is the autobiography of India's ambassador stationed in Beijing, Kavalam M. Panikkar.

[73] Quoted in Alice Langley Hsieh, "China's Secret Military Papers: Military Doctrine and Strategy," *China Quarterly* 18 (1964): 90.

[74] Chen Jian, *Mao's China and the Cold War* (Chapel Hill: University of North Carolina Press, 2001), 71 and 189. These discussions occurred in the late 1950s, at which point the Chinese had significantly hardened their views toward nuclear weapons. That Zhou would nevertheless discourage Soviet retaliation at that late point only emphasizes how little he feared nuclear weapons in general.

[75] Ibid., 189.

[76] Quoted in Lewis and Xue, *China Builds the Bomb*, 66.

use "all means at its disposal" (which Gromyko understood as Soviet nuclear weapons) to destroy them.[77]

Nuclear weapons clearly received little or no serious analytical study in China until long after the Korean War. Chinese consideration of the dangers of nuclear weapons in the Korean War was extremely simplistic.[78] Before 1955, there was no formal analytical study of what atomic weapons could do against China. Only in July 1955 did the top two hundred leaders in the CCP finally receive a briefing on the subject, and even then it consisted of a scant twenty-five-page document on different aspects of nuclear war, such as what the weapons could do to cities and to forces in the field.[79] Before 1957, the PLA did not engage in training that would allow it to survive a nuclear attack.[80] As late as 1961, the Chinese discussions of U.S. nuclear doctrine appear exceedingly superficial.[81] This is quite shocking compared to the detailed study such matters received in the United States and the Soviet Union.

There are alternate views regarding Mao's thoughts on nuclear weapons. For example Mark A. Ryan, in his 1984 book, *Chinese Attitudes toward Nuclear Weapons,* argues that the Chinese, contrary to their public statements, recognized the importance of nuclear weapons. Ryan's evidence on the post–Korean War period is strong.[82] However, he himself notes that evidence on Mao's private position in this early period is quite slim.[83] In one passage on the pre–Korean War period, even Ryan confirms Mao's denigration of such weapons.[84] Although Ryan presents clear evidence that by the early and mid-1950s, Mao's China was on its way to recognizing the importance of nuclear weapons, his position on the period of interest to this book—1950—is more nuanced.

[77] Chen, *Mao's China and the Cold War,* 189.

[78] This point is discussed further in chapter 4.

[79] Interview with Shen Zhihua, Beijing, September 2002. Shen is one of only a few historians of Chinese foreign policy outside the government and government-controlled research centers who has access to the Chinese archives.

[80] Lewis and Xue, *China Builds the Bomb,* 217.

[81] See Hsieh, "China's Secret Military Papers," 84.

[82] Ryan, *Chinese Attitudes toward Nuclear Weapons,* for specific reference to the pre–Korean War period, see 21. Note, however, that even after China recognized the importance of nuclear weapons, it continued to think of them in ways rather different from the United States or Soviet Union. See Christopher P. Twomey, ed., *Perspectives on Sino-American Strategic Nuclear Issues* (New York: Palgrave Macmillan, 2008).

[83] In particular, Ryan notes the limitations of his key source on the question, Morton Halperin. Ryan, *Chinese Attitudes toward Nuclear Weapons,* 18.

[84] Ibid., 21.

PEOPLE'S WAR

In the wake of the Communist victory in the civil war, Chinese tactical and operational doctrine was focused on a form of "People's War" that encapsulated "a vision of a highly politicized guerrilla army."[85] "The Chinese were different not simply [due to] inferior equipment...but more generally, by virtue of a different approach to warfare."[86] Blending tactical and strategic-level thought, Mao's military philosophy emphasized guerrilla warfare, the strategic depth that China's geography provided, and mobile warfare.[87] It had many specific components.

*Individual Tactics*

Perhaps the main emphasis of People's War was on morale and manpower over material. Mao declared that "weapons are an important factor in war, but not the decisive factor; it is people, not things, that are decisive."[88] Similarly, he wrote that "the richest source of power to wage war lies in the masses of the people."[89] Zhang, a Chinese scholar who has carefully studied Maoist doctrine, summarized Mao's thinking:

> Mao firmly believed that a weak army could win in a war against a strong enemy because he was convinced that "man" could beat "weapon." Given Mao's confidence in a human being's *subjective capability* to determine defeat or victory in war, the CCP chairman *romanticized* military affairs. Yet as he calculated the probability of victory for a weak army, he found his theory logical, realistic, and plausible.[90]

William Whitson, a leading scholar of the PLA, refers to Mao's view disparagingly as an "infantry small-arms syndrome."[91]

For Mao, it was not only sheer numbers, although these were clearly important, but the motivation of his soldiers that would guarantee victory. He

---

[85] Jencks, *From Muskets to Missiles*, 69.

[86] Eliot A. Cohen, "'Only Half the Battle': American Intelligence and the Chinese Intervention in Korea, 1950," *Intelligence and National Security* 5, no. 1 (1990): 143.

[87] On the tactical and strategic elements of People's War, see Chen-Ya Tien, *Chinese Military History: Ancient and Modern* (Oakville, Ontario: Mosaic Press, 1992), 223–45; William W. Whitson and Zhenxia Huang, *The Chinese High Command: A History of Communist Military Politics, 1927–71* (New York: Praeger, 1973).

[88] Mao, "On Protracted War [May 1938]," 219.

[89] Ibid., 261.

[90] Zhang, *Mao's Military Romanticism*, 29. Emphasis in the original.

[91] Whitson and Huang, *Chinese High Command*.

had written that, against Japan, China's "advantages lie in the progressive and just character of her war."[92] Mao thought Japanese soldiers inferior, not for racist reasons, but because Japan's "weapons are not in the hands of politically conscious soldiers"[93]: "We must make full use of this move, political mobilization, to get the better of him. This move is crucial; it is indeed of primary importance, while our inferiority in weapons and other things is only secondary."[94]

Mao also stressed the centrality of surprise in People's War. Although he recognized that it played a role in conventional warfare as well, "there are fewer opportunities to apply it [in conventional battles] than there are in guerrilla hostilities. In the latter speed is essential."[95]

In addition, Mao utilized a fluid, mobile style of warfare. He urged concentration of forces while on the offensive, but dispersal while on the defensive.[96] The Maoist view of "People's War" also emphasized the importance of troops reducing their logistical requirements substantially by providing for their own sustenance while in the field and by relying on simple means for shelter. The emphasis on light arms further supported this advantage. These factors meant that logistical lines were far less vulnerable to airpower or fast-moving ground forces. It was "based on the CCP's civil war experience in which the Communists had scored constant victories by fighting mobile warfare."[97]

*Integration of the Various Tactics*
Weaving together these various strands of People's War theories, Mao's emphasized guerrilla tactics: "The enemy advances, we retreat; the enemy camps, we harass; the enemy tires, we attack; the enemy retreats, we pursue."[98] In practice, this meant that mobile Chinese operations were characterized by the "use of relatively untrained and under-armed soldiers against a more sophisticated enemy. By using impressive deception and stealth the Chinese overcame technological inferiority. By using remarkable mobility, mostly by foot over rough terrain, the Chinese overcame logistical inferiority."[99]

---

[92] Mao, "On Protracted War [May 1938]," 197.
[93] Ibid., 259.
[94] Ibid., 228.
[95] Mao Tse-tung, *On Guerrilla Warfare* (New York: Praeger, 1961), 97.
[96] Tien, *Chinese Military History*, 238–41.
[97] Zhang, *Mao's Military Romanticism*, 118.
[98] Mao, "Problems of Strategy in China's Revolutionary War [December 1936]," 111.
[99] Segal, *Defending China*, 101.

Mao's high-morale forces could concentrate in large numbers to over-whelm or annihilate entire enemy units. He advised that "in every battle concentrate an absolutely superior force (two, three, four, and sometimes even five or six times the enemy's strength), encircle the enemy forces com-pletely, strive to wipe them out thoroughly, and do not let any escape from the net."[100] A definitive survey of the PLA by William Whitson and Zhenxia Huang, *The Chinese High Command*, suggests that this represented not just Mao's strategic thought, but a consensus of the senior military leadership at the time.[101]

The Chinese Communists had used this strategy many times with great success during the civil war.[102] The West referred to it as a "human wave" or "human sea" tactic.[103] Chinese Communist forces would gather four or five times as many troops as their opponent, or even more.[104] They would surround an isolated opponent (often by luring them to the end of a long supply line) and overwhelm their forces. This was ambush on a very large scale. Such tactics substituted for more complex "fire and maneuver" infantry practices that have dominated infantry warfare in the West since World War I; the Chinese Communist forces lacked the noncommissioned officers necessary to lead such challenging tactics.[105] Although the material shortcomings discussed elsewhere also limited Chinese strategic choice in other areas, with regard to fire and maneuver tactics, simple technology had allowed for German infantry infiltrations at the end of World War I. The Chinese could have pursued something similar, if only they had chosen to develop sufficient small-unit leadership.

Instead, during the civil war:

[The Chinese] attacked mainly by night, using large quantities of hand grenades, light machine gun and mortar fire...from very close ranges. They usually approached from the rear, after drawing enemy fire by sniping and bugle or pipe music. Operationally, the Chinese had a

---

[100] Mao, "The Present Situation and Our Tasks [December 25, 1947]," 349. On the importance of this document to Maoist thought, see Whitson and Huang, *Chinese High Command*, 492.

[101] Whitson and Huang, *Chinese High Command*, 492.

[102] For examples, see Edward L. Dreyer, *China at War, 1901–1949* (New York: Longman, 1995); Wilson, *China's Revolutionary War*.

[103] Joffe, *Party and Army*, 11.

[104] See Gary J. Bjorge, *Moving the Enemy: Operational Art in the Chinese PLA's Huai Hai Campaign*, Leavenworth Paper Number 22 (Fort Leavenworth, Kans.: Combat Studies Institute, 2004), 43.

[105] Whitson and Huang, *Chinese High Command*, 13.

more supple approach…feinting, probing, or withdrawing…in order to test enemy reactions or to confuse and intimidate them.[106]

The PLA went on to employ similar tactics during the Korean War:

> Since the CCF had no close air support, no tanks, and very little artillery, it specialized in fighting under cover of darkness. The whistles, bugles, and horns were not only signaling devices (in place of radios) but also psychological tools, designed to frighten the enemy in the dark and cause him to shoot, thereby revealing the position of men and weapons. The fighting tactics were relatively simple: frontal assaults on revealed positions, infiltration and ambush to cut the enemy's rear, and massed manpower attacks on the open flanks of his main elements. War correspondents were to describe the attacking waves of the CCF as a "human sea" or "swarm of locusts."[107]

Thus, the Chinese infantry doctrine centered on the provision of mobile manpower armed with high morale more so than sophisticated weapons. Complex tactics were also forgone, replaced by simple but effective human wave stratagems. Limited command and control and fire support demanded close contact with the enemy and high-morale forces. These were all hallmarks of People's War.

*Implementation in Practice*

These doctrines were not just theoretical for the Chinese but were put into practice throughout the military. The PLA was an exceptionally large, underequipped force. Late in the civil war it had grown quite rapidly.[108] By the outbreak of the Korean War, it was a large infantry force of over five million men in some 250 divisions, but was still very poorly outfitted:[109]

> In terms of equipment, the Chinese Communist Army of 1950 was primitive by any standards. It has been compared to an army of 1914, without the trucks and the artillery, primarily an army of infantrymen. There were few trucks, little artillery, very limited communication (particularly

---

[106] Cohen and Gooch, *Military Misfortunes,* 177.
[107] Blair, *Forgotten War,* 382.
[108] Dreyer, *China at War, 1901–1949,* 317.
[109] Patrick C. Roe, *The Dragon Strikes: China and the Korean War, June–December 1950* (Novato, Calif.: Presidio, 2000), 415.

via radio), no air support, and no antiaircraft defense. Logistical support in the civil war had been provided by the local population.[110]

Another scholar similarly emphasizes its backwardness:

On the eve of the Korean War, the PLA remained an infantry army with acute deficiencies in heavy artillery, armored vehicles, and ammunition. Military officers still lacked technological know-how as well as familiarity with operational tactics such as coordination of joint operations, armor-infantry-artillery team work, and close air support. There was, at that time, no sign of plans to modernize and regularize the PLA.[111]

Indeed, as they entered the Korean War, many Chinese noted that their armament was not even up to North Korean standards, let alone Western ones. A Chinese liaison office to the North Korean military noted that "by Chinese standards, the North Koreans themselves had been magnificently equipped by the Soviets."[112] In the standard TOE for divisions, North Korea had nearly twice as many light machine guns as China, three times as many heavy machine guns, and six times as many trucks.[113] On the other hand, China held the advantage in horses and mules.[114] The PLA was well suited for a People's War strategy.

By the later stages of the Korean War, the PLA was able to arm the poorly equipped force from China with substantial advanced material from the Soviets. However, at the time that the initial decisions were being made regarding involvement in the war, no such capabilities existed.

## THE PLA AIR FORCE

While it is not necessary to evaluate each service individually, it is worth describing the People's Liberation Army Air Force (PLAAF) briefly, given the importance that airpower played in American strategic thought at that time. Airpower played only a trivial role in Chinese Communist military history.

---

[110] Ibid., 417.

[111] Melvin Gurtov and Byong-Moo Hwang, *China under Threat: The Politics of Strategy and Diplomacy* (Baltimore: Johns Hopkins University Press, 1980), 33.

[112] See Russell Spurr, *Enter the Dragon: China's Undeclared War against the U.S. in Korea, 1950–51* (New York: Newmarket Press, 1988), 16.

[113] Charles R. Shrader, *Communist Logistics in the Korean War* (Westport, Conn.: Greenwood Press, 1995), 93, table 5.2.

[114] Ibid., 95.

The CCP had faced a substantial air force in its Kuomintang opponents in the civil war.[115] However, the Communists never fielded airpower of any consequence. Their fledgling air force was grounded a number of times before 1945: by attrition in the early 1930s, by the arrest of all the members of the Xinjiang Aviation unit in a political purge in 1942, by financial pressures in 1943 that forced the student pilots to "terminate their studies and cultivate the land or work in shops," and by bureaucratic fiat by senior military leaders in 1945.[116]

Once the Chinese began to create their own air force, they exported a People's War philosophy from the ground-based, guerrilla context in which it had originated. This manifested itself in several ways. First, the early Chinese doctrine regarding airpower viewed it as primarily a defensive asset, a component of People's War in the sky.[117] Second, the morale of pilots was emphasized to an extreme degree: "The PLAAF still believed in the efficacy of its man-over-weapons doctrine. Young Chinese pilots would be able to defeat the enemy, they argued, because they had come from ground forces accustomed to difficult situations and were willing to sacrifice themselves for China."[118] One of the official histories of the Chinese air force extolled the bravery of the Chinese pilots and wistfully concluded: "The experience of the People's Volunteer Air Force in the war to resist America and support Korea revealed a single truth for all to see: Under the conditions of modern warfare, human factors are the determining factor for victory or defeat."[119] The Chinese emphasis on morale, bravery, and élan turned out, however, to be found ill-suited to modern air combat:

> Inflated combat morale, while welcomed, also caused anxiety among Chinese pilots, who were eager to redeem themselves with personal glory and individual success. The basic principles of air operations—teamwork, protecting each other, and tactics—were often ignored. According to PLAAF records, five of eight regimental commanders were killed in action over Korea because of their brashness.[120]

---

[115] Zhang Xiaoming, *Red Wings over the Yalu: China, the Soviet Union, and the Air War in Korea*, 1st ed. (College Station: Texas A&M University Press, 2002), 17.
[116] Ibid., 19, 21, and 23, respectively.
[117] Ibid., 48 and 103.
[118] Ibid., 205.
[119] 王定烈、主编、《当代中国空军》(北京:中国社会科学出版社、1989) [Wang Dinglie, *Contemporary China's Air Force* (Beijing: Contemporary China Publishing/Chinese Social Science Press, 1989), 207].
[120] Zhang, *Red Wings over the Yalu*, 179.

Third, the Chinese continued to deemphasize training and education. In general, Mao had emphasized instead experiential learning: "Reading is learning, but applying is also learning and the more important kind of learning at that. Our chief method is to learn warfare through warfare."[121] Although this might be appropriate for a guerrilla or light infantry army, it posed significant problems for the development of an air force. The poor education level of the Chinese soldiers impeded the Communists' ability to create a viable air force throughout the revolutionary period.[122] Indeed, some Chinese apparently viewed the Soviet training standards for pilots as too rigorous, suggesting that their leaders placed little emphasis on the quality of training.[123]

In sum, the Chinese air force exhibits sharp contrasts with that of the United States. Airpower played a minor role in PLA thinking about warfare, and even that small role was characterized by a different understanding of its uses.

## CONTRARY DOCTRINAL CURRENTS

There were dissenters to this Chinese theory of victory, and there were contrary trends in Chinese military history. Although the characterization above is accurate in describing the dominant element in CCP military thought, it is worthwhile to consider some of the exceptions to this overall trend.

A number of PLA leaders did not buy in to the People's War thinking; these were leaders who had been trained extensively at the Yunnan Military Academy or at the Whampoa Military Academy, where they studied Japanese and German military science.[124] The Yunnan Military Academy was already notable for its high quality in the waning days of the Qing Dynasty. Whampoa, the military institute created by Sun Yat-sen and led by Chiang Kai-shek, created the first professional army in postdynastic China. These academies stressed the role of firepower, professionalized divisional-level leaders, the utility of the technical branches, and many other concepts that were inconsistent with Maoist People's War. The roles played by some leaders trained here are discussed in the next two chapters.

---

[121] Bjorge, *Moving the Enemy*, 32.
[122] Zhang, *Red Wings over the Yalu*, 17–27, 41, 119–20, and 181; he also emphasizes the student pilots' "limited reading and writing skills," 26.
[123] Ibid., 44.
[124] Dreyer, *China at War, 1901–1949*, 124. Jencks, *From Muskets to Missiles*, 39.

Additionally, by the final stages of the civil war, People's War no longer had a monopoly on Chinese strategic thought. Whitson writes that, in 1947, Chinese doctrine represented a compromise between the Maoist "peasant ethic" and Soviet or Westernized warlord strategies.[125] Also, by the end of the civil war, battles had become much more conventional.[126] However, this mostly applies after 1948, when the tide of the civil war had swung dramatically in favor of the CCP. The lessons of this latter period seemed relevant primarily to "mopping up" campaigns, not to future intense wars against China's most daunting adversaries. Further, even at this period, the PLA was not a very well mechanized force, quite lacking in artillery and tanks, especially in comparison to the KMT.[127] For instance, in the pivotal HuaiHai Campaign of late 1948, the CCP force overcame a force of similar size in which "most... [troops] were better trained and better equipped than the CCP forces."[128] The disparity in aircraft was even wider. Thus, it is important not to overstate the importance of these late battles after the tide of the civil war had turned in terms of their lasting legacy on CCP thinking.

## SOURCES OF CHINESE DOCTRINE

The PLA's doctrinal and strategic beliefs had many sources. Many of these elements can be traced to Sun Tsu and other statements of classical military thought in Chinese history.[129] Some strategies were, at least in part, forced on China by external pressures.[130] For instance, the limitations of the Chinese economy played a role: "The persistence of the 'People's War' concept, of the commissar system, and, indeed, of the whole 'Maoist' approach to military affairs, has been largely a result of China's relatively low level of industrial development."[131] However, some elements trace their roots to centuries of factor endowments in Chinese civilization: a massive

[125] Whitson and Huang, *Chinese High Command*, 89, and chapter 11, "Strategy and Tactics."
[126] Dreyer, *China at War, 1901–1949*, 353; Whitson and Huang, *Chinese High Command*, 82–93.
[127] See Mao's concerns regarding tanks and aircraft in Mao Tsetung, "Carry the Revolution through to the End [December 30, 1948]," in *Selected Military Writings of Mao Tse-Tung* (Beijing: Foreign Languages Press, 1966), 384.
[128] Odd Arne Westad, *Decisive Encounters: The Chinese Civil War, 1946–1950* (Stanford: Stanford University Press, 2003), 206.
[129] As with many classic strategic texts, many different lessons could be drawn from Sun Tsu. See discussion of this point in Tien, *Chinese Military History*, 212–13; Georges Tan Eng Bok, "Strategic Doctrine," in *Chinese Defence Policy*, ed. Gerald Segal and William T. Tow (London: Macmillan, 1984), 5.
[130] Dreyer, *China at War, 1901–1949*, 321. Echoing this is Hsieh, "China's Secret Military Papers."
[131] Jencks, *From Muskets to Missiles*, 26.

population. The importance placed on manpower has had a long history in Chinese military thought.[132] Reliance on defections for victory, and therefore the importance of the justness of one's own cause, also can trace its roots through millennia of Chinese history and strategic thinking. Whitson refers to many elements of People's War as stemming from a "peasant ethic" of warfare, distinct from warlordism and from Soviet advisers and training, the other major influences on Chinese strategic thought.[133]

China's more recent history had confirmed these ancient themes. Such principles had stood the CCP in good stead against the better-armed and better-equipped KMT in the civil war.[134] Mao had consistently argued on behalf of these strategies throughout that conflict.[135] Immediately before the collapse of the KMT forces, he wrote that "none of [its] efforts can save the Chiang Kai-shek bandit gang from defeat. The reason is that our strategy and tactics are based on a People's War; no army opposed to the people can use our strategy and tactics."[136] Immediately after his civil war adversaries collapsed, Mao attributed the victory to the People's War strategy.[137] These views remained dominant in the PLA for years afterward. In 1961, one of the most senior military leaders of the PLA wrote confidently that "if there is a war within three to five years, we will have to rely on hand weapons.... In the event of war within the next few years we can defeat the enemy by using close combat although we have no special [i.e., nuclear] weapons."[138]

The organizational culture of the Chinese military, too, influenced China's military doctrine:

> For many reasons, the Soviet and Chinese armies have not responded to the technological imperative the same way [as Western militaries had]. Perhaps the most important single factor has been the makeup of the respective officer corps. By the outbreak of the Chinese civil

---

[132] Tien, *Chinese Military History*, 214–15.

[133] Whitson and Huang, *Chinese High Command*, passim, esp. 22–23.

[134] For Mao's view on the better equipped KMT army, and ways to overcome it, see Mao Tsetung, "Problems of Strategy in China's Revolutionary War [December 1936]," 95–97. Also on this point, see Bjorge, *Moving the Enemy*, 22.

[135] Mao, "Problems of Strategy in China's Revolutionary War [December 1936]," 112–13, 141.

[136] Mao, "The Present Situation and Our Tasks [December 25, 1947]."

[137] Mao Tsetung, "On the Great Victory in the Northwest and on the New Type of Ideological Education Movement in the Liberation Army [March 7, 1948]," in *Selected Military Writings of Mao Tse-Tung* (Beijing: Foreign Languages Press, 1966), 358–59.

[138] Marshal Yeh Chien-ying, quoted in Hsieh, "China's Secret Military Papers," 85. See also 84 and 90.

war, PLA officers were tested, experienced, and thoroughly reliable both politically and military.... During their civil wars, both the Soviet and Chinese communists engaged in a type of warfare which was more concerned with winning over populations than with destroying enemy forces. The "dual-command" system of a military commander and a coequal political commissar can work very well in such a situation.[139]

The organizational structure of the PLA was deeply intertwined with its guerrilla roots, and therefore emphasized the political aspect of warfare.[140] This organizational structure could be expected to oppose any attempt at fundamental reform. The cadres in the organization focused on issues beyond military effectiveness as being central for final victory. The senior leaders had risen through the organization by excelling in such work. Change would threaten the core culture of the organization.

Thus, the Chinese theory of victory had its roots in a number of factors: material and strategic constraints, historical experience, and organizational politics. Relying on a single one of these would oversimplify.

## PERCEPTIONS OF THE ADVERSARY'S DOCTRINE

China and the United States had very different military capabilities and very different beliefs about how best to use them. The two sides' views on nuclear weapons were about as opposite as could be. There was wide variance in emphasis in conventional forces as well: on tactical air and combined arms on the U.S. side and on People's War on the Chinese side. In short, there was a very large doctrinal difference, a high value on this book's independent variable: the two nations' theories of victory could hardly have been more distinct.

However, beyond this mere difference, China and the United States each showed only a limited understanding of their adversary's doctrine and the dangers it would pose to their own forces. Given the substantial differences in their doctrines, this is not surprising and supports the doctrinal-difference misperception hypothesis (DDM) and the associated Misperception, Discounting, and Superficial Views Predictions.

---

[139] Jencks, *From Muskets to Missiles*, 25.
[140] Bjorge, *Moving the Enemy*, 18–21.

THE VIEW OF PEOPLE'S WAR FROM THE UNITED STATES

As would be expected by doctrinal-difference theory, there was little understanding of Chinese doctrine in Washington, or even in Tokyo. Prior to the war, Americans viewed the Chinese doctrine as militarily ineffective, and this directly shaped their assessments of Chinese capabilities. The results of a comprehensive Joint Intelligence Committee (JIC) report were sweeping:

> The past combat experience of the PLA soldiers was inappropriate to the operations in Korea. Their previous fighting had involved "hit and run" guerrilla tactics; they had never met "a well-trained force with high morale equipped with modern weapons and possessing the will and the skill to use those weapons." In addition, China had "practically no capability" of reinforcing or supporting the North Korean navy and not much in the way of an air force either.[141]

As war with China drew closer, such incomprehension shows up repeatedly at the tactical level. One recurring theme was an inability to understand that nonmechanized forces could move quite rapidly if their logistics tail was minimal, as was the case in People's War doctrine. For instance, on the eve of the main Chinese attack in November, the intelligence chief of the U.S. X Corps, Colonel William Quinn, wrote:

> Several recent unconfirmed reports, primarily from civilian sources, indicate a possible concentration and build up of enemy forces in the area west and southwest of Choshin Reservoir. Considerable number of CCF troops have been reported in this locality and air observers have sighted at least one convoy moving southwest from Yudam-ni toward Chang-ni.... The enemy is in position to attempt a penetration of the UN front between the X Corps and Eighth Army, although such an operation would be faced by extremely difficult cross country movement. The enemy's capability to launch an attack against the X Corps from the west is restricted by the mountainous terrain through which such an attack would have to be made. Winter weather will still further limit this capability.[142]

[141] Foot, *Wrong War*, 81. The JIC report was dated July 6, 1950.
[142] G-2 (Colonel William Quinn), "Headquarters X Corps, Periodic Intelligence Report #50 (November 15, 1950)," in Military History Institute Library, U.S. Army War College, Carlisle, Penn.

Even twenty-five years later, the commander of the X Corps, General Ned Almond, still had trouble acknowledging the mobility of the light Chinese forces on foot: "I have already said that the gap between the two forces [X Corps and Eighth Army] was interrupted by a difficult mountain range or series of mountain ranges and no road system between. *It would have been impossible* for any force to break the gap and supply itself except by air which the Chinese didn't possess."[143]

In fact, it was not impossible: breaking the gap was precisely what the PLA's 42nd and 38th armies eventually did.[144] Similarly, at the end of November 1950, General Dutch Keiser, commander of the 2nd Infantry Division, found it hard to believe that Chinese soldiers who lacked motor transport could outflank him while his (more mechanized) division was on the move: "Keiser continued to misread his situation grossly. He persisted in the belief that the roadblock was shallow or 'local,' that with a concerted 'push' and with FEAF [Far East Air Force] help it could be overcome, that the road beyond the block was 'clear.'"[145]

The inability of U.S. military leaders to anticipate the mobility that a minimal logistics tail provided led to repeated battlefield defeats, as the next chapter chronicles in detail. These examples show an inability to understand a core element of China's doctrine, that lightly armed soldiers were quite mobile.

The bewilderment about another aspect of Chinese doctrine is apparent in comments from the deputy head of logistics for the United States, General Darr H. Alkire, who was explicit in his respect for the Chinese ability to keep the supplies moving:

It has frequently been stated by commanders in Korea that the one man they would like to meet when the war is over is the G-4 [logistics commander] of the Communist forces. How he has kept supplies moving in the face of all obstacles is a real mystery. He has done it against air superiority, fire superiority, guts, and brawn.[146]

[143] Emphasis added. Captain Thomas G. Fergusson and Lt. General Edward M. Almond, "Interview with General Almond: Transcriptions of the Debriefing of General Edward M. Almond by Captain Thomas G. Fergusson (Interview Section 4)," 1975, in the Edward M Almond Papers, Box: "Recollections and Reflections," Military History Institute Library, U.S. Army War College, Carlisle, Penn., 70.

[144] For description of the Chinese strategy here, see 沈宗洪、孟照辉、等《中国人民志愿军抗美援朝战史》(北京:军事科学出版社、版次 1990、印次 1999) [Shen Zonghong, Meng Zhaohui, and others, *The History of the War to Resist America and Support Korea by the Chinese People's Volunteer Army* (Beijing: Military Science Press, 1999), 29–37].

[145] Blair, *Forgotten War*, 482.

[146] Shrader, *Communist Logistics in the Korean War*, 225–26.

While use of animals and human porters as its primary logistics train certainly had drawbacks for the Chinese forces, it also had advantages in "the relative invulnerability of marching troops to enemy air and armored attack"; moreover, "the lack of motorized transport was something of an advantage in that it permitted off-road movement over difficult terrain and thus increased the ability of the CCF to avoid detection and attack by UNC [United Nations Command] air forces."[147] Further, in this conflict, with less emphasis on logistics by the enemy, airpower aimed at interdiction inevitably had less effect.[148] These are precisely the sort of conceptual struggles that doctrinal-difference theory predicts: the air force struggled to understand the basics of the adversary's doctrine.

The U.S. Air Force had not anticipated substantial challenges trying to find Chinese troops themselves who used "excellent camouflage discipline...in the heavily wooded mountainous terrain."[149] Months after war was joined, an independent evaluation of the difficulties faced by the Air Force concluded that "joint doctrine and communications had to be improved, and a better antipersonnel air weapon would be useful against masses of enemy manpower."[150]

## THE VIEW OF AMERICAN DOCTRINE FROM BEIJING

Unsurprisingly from the perspective of this book, the Chinese were just as prone to ignorance of the dangers posed by their adversary as the Americans were. Several Chinese assessments of U.S. military capabilities display a fundamental misunderstanding of the advantages posed by American doctrine. In August, Zhou had conducted research into the U.S. Army at Mao's request. He reported weaknesses such as "the heavy American dependence on logistical support."[151] Similarly, a detailed assessment made by field commanders from late September fails to grapple with core advantages from the U.S. theory of victory; a summary of that report quotes from the actual document:

First, the U.S. forces were politically unmotivated because "they are invading [an]other people's country, fighting an unjust war, and thus

---

[147] Ibid., 143 and 173, respectively.
[148] Even the official Air Force history admits as much. See Robert Frank Futrell, *The United States Air Force in Korea, 1950–1953*, rev. ed. (Washington, D.C.: Office of Air Force History United States Air Force, 1983), 228. See also Pape, *Bombing to Win*, 145. A more appropriate strategy would have focused much more on close air support rather than deep interdiction.
[149] Futrell, *United States Air Force in Korea, 1950–1953*, 228.
[150] Crane, *American Airpower Strategy in Korea, 1950–1953*, 61.
[151] Goncharov, Lewis, and Xue Litai, *Uncertain Partners*, 337, note 19.

encountering opposition not only from the American but other peace-loving peoples around the world," whereas the Chinese forces would "fight against aggression, carrying on a just war, and thus will have the support of our people and other peace-loving peoples; and more important our troops have a stronger political consciousness and higher combat spirit." Second, the U.S. troops were inferior in terms of combat effectiveness, because, "although they have excellent modern equipment, their officers and soldiers are not adept in night battles, close combat, and bayonet charges." By contrast, the CCP troops "have had rich experience over the past ten years in fighting an enemy of modern equipment...and are good at close combat, night battles, mountainous assaults, and bayonet charges." Third, the U.S. forces were not tactically flexible, since "American soldiers always confine themselves to the bounds of military codes and regulations, and their tactics are dull and mechanical." On the other hand, the CCP forces were "good at maneuvering flexibility and mobility and, in particular, good at surrounding and attacking the enemy's flanks by taking tortuous courses, as well as dispersing and concealing [our own] forces." Fourth, American soldiers were not capable of enduring hardship. "They are afraid of dying and merely rely[ing] on firepower [in combat, while]...on the contrary our soldiers are brave and willing to sacrifice life and blood and capable of bearing hardship and heavy burdens," attributes that would remedy the disadvantage of inferior Chinese firepower. Finally, the U.S. forces had greater logistical problems. The U.S. was "carrying on a war across the [Pacific] Ocean and has to ship most of the necessities from the American continent—even if it can use supply bases in Japan, [for instance], it is transporting drinking water from Japan—and therefore its supply lines are much longer, eventually making it difficult for them to reinforce manpower and supplies." Meanwhile, the Chinese would be close to rear bases and "back[ed] by [their] fatherland." The organization of supplies would also be much easier; because "we have less trucks and artillery, we won't consume that much gasoline and ammunition."[152]

In this summary, the United States is viewed as militarily weak because of long supply lines, tactical inflexibility, and lack of appropriate political motivation. The Chinese gave little credit to potential U.S. strengths such as

[152] Zhang, *Mao's Military Romanticism*, 76–77. The report evidently comes from late September 1950.

nuclear weapons and tactical mobility. The Chinese side was thought to benefit from the justness of its cause, ability to move on foot, aptitude for hand-to-hand fighting, and light logistics tail. The Chinese military lens distorted Beijing's ability to thoroughly understand American doctrine.

When Mao considered the prospect of an expanded war, once again his engagement with the American way of war was superficial. He expressed great optimism regarding China's ability to withstand American attacks in early October 1950: "We have to prepare for America to declare and get into war with China. We also must prepare, at least, for the United States to bomb large cities and industrial bases within China and of the navy attacking our coastal zone."[153] Mao downplayed this danger, however, suggesting that the Chinese population could be mobilized to create air defense forces.[154] It is unclear how the local peasantry could do any better at air defense than the PLA, which at least had some antiaircraft artillery.

Mao's confidence in China's ability to destroy the 8th Army seems excessive as well; Mao's writing on this topic echoes his writing in 1947 about the Communists' prospects against the corrupt and inept KMT army in a previous era. In 1950, he called for overwhelming numerical superiority—"my army needs four times [as much] troop strength as the enemy's"—in order to "thoroughly annihilate one army of the enemy."[155] The similarities of Mao's strategies against vastly different military adversaries suggest how persistent was the influence of China's theory of victory on his analysis and how superficial was his engagement with American doctrine. (Mao's optimism was not unalloyed; see the discussion below.)

With regard to conventional bombing, China's senior leaders consistently discounted the value of airpower.[156] Throughout this period, material factors restrained the Communists from planning a modern air force, but Mao's attitude discounted any perceived costs of this lack:

In June 1950, while discussing the air force issue with other Chinese leaders, an emotional Mao remarked that the Communist way to deal

[153] 沈、孟、等、《抗美援朝战史》 [Shen Zonghong, Meng Zhaohui, and others, *History of the War*, 9].

[154] 沈、孟、等、《抗美援朝战史》 [ibid.].

[155] See 毛泽东、"关于决定派军队人朝作战给斯大林的电报"、1950年十月二日、《建国以来毛泽东文稿》、第一册:9/1949–12/1950(北京:中央文献出版社、1987) 第539页。 [Mao Zedong, "Telegram to Stalin Regarding the Decision to Send Troops to Korea for Combat (October 2, 1950)," in *Mao Zedong's Manuscripts since the Founding of the State* (Beijing: Central Party Documents Publishers, 1987), 541].

[156] Zhang, *Red Wings over the Yalu;* see, for instance, 22, 46, and 115.

with enemy airpower was to "not fear death, but be brave, and dare to sacrifice lives." The hardships Mao experienced during his revolutionary career unquestionably contributed to his determination to build a strong air force when the time came. However, his experiences also influenced him to maintain the view that the human factor could overcome the machine.[157]

Indeed, even after military conflict began, Mao continued to express skepticism regarding airpower. When a general was visiting Beijing during the early months of the war, "Mao invited him to his office and asked for [General] Zhu's opinion about how serious a threat UN airpower was to ground operations, and how many casualties were actually inflicted upon Chinese forces by aircraft. The chairman appeared displeased with those he thought exaggerated the role of enemy airpower."[158]

China's emphasis on airpower as a defensive asset took no lessons from the way in which airpower was used by nearly every great power in the Second World War, basically ignoring the relevance of strategic bombing from both the European and Pacific theaters. Thus, both financial reasons and Mao's attitude played a role in the slow growth of the Chinese air force.

On the nuclear front as well, there was no detailed consideration of the dangers posed by the American approach. A 1994 scholarly assessment from the Chinese Academy of Social Sciences is critical of the depth of the leadership's knowledge: "In the case of Sino-U.S. conflict, we can see that Chinese leaders, particularly Mao Zedong, and the American leaders used different criteria to assess atomic bombs or atomic warfare. They lacked the basis to reach a common understanding."[159]

At a meeting of the commanders at divisional level and above of the Northeast Military Region on August 13, 1950, one senior participant recalled, the military leaders believed that international popular opposition would prevent the United States from using the weapons:

We then explicitly assessed the factor of nuclear weapons and concluded that it was men, not one or two atomic bombs, that determined the outcome of war. And an atomic bomb use on the battlefield

---

[157] Ibid., 28. See the discussion in 廖国良、李士顺、徐焰、《毛泽东军事思想发展史》 (北京: 解放军出版社、2001) [Liao Guoliang, Li Shishun, and Xu Yan, *The Development of Mao Zedong's Military Thought* (Beijing: People's Liberation Army Press, 2001)].

[158] Zhang, *Red Wings over the Yalu*, 115.

[159] He Di, "Paper Tiger or Real Tiger: America's Nuclear Deterrence and Mao Zedong's Response," *American Studies in China* 1 (1994): 14.

would inflict damage not only on the enemy's side but also on friendly forces. Furthermore, the people of the world opposed the use of nuclear weapons; the United States would have to think twice before dropping them.[160]

Such thinking would be less surprising coming from pacifist idealists or political propagandists than, as here, from hardheaded military line-unit commanders. Senior leaders at the same meeting also focused on China's ability to prevail in spite of atomic weapons: "Top CCP leaders speculated... that the atomic bomb might be used. They understood that if the United States were to use the atomic bomb in Korea China had no way to stop it. But they would not be scared by such a prospect and would try to use conventional weapons to fight the Americans."[161] In all these cases, the shallowness of the consideration given to the most powerful weapons known to mankind provides prima facie evidence for the Discounting and Superficial Views Predictions.

Once the battle was joined, Beijing's shock further emphasizes its lack of understanding of the dangers posed by American doctrine. When U.S. and Chinese forces met in November 1950, the experience proved disastrous for Maoist military thought. Whitson writes that after the initial period of the war, the role of the "peasant ethic" in Chinese military thought declined:[162]

The first year of the Korean War thus challenged the 1947 [statement on the nature of war agreed to] between Mao and his generals. On the strategic level, the belief of senior Communist officials that a quick battlefield victory would demoralize the United Nations troops proved not only erroneous but terribly costly in trained manpower. At the tactical level, commissar emphasis on political ideology soon rang false, as officers and men rediscovered the virtues of small-unit professional leadership as the greatest assurance of battlefield performance and loyalty.[163]

As a result, Whitson continues, "They learned other disheartening lessons about the efficacy of guerrilla warfare, Mao's thought, and 'People's War.'"[164] Statements by senior Chinese leaders emphasize this point. Even

---

[160] Du Ping, "Political Mobilization and Control," in *Mao's Generals Remember Korea*, ed. Li Xiaobing, Allan Reed Millett, and Yu Bin (Lawrence: University Press of Kansas, 2001), 62.
[161] Chen Jian, *China's Road to the Korean War: The Making of the Sino-American Confrontation* (New York: Columbia University Press, 1994), 142–4.
[162] Whitson and Huang, *Chinese High Command*, 459.
[163] Ibid., 95.
[164] Ibid., 462.

Mao would say that "the War to Resist America and Support Korea served as a large classroom for us. At that time we engaged in a big practice exercise. This exercise was much more useful than ordinary military training."[165]

Zhou Enlai similarly wrote in 1952:

> Although in terms of equipment, weapons, and firepower we were weak compared to the American imperialists, we learned many things from our enemy's side. Now we have practiced, and we know how to drive back their attacks.... If this war had not occurred, we would not have been able to learn from these experiences.[166]

Thus, they implicitly conceded that the United States taught the Chinese forces some lessons in Korea. Given that archival material is only selectively released by a CCP bureaucracy that uses historiography (and hagiography) to justify the party's continued authoritarian rule, one should not expect much more explicit evidence. (Indeed, at a general level, even now one rarely sees critiques of Mao's conduct of the war. In a rare instance, one Chinese scholar writes that Mao's "rash determination to entirely destroy the UN Army" following the successful second campaign begun in November 1950 led to "many serious setbacks in subsequent campaigns."[167]) Nevertheless, all these comments emphasize the degree to which the Chinese leadership was ignorant of the advantages posed by American doctrines.

Outsiders can be more honest. In his memoirs, Nikita Khrushchev writes of the persistent and mistaken optimism of the Chinese forces as they entered the Korean War:

> In the archives you can find documents in which P'eng Te-huai gave his situation reports to Mao-Tse-tung. P'eng composed lengthy telegrams expounding elaborate battle plans against the Americans. He declared categorically that the enemy would be surrounded and finished off by decisive flanking strikes. The American troops were crushed and the war ended many times in the battle reports which P'eng sent to Mao, who then sent them along to Stalin.

---

[165] 廖、等、《毛泽东军事思想发展史》 [Liao et al., *Mao's Military Thought*, 452].

[166] 周、《周恩来军事文选》 [Zhou Enlai, *Zhou Enlai's Selected Military Writings* (Beijing: People's Publishers, 1997), 297].

[167] 时殷弘、《关于台湾的几项必须正视的大战略问题》战略与管理宗弟39期、第2期(2000) [Shi Yinhong, "Several Major Strategic Problems Regarding Taiwan That Must Be Addressed," *Strategy and Management* 39, no. 2 (2000): 29].

Unfortunately, the war wasn't ended quickly at all. The Chinese suffered many huge defeats....China bore terrible losses because her technology and armaments were considerably inferior to those of the Americans. On both the offensive and the defensive, Chinese tactics depended mostly on sheer manpower.[168]

All of this suggests that, at a strategic level, the Chinese were surprised by the prowess of the American military against the People's War strategy. Such surprise at the adversary's capabilities on the battlefield is what the theory predicts (the Startling Battlefield Outcomes Prediction) and is inconsistent with a detailed understanding of American doctrine.

The above discussion highlights the thinking in Beijing regarding the American theory of victory at the highest levels. The picture painted is one of only a superficial understanding of the strategies that the U.S. military would employ against the PLA. The subsequent chapter supplements this high-level discussion with extensive data on specific tactics that Beijing had not anticipated, such tactical mobility, the robust defensive capabilities of even surrounded units, and the unexpected dangers of the U.S. Air Force. But the evidence presented here lays a foundation in support of the doctrinal-difference misperception hypothesis that underestimation was linked to differences in the two countries' theories of victory.

The evidence presented in this chapter strongly supports a characterization of two countries facing each other with vastly different theories of victory. Furthermore, the two sides each struggled to understand the other side's theory with any degree of sophistication.

It is a truism that no plan survives contact with the enemy. It is certainly the case that as war was joined and intensified both sides adjusted their doctrines and fought accordingly. Nevertheless, the key issue for this book is the signaling that *preceded* the Sino-American phase of the war. Had that signaling been more effective, a great tragedy might have been avoided. That signaling and interpretation process was greatly impeded, as the next chapter will show, by the doctrinal difference with which the two sides approached the war in the middle of 1950.

At a very fundamental level, therefore, the two sides faced off with different views of warfare and limited understanding of the implications. The

---

[168] Nikita Sergeevich Khrushchev, *Khrushchev Remembers* (Boston: Little, Brown, 1970), 372.

book now turns to examining the tragic effects of this difference on perception, misperception, and two critical decisions that escalated the conflict during the Korean War: the U.S. decision to go north across the 38th parallel (chapter 4) and the Chinese decision to go south across the Yalu River (chapter 5).

# 4

# THE UNITED STATES CROSSES
# THE 38TH PARALLEL

AFTER THE NORTH KOREAN attack across the 38th parallel of June 25, 1950, the United States rushed to aid the collapsing South Korean forces. Through the summer of 1950, the ground war went poorly for the South Korean and U.S. forces, which were pushed back in a long retreat to the Pusan Perimeter. After that line solidified in early August, however, the Inchon landings of September 15 were a success, forcing the United States to consider more directly whether to cross the 38th parallel, how to do so, and what the strategic goals would be once it did so. The Chinese sent a large number of signals—both explicit and implicit—to the United States, warning it against continuing its offensive. Washington, however, disregarded these signals in the belief that the Chinese would not get involved. The Americans drove north. The PLA attacked, first in late October and early November in modest scale, and second in late November with a massive force (the first and second offensives, in the Chinese parlance). These attacks fundamentally altered the course of the conflict, which would over the next three years take more than a million lives. It also further hardened the Cold War.[1] The failure of Chinese attempts to coerce the United States into staying south of the 38th parallel, then, merits careful consideration.

In this chapter I outline the role that the two sides' theories of victory played in this colossal failure of communication and perception. Although

---

[1] Robert Jervis, "The Impact of the Korean War on the Cold War," *Journal of Conflict Resolution* 24, no. 4 (1980).

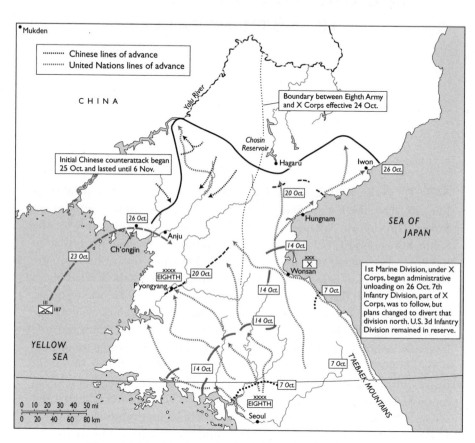

**Figure 4.1.** The American offensive in Korea, October 7–26, 1950.

there were other factors that played a role, most of which are subsumed under the Weakness Hypothesis in this book, doctrinal difference is a critical part of this story that has gone unappreciated. Key elements of the conventional wisdom have been overstated: MacArthur's complacency was not unique and indeed was shared by many military leaders. Nor can poor signals intelligence or Chinese deception account for the failures. The evidence presented below suggests that doctrinal difference were a necessary condition for this tragedy. In short, this chapter tells of "a time of signals sent but not received."[2]

## HISTORICAL BACKGROUND

Among scholars of the Korean War, there had long been a debate over the role of the Soviets and the Chinese in the outbreak of the Korean War. There is now enough evidence to end the debate. Scholars have long known that Beijing, like Moscow, had been a strong supporter of the Communists in the North.[3] Kim Il Sung consulted regularly with the Chinese leadership and in early 1950 the CCP's Central Committee ordered that three divisions who had been fighting on the Communist side in the Chinese civil war should return to Korea, keeping their weapons.[4] Even more critical than this direct military support for the North was Mao's formal approval of Kim Il Sung's attack, an issue upon which there is now widespread consensus.[5] (The following chapter

[2] David Halberstam, *The Coldest Winter: America and the Korean War* (New York: Hyperion, 2007), 334.

[3] On this support in general, see 宋连生、《抗美援朝在回首》(昆明、云南人民出版社、2002) [Song Liansheng, *Recollections on the Korean War* (Kunming: Yunnan People's Press, 2002), 172–73].

[4] 蔡仁照、《中国元帅聂荣臻》(北京:中共中央党校出版社、1994). pp. 445–46. [Cai Renzhao, *Nie Rongzhen: China's Principal Military Chief* (Beijing: Central Party School of the CCP, 1994)]. See also Chen Jian, *China's Road to the Korean War: The Making of the Sino-American Confrontation* (New York: Columbia University Press, 1994), 106–7. Liu Shaoqi attributes the decision to let them take their weapons to Mao. 刘少奇、"军委同意第四野战军中朝鲜营兵会朝鲜的电报"、1950年一月十一日《建国以来刘少奇文稿》、第一册:7/1949–3/1950(北京:中央文献出版社、1998) [Liu Shaoqi, "Telegrams Regarding the CMC Concurring with the 4th Field Army Regarding the Return of the Korean Battalions to Korea (January 17, 1950)," in *Liu Shaoqi's Manuscripts since the Founding of the State* (Beijing: Central Party Documents Publishers, 1998)].

[5] William Whitney Stueck Jr., *The Korean War: An International History* (Princeton: Princeton University Press, 1995), 37, 39–40; Sergei Goncharov, John Lewis, and Xue Litai, *Uncertain Partners: Stalin, Mao, and the Korean War* (Stanford: Stanford University Press, 1993), 145–46; Chen, *China's Road*, 112–13; Shen Zhihua, "Sino-Soviet Relations and the Origins of the Korean War: Stalin's Strategic Goals in the Far East," *Journal of Cold War Studies* 2, no. 2 (2000): 67.

describes the role of perceptual dynamics in shaping that and subsequent decisions.)

The U.S. decision to cross the 38th parallel was contingent on a belief that, if it did so, the Chinese and Soviets would not get directly involved.[6] In fact, however, by crossing the 38th parallel, the United States greatly reduced its opportunities to avoid a Sino-American war. As the Chinese finalized their decision to intervene in early October 1950, the U.S. crossing of the 38th parallel loomed large in their deliberations. Thus, the signaling and interpretation regarding this issue had enormous consequences. If doctrinal-difference theory deepens the understanding of this catastrophic U.S. error, it teaches something valuable.

The U.S. advance against North Korea moved very rapidly beginning in early September. Planning for crossing the 38th parallel began only days before the actual Inchon landings took place. "The decision [to cross the 38th] was embodied in NSC-81, written mostly by [Assistant Secretary of State Dean] Rusk, which authorized MacArthur to move into North Korea if there were no Soviet or Chinese threats to intervene."[7] Although NSC-81/1, signed on September 11, 1950, did pave the way for the general invasion of North Korea, it postponed a specific decision on that point:

> It would be expected that the U.N. Commander would receive authorization to conduct military operations, including amphibious and airborne landings or ground operations in pursuance of a roll-back in Korea north of the 38th parallel, for the purpose of destroying the North Korean forces, provided that at the time of such operations there has been no entry into North Korea by major Soviet or Chinese Communist forces, no announcement of intended entry, nor a threat to counter our operations militarily in North Korea.[8]

On October 1, MacArthur demanded in sweeping terms that the North Koreans surrender; obtaining no such response, MacArthur received final

[6] A thorough review of the literature on this episode as of the early 1990s can be found in Rosemary Foot, "Making Known the Unknown War: Policy Analysis of the Korean Conflict in the Last Decade," *Diplomatic History* 15, no. 3 (1991). Updating that is Allan R. Millett, "The Korean War: A 50-Year Critical Historiography," *Journal of Strategic Studies* 24, no. 1 (2001).

[7] Bruce Cumings, *The Origins of the Korean War: The Roaring of the Cataract, 1947–1950*, vol. 2 (Princeton: Princeton University Press, 1981), 711.

[8] National Security Council, "Report by the National Security Council to the President (September 9, 1950)," in *FRUS, 1950*, ed. United States Department of State (Washington, D.C.: U.S. GPO, 1976).

authority to cross the 38th parallel on October 2.[9] By October 3, "the ROK [Republic of Korea] I Corps was well inside North Korea on the east coast."[10] Four days later, the UN passed a "go anywhere" resolution, authorizing the UN force to engage in ground operations in North Korea. The first U.S. troops crossed the 38th parallel on that same day. Throughout these incremental escalations, it is very clear that U.S. decisions were based on the presumption that China and the Soviet Union would not get involved in a significant way.[11]

The U.S. decision to cross the 38th parallel into North Korea greatly reduced the prospects for avoiding war between the two great powers. This chapter begins by assessing the Chinese signals, both diplomatic and, more important, military. It then turns to an examination of the interpretation of those signals by the United States, noting the substantial misperceptions and their links to the causal chains as predicted by doctrinal-difference theory. Then it reviews additional evidence from subsequent U.S. analysis of these events that supports doctrinal-difference theory. In short, this case provides robust evidence for the theory.

## SIGNALING BY CHINA

A large number of Chinese signals were aimed directly at the United States. This section surveys both the public and private diplomatic signals, and then examines China's contemporaneous military signals.

### DIPLOMATIC AND PUBLIC SIGNALS

Propaganda served (and still serves) many purposes for the Chinese regime, addressing both domestic and international audiences.[12] The propaganda department recognized the importance of the Korean War for Chinese Communist Party (CCP) domestic politics:

> This is an important event at the present time. The United States has thus exposed its imperialist face, which is not fearsome at all but is favorable

---

[9] James F. Schnabel, *United States Army in the Korean War,* vol. 3: Policy and Direction: The First Year (Washington, D.C.: Office of the Chief of Military History United States Army/GPO, 1972), 181 and 193.

[10] Ibid., 202.

[11] Ibid., 178.

[12] Jonathan D. Spence, *The Search for Modern China,* 1st ed. (New York: Norton, 1990), 514–19.

for the further awakening of the Chinese people and the people of the whole world. All over China, we have to use this opportunity to echo Foreign Minister Zhou's statement and to start a widespread campaign of propaganda, so that we will be able to educate our people at home and to strike firmly the arrogance of the U.S. imperialist aggression.[13]

However, following the withdrawal of Ambassador John Leighton Stuart in 1949, the United States had no formal lines of communication with the Chinese. Propaganda was therefore an important means of international communication.[14] Public statements were the primary remaining means of direct communication between China and the West, which certainly exacerbated the two sides' potential for misunderstanding.

Immediately after U.S. intervention in the Korean War, Chinese signals were rather mild: "China's initial public reaction demonstrated its caution, watchfulness, and explicitly defensive posture."[15] However, by the week of July 17–24, 1950, a "Hate the United States" campaign began in China.[16] Furthermore, "August marked the start of [China's] more aggressive stance" in terms of propaganda.[17]

Indeed, by the end of the summer, Chinese diplomacy as well had shifted, from a search for negotiated solutions (such as support for the Soviet peace initiative in early August) to explicitly threatening the United States that it would intervene. These warnings began in mid-August.[18] Initially, China made two rather oblique warnings. First:

On 20 August [1950] Chinese foreign minister Zhou Enlai sent a message to the United Nations that deviated from past statements

---

[13] "Instruction, General Information Agency, 'On the Propaganda about U.S. Imperialists' Open Intervention in the Internal Affairs of China, Korea, and Vietnam,' 29 June 1950," in Zhang Shuguang and Chen Jian, eds., *Chinese Communist Foreign Policy and the Cold War in Asia: New Documentary Evidence, 1944–50* (Chicago: Imprint Publications, 1996), 153. This instrumental use of the crisis parallels Mao's use of other crises in Sino-American relations. See Thomas J. Christensen, *Useful Adversaries: Grand Strategy, Domestic Mobilization, and Sino-American Conflict, 1947–1958* (Princeton: Princeton University Press, 1996), chapter 6.

[14] Yuan Ming, "The Failure of Perception: America's China Policy, 1949–50," in *Sino-American Relations, 1945–1955: A Joint Reassessment of a Critical Decade*, ed. Harry Harding and Ming Yuan (Wilmington, Del.: SR Books, 1989), 145.

[15] Zhang Shuguang, *Deterrence and Strategic Culture: Chinese-American Confrontations, 1949–1958* (Ithaca: Cornell University Press, 1992), 90.

[16] Stueck, *Korean War,* 52.

[17] Rosemary Foot, *The Wrong War: American Policy and the Dimensions of the Korean Conflict, 1950–1953* (Ithaca: Cornell University Press, 1985), 79.

[18] Rosemary Foot, *A Substitute for Victory: The Politics of Peacemaking at the Korean Armistice Talks* (Ithaca: Cornell University Press, 1990), 26.

emanating from Beijing in its emphasis on Korea rather than Taiwan. Because "Korea is China's neighbor," Zhou declared, "the Chinese people cannot but be concerned about the solution of the Korean question."[19]

Within a week of that warning, on August 26, the government mouthpiece magazine *World Knowledge* stated more explicitly that China viewed potential U.S. intervention in Korea as a potential security threat.[20] Later, "On September 25, Nieh Jung-chen, acting chief of staff of the PLA, told [Indian Ambassador to Beijing Kavalam M.] Panikkar that the Chinese would not 'sit back with folded hands and let the Americans come up to the border.'"[21] (Both sides often used Ambassador Panikkar as a vehicle for passing messages.) Zhou Enlai chimed in on September 30: "The Chinese people absolutely will not tolerate foreign aggression, nor will they supinely tolerate seeing their neighbors being savagely invaded by the imperialists."[22] The Chinese stepped up their diplomacy once again:

> Even more dramatic was Chou En-lai's late-night meeting with Panikkar on October 3 in which the Chinese premier made it unmistakably clear that if U.S. troops crossed into North Korea, Chinese contingents would enter the war. "The South Koreans did not matter," Chou explained, "but American intervention into North Korea would encounter Chinese resistance."[23]

On October 10,[24] China's official government newspaper, the *Renmin Ribao,* published a statement relaying Zhou's Foreign Ministry warning issued the same day:

> The American war of invasion in Korea has been a serious menace to the security of China from its very start.... *The Chinese people cannot stand idly by* with regard to such a serious situation created by the invasion of Korea by the United States and its accomplice countries and to the dangerous trend toward extending the war.... The Chinese people firmly advocate a peaceful solution to the Korean problem and are firmly opposed to the

[19] Stueck, *Korean War,* 64.
[20] Ibid.
[21] Foot, *Wrong War,* 79.
[22] Schnabel, *United States Army in the Korean War,* 197.
[23] Foot, *Wrong War,* 79.
[24] By this time, however, both South Korean and American troops had already crossed the border, although they had only just begun their advance northward.

extension of the Korean war by America and its accomplice countries. And they are even more firm in holding that *aggressors must be answerable for all consequences* resulting from their frantic acts in extending aggression.[25]

Blair interprets this as "very close to a declaration of war."[26]

Thus, throughout this period, diplomatic warnings were numerous and—over time—increasingly insistent and explicit.

## MILITARY SIGNALS AND POLICY

Complementing the above signaling, "the Chinese reinforced that policy with active preparations for military intervention in Korea."[27] Chinese military moves had begun quite early. As Mao explained several years later to a Soviet delegation, "After the war broke out, we first shifted three armies and later added another two, putting a total of five armies on the edge of the Yalu River" and the border with China.[28] The Central Military Commission (CMC) meeting of July 7 (discussed in the next chapter) ordered forces redeployed from Fujian to Manchuria.[29] At CMC meetings August 7 through August 10, Chinese leaders continued to lay the groundwork for defensive deployments to the Korean-Chinese border, including significant troop deployments.[30] The gathered forces would number 225,000 by the end of the summer.[31] These were reinforced further as the United States solidified the Pusan perimeter in early August: "[Mao] informed his generals in the northeast that they must be prepared to fight within a month. Later in August he extended the period of preparation to the end of September, but he also called for twelve armies to be stationed along the Yalu, an increase of eight over his order of early July."[32]

---

[25] Emphasis added. Quoted in editorial comments in United States Department of State, *FRUS, 1950*, vol. 7: Korea (Washington, D.C.: U.S. GPO, 1976), 914.

[26] Clay Blair, *The Forgotten War: America in Korea* (New York: Times Books, 1988), 340.

[27] *World Knowledge* 23, no. 8 (August 26, 1950).

[28] 廖国良、李士顺、徐焰,《毛泽东军事思想发展史》修订版(北京:解放军出版社、2001) [Liao Guoliang, Li Shishun, and Xu Yan, *The Development of Mao Zedong's Military Thought* (Beijing: People's Liberation Army Press, 2001), 372].

[29] Zhang Shuguang, *Mao's Military Romanticism: China and the Korean War, 1950–53* (Lawrence: University Press of Kansas, 1995), 59; Chen, *China's Road*, 132. China's Central Military Commission (CMC) is the institution that exerts control over the military for the CCP and also integrates political factors into military decision making.

[30] Chen, *China's Road*, 136.

[31] Zhang, *Deterrence and Strategic Culture*, 91.

[32] Stueck, *Korean War*, 65. See also Zhang, *Deterrence and Strategic Culture*, 91–92; Edwin Palmer Hoyt, *The Day the Chinese Attacked: Korea, 1950: The Story of the Failure of America's China Policy* (New York: Paragon House, 1993), 72.

These decisions percolated through the Chinese chain of command. As the PLA Chief of Staff later wrote:

[China expected that] North Korea would very likely experience a setback and some complications in the war. Thus, according to the CMC's decision, I telegraphed an order to the strategic reserve forces on August 5: "Complete all the necessary preparations within this month. Be ready for the order of new movement and engagement."[33]

These strategic reserve forces consisted of three multidivision armies totaling nearly one hundred thousand troops).

While the United States was preparing for the Inchon landings, Chinese preparations intensified even further. On August 23, Mao and Zhou Enlai "decided to reiterate to the NEBDA [China's Northeast Border Defense Agency] that no matter what the difficulties, all preparations for operations should be completed by the end of September."[34] In early September, the Chinese moved the headquarters of the crack Fourth Field Army to Shenyang so that it would be closer the North Korean border.[35] Logistics preparations were made at the same time.[36] China sent military observers to North Korea to assess the tactical situation in late September.[37]

Many of these steps were meant primarily to create the material conditions that would allow the Chinese to intervene. However, such military moves also had communicative goals and were intended to bolster the diplomatic warnings that were being issued at the same time. Allen Whiting and Zhang Shuguang, like most other historians of the period, believe that Beijing intended with these military moves to send deterrent signals.[38]

Indeed, it had been Mao's practice to do precisely this—to use military deployments to send deterrent signals to the Americans: he believed, for example, that his large deployment of troops to coastal regions in Northern China in 1949 had deterred the United States from getting involved in the

---

[33] Nie Rongzhen, "Beijing's Decision to Intervene," in *Mao's Generals Remember Korea*, ed. Li Xiaobing, Allan R. Millett, and Yu Bin (Lawrence: University Press of Kansas, 2001), 40.

[34] Chen, *China's Road*, 148.

[35] Russell Spurr, *Enter the Dragon: China's Undeclared War against the U.S. in Korea, 1950–51* (New York: Newmarket Press, 1988), 70–71.

[36] Charles R. Shrader, *Communist Logistics in the Korean War* (Westport, Conn.: Greenwood Press, 1995), 170.

[37] Chen, *China's Road*, 163.

[38] See Zhang, *Deterrence and Strategic Culture*, 90–94; Allen S. Whiting, *China Crosses the Yalu: The Decision to Enter the Korean War* (New York: Macmillan, 1960), 64–67.

civil war in its waning days.[39] Then, the Central Military Committee empha-sized the deterrent nature of the deployment, declaring that "with [these preparations] we can dissuade the United States from realizing its ambition of armed intervention [in China]."[40]

According to the conventional wisdom in the deterrence literature, tested here as the Weakness Hypothesis, these strong signals should have had a high probability of leading to coercive success. However, as this book argues, China's signals—large-scale infantry deployments—were fundamen-tally shaped by the Chinese theory of victory (i.e., supporting the Nature of Signaling Prediction). Instead of strong signals leading to coercive success, they failed—as predicted by doctrinal-difference theory. Despite China's sig-nals, both diplomatic and military, the United States crossed the 38th paral-lel; the Chinese involvement in the war followed.

The following section outlines the U.S. perception of the strong Chinese signals and explains why it did not understand them.

## INTERPRETATION BY THE UNITED STATES

This section addresses the questions of whether American decisionmakers were aware of the Chinese threats; how they interpreted them; and what role U.S. beliefs about the nature of war played in that process.

The primary conclusion both in Washington and at MacArthur's head-quarters in Tokyo was that China would not intervene. This supports the Downplaying Prediction, which suggests that leaders will downplay the likelihood of an adversary getting involved. At a Wake Island meeting on October 15, only a few weeks before the first battle with the PLA, Truman and MacArthur discussed this issue explicitly. In that exchange, as in many instances discussed in this book, the assessments of China's capability and of its intent were intertwined, each mutually supporting the other:

---

[39] Zhang, *Mao's Military Romanticism*, 54, see also 13–33. U.S. forces of over one hundred thou-sand in 1945 had been reduced to four thousand in 1948; they were completely withdrawn from mainland China in June 1949. Although there had been some skirmishing between the Red Army and U.S. Marines (leading to over forty American casualties) in the late periods of the Chinese civil war, the last significant action had occurred in April 1947. Henry I. Shaw Jr., *The United States Marines in North China, 1945–1949* (Washington, D. C.: Historical Branch, G-3 Division, Headquarters, U. S. Marine Corps, 1968).

[40] Zhang, *Mao's Military Romanticism*, 36.

THE PRESIDENT: What are the chances for Chinese or Soviet inter-
ference?

GENERAL MACARTHUR: Very little.... The Chinese have 300,000 men in
Manchuria.... Only 50–60,000 could be gotten across the Yalu River.
They have no Air Force. Now that we have bases for our Air Force in
Korea, if the Chinese tried to get down to Pyongyang there would be
the greatest slaughter.[41]

This section examines a range of reasons for this confidence. It begins
by addressing the conventional argument that the messenger who delivered
several of the signals, Ambassador Panikkar, was not trusted. This argument
generally is used to bolster the Weakness Hypothesis, which centers on the
objective quality of the signal to explain deterrence success or failure. If the
signals were not clear, then the alternate (weakness) hypothesis would indeed predict the resulting deterrence failure. However, as will be shown, this
is not the case. Panikkar cannot be blamed for the deterrence failure because
the military threats were heard in Washington; they simply were not viewed as
threatening. The last section of the chapter evaluates the acute and pervasive
surprise that the U.S. leadership felt when the Chinese did in fact intervene,
at great cost to American soldiers and Marines.

### ROLE OF PANIKKAR

In the conventional interpretation, Beijing's message did not get through
to Washington because of the latter's mistrust of the chosen messenger, the
Indian ambassador stationed in Beijing, Kavalam M. Panikkar. The argument
is that Washington viewed him as a self-promoter and a Communist sympa-
thizer.[42] Britain was also said to consider him unreliable.[43]

However, Panikkar's reliability was not as suspect as the later historiography indicated. Although the United States was looking for alternate lines
of communication to use with Beijing,[44] it had long used India as a way to

---

[41] "Substance of Statements Made at Wake Island Conference on 15 October 1950," in *FRUS,
1950, Vol. 7*, 953. Although the operational order to cross had been given days before, this passage is indicative of the views held in the United States about the relevant dangers.

[42] Foot, *Wrong War*, 79.

[43] Peter Lowe, *The Origins of the Korean War*, 2nd ed. (New York: Longman, 1997), 215.

[44] See the concerns expressed in "Memorandum by the Director of the Office of Chinese
Affairs (Clubb) to the Assistant Secretary of State for Far Eastern Affairs (Rusk)," October 26,
1950, in *FRUS, 1950, Vol. 7*, 1000–1002.

send signals to and receive them from Beijing.[45] Indeed, only a few days before presenting the first warning, Panikkar had been suggesting, based on his conversations with Zhou Enlai and other forms of information, that China would not intervene, and this message was given credence by the United States.[46] After the outbreak of war between the United States and China, Washington continued to use Indian emissaries as intermediaries to Beijing.[47] Thus, the United States had a history of using Panikkar and India as conduits for messages; moreover, it is indisputable that the warnings were conveyed to Washington: "The State Department got word of this threat early the following day."[48]

Moreover, it was not only isolated warnings from Panikkar that got through, but a wide range of other sources of information. One report in early September gives essentially the same warning that was repeated frequently later: James Wilkinson, the U.S. consul general in Hong Kong, received a letter purporting to reproduce discussions of a "Peking conference," quoting Zhou Enlai as follows: "When asked [about the] position of China should North Korean troops be pushed back to Manchurian border, Chou [Zhou Enlai] replied China would fight [the] enemy outside China's border and not wait until enemy came in."[49] Other warnings abounded: "From Hong Kong and Taipei, word did filter into the State Department that Beijing would commit troops to Korea if U.S. soldiers advanced north of the 38th parallel."[50] In addition:

Indications of Chinese intentions grew increasingly disturbing. On [September 29], the State Department received word, indirectly through the embassy in Moscow, that the Dutch chargé in Beijing believed Chinese officials were considering military intervention in Korea if U.S. troops entered the North. On 2 October [Consul

---

[45] Foot, *Wrong War*, 83; Dean Acheson, *Present at the Creation: My Years in the State Department* (New York: Norton, 1969), 452.

[46] This message was relayed to Washington on September 21, 1950. Stueck, *Korean War*, 90.

[47] Indian prime minister Jawaharlal Nehru was involved as a conduit for information as late as the Panmunjom negotiations in 1953. Robert Pape, *Bombing to Win: Air Power and Coercion in War* (Ithaca: Cornell University Press, 1996), 166. During the early part of the war, Indian diplomats played this messenger role several times. See "Memorandum by the Deputy Assistant Secretary of State for Far Eastern Affairs (Merchant) to the Assistant Secretary of State for Far Eastern Affairs (Rusk)," November 16, 1950 in *FRUS, 1950, Vol. 7*, 1164.

[48] Stueck, *Korean War*, 94, see also 91.

[49] "The Consul General at Hong Kong (Wilkinson) to the Secretary of State (September 5, 1950)" in *FRUS, 1950, Vol. 7*, 698.

[50] Stueck, *Korean War*, 90.

General] Wilkinson in Hong Kong sent a partial text of a Zhou Enlai speech of 30 September, which included the assertion that "the Chinese people absolutely will not tolerate foreign aggression nor will they supinely tolerate seeing their neighbors being savagely invaded by foreigners."[51]

The report from the Moscow embassy was passed through the CIA, suggesting that this warning got wide distribution in the U.S. government, as had the others discussed above.[52] Beijing's most ominous October 10 warning from the Foreign Ministry clearly found its way to senior leaders in Washington.[53] All of these messages corroborated Panikkar's warnings, yet they too were ignored.

When Panikkar conveyed messages Washington wanted to hear, they were treated as credible. When he passed on messages that Washington did not want to hear, it labeled him as unreliable. Panikkar's warnings were not the only ones ignored. His role in the miscalculations is not causal.

### IGNORANCE OF THE MILITARY SIGNALS WAS NOT AN EXCUSE

Throughout this period, the United States was also aware that Beijing was conducting extensive military movements in the region. Thus the failure of the Chinese signals cannot be accounted for by purported American ignorance of these moves.

A few examples will help make the case. On the military side: "U.S. intelligence picked up the steady movement of Chinese forces northward toward Korea."[54] General Charles Willoughby, MacArthur's G-2 (intelligence) officer, estimated on July 3 that "the Chinese had stationed two cavalry divisions and four armies in Manchuria."[55] This would have been a force totaling approximately 140,000 men. By the end of August, he noted that "sources have reported troop movement from Central China to Manchuria for some time which suggest movements preliminary to entering the Korean theater."[56]

---

[51] Ibid., 93–94.

[52] Central Intelligence Agency, "Document 197. ORE 58–50 Excerpt, 12 October 1950, Critical Situations in the Far East," in *Assessing the Soviet Threat: The Early Cold War Years,* ed. Woodrow J. Kuhns (Washington, D.C.: Central Intelligence Agency, 1997).

[53] "Memorandum of Conversation, by the Ambassador at Large (Jessup) (October 12, 1950)," in *FRUS, 1950, Vol. 7,* 931.

[54] Stueck, *Korean War,* 65.

[55] Schnabel, *United States Army in the Korean War,* 198. See also Foot, *Wrong War,* 79.

[56] This is a summary of the contents in "Daily Intelligence Summary No. 2913 (August 31, 1950)," as described in General Charles Willoughby, "The Chinese Communist Potential for

At that point, he estimated that some 246,000 Chinese soldiers were in Manchuria, and of those 80,000 were in the Chinese village of An-tung, just across the Yalu.[57] Following the U.S. landings at Inchon, Willoughby raised his estimate of Chinese forces in Manchuria to 450,000.[58] His staff reported that there were some thirty-eight divisions in Manchuria on October 4.[59]

Although some of these Chinese moves might have been explained away as defensive deployments, other specifics should have been less easily dismissed. On October 5, Willoughby prepared a Daily Intelligence Summary (DIS):

[The DIS] contained the raw data for MacArthur's intelligence assessment. The DISs, which could be 30 pages long and frequently longer, contained detailed accounts of the day's fighting in Korea, a good deal of political material on all countries in the FEC [Far East Command] region (including Japan and China), as well as special appreciations and order of battle annexes.[60]

The October 5 DIS was immediately telexed to Washington; in it, Willoughby noted that many of these troops were massing at border crossings:

A build-up of Chinese forces along the Korean-Manchurian border has been reported in many channels, and while exaggerations and canards are always evident, the potential of massing at the Antung and other Manchurian crossing appears conclusive. This mass involves a possible

Intervention in the Korean War (Undated)," in the Charles A. Willoughby Papers, Box 10, Military History Institute Library, U.S. Army War College, Carlisle, Penn., 2.

[57] Schnabel, *United States Army in the Korean War,* 179.

[58] Ibid., 199.

[59] See "Joint Daily SITREP, No. 99 (October 4, 1950)," in *Joint Daily Sitrep Collection,* (Carlisle, Penn.: Military History Institute Library, U.S. Army War College, 1950). This collection consists of the daily situation reports for the entire Far Eastern Command. Chinese divisions varied in size widely, from as few as three thousand to more than six thousand soldiers. Further, support troops outside a division might account for additional troops in the amount of 50 percent to 100 percent of the combat formations.

[60] Eliot A. Cohen, "'Only Half the Battle': American Intelligence and the Chinese Intervention in Korea, 1950," *Intelligence and National Security* 5, no. 1 (1990): 132. Cohen notes that "three copies of the DIS [the Daily Intelligence Summary, the key intelligence document put out by Willoughby's office] were sent every day to Washington by courier from Tokyo taking three to five days, apparently, to arrive there. Another 54 copies went by registered mail" (146, note 7). The State Department staff on the ground in South Korea also had access to Eighth Army and X Corps intelligence reports as they were produced. They often cabled summaries of these to Acheson in Washington. See, for instance, "The Chargé in Korea (Drumright) to the Secretary of State (November 1, 1950)," reprinted in *FRUS, 1950, Vol. 7,* 1022.

9–18 divisions organized into 3–6 armies of the total strength of 38 divisions and 9 armies now carried in all Manchuria.... The potential exists for Chinese Communist forces to openly intervene in the Korea War if UN forces cross the 38th Parallel.[61]

Some reports also circulated in the American national-security bureaucracy that Chinese forces had crossed the Yalu on October 5, although these reports turned out to be inaccurate.[62] By mid-October, Willoughby was reporting that scores of Chinese divisions were being forward deployed, not just moved to Manchuria in general: "Intervention is a decision for war, on the highest level, i.e., the Kremlin and Peiping. However, the numerical and troop potential in Manchuria is a *fait accompli*. A total of 24 divisions are disposed along the Yalu River."[63] Two weeks later, his staff estimated the number of forward-deployed divisions along the river at twenty-nine.[64]

Throughout this period, the United States remained confident of its ability to monitor Chinese movements through Air Force reconnaissance and intelligence assets.[65] When convoys were sighted coming south from the border (a very common occurrence[66]), the standard operating procedure was to continue to monitor the road with aircraft, to guarantee information. For instance, "The most significant enemy activity was the unconfirmed sighting of extensive vehicular convoy movements south, toward and through Pyongyang. Constant air surveillance of the routes between Sariwon and Sunchon is now being maintained."[67]

Other intelligence sources, outside of the military chain of command, echoed these reports through State Department reports from Moscow, Hong Kong, and Taipei, as well as through the reporting of other allied nations' foreign ministries and military attachés. For instance, "Earlier intelligence

---

[61] "Daily Intelligence Summary No. 2948 (October 5, 1950)," quoted in Willoughby, "Chinese Communist Potential," 3. The Daily Intelligence Summary of four days later reinforced that conclusion. See also Schnabel, *United States Army in the Korean War,* 200.

[62] Schnabel, *United States Army in the Korean War,* 200.

[63] "Daily Intelligence Summary No. 2957 (October 14, 1950)," quoted in Willoughby, "Chinese Communist Potential," 3.

[64] "Daily Intelligence Summary No. 2971 (October 28, 1950)," summarized in ibid., 4.

[65] Dennis D. Wainstock, *Truman, MacArthur, and the Korean War* (Westport, Conn.: Greenwood Press, 1999), 88.

[66] Such reports litter the SITREPs beginning in September and continuing through the Chinese offensives. See, for instance "Joint Daily SITREP No. 69 (September 4, 1950)"; "Joint Daily SITREP No. 98 (October 3, 1950)"; "Joint Daily SITREP No. 102 (October 7, 1950)," all in *Joint Daily Sitrep Collection.*

[67] "Joint Daily SITREP No. 99 (October 4, 1950)," in ibid.

reports had indicated that, since July, sizable Chinese ground forces had been moving into Manchuria from distant regions of the country."[68] The CIA, in a major survey regarding the prospect of Chinese entry in early September 1950, also noted the enormous force in Manchuria:

> Following the fall of Manchuria there were approximately 565,000 Military District [MD] troops in Manchuria (including 165,100 ex-Nationalists), and possibly 100,000 to 125,000 of these MD troops have now been integrated into the regular army and organized as combat forces. These units, as well as the remaining MD troops, probably are Soviet-equipped. In addition, reports during the past three months have indicated a considerable increase in regular troop strength in Manchuria. It is estimated that the major elements of Lin Piao's 4th Field Army—totaling perhaps 100,000 combat veterans—are now in Manchuria and are probably located along or adjacent to the Korean border, in position for rapid commitment in Korea. Approximately 210,000 Communist regulars under Nieh Jung-chen's command are presently deployed in the North China area. Some of these troops have been reported enroute to Manchuria.[69]

Indeed, in some cases intelligence falsely suggested that the Chinese had already entered North Korea in the days immediately before the United States crossed the 38th parallel. Two separate Daily Intelligence Summaries (DIS) for the UN Command made this point. The first on October 3 "reported some evidence that twenty Chinese communist divisions were in North Korea and had been there since September 10."[70] The second on October 5 "noted the purported entry into North Korea of nine Chinese divisions."[71] Based on evidence from the Chinese side, it is clear these reports were false; indeed, the DIS conveys some skepticism about them. Nevertheless, their inclusion in the final reports would have shaped American leaders' understandings at the time.

Some of this evidence might, it is true, have been explained away as primarily defensive deployments. However, not all of it could. The massing of

---

[68] Stueck, *Korean War*, 90.

[69] Central Intelligence Agency, "Document 190. Intelligence Memorandum 324, 8 September 1950, Probability of Direct Chinese Communist Intervention in Korea," in *Assessing the Soviet Threat: The Early Cold War Years*, ed. Woodrow J. Kuhns (Washington, D.C.: Central Intelligence Agency, 1997), 434–35.

[70] Schnabel, *United States Army in the Korean War*, 199.

[71] Ibid., 200.

troops at border crossings would be a clear sign of offensive capability, as would reports of Chinese troops in North Korea (although these later turned out to be mistaken): moving large numbers of troops to forward positions does not make sense for a military force geared toward defense. Finally, the numbers were of a scale that should have raised U.S. eyebrows: at the time that Chinese troop numbers in Manchuria were thought to be nearly half a million, there were fewer than 150,000 U.S. troops on the Korean Peninsula.[72]

Nevertheless, MacArthur continued to insist that there was no sign of "present entry into North Korea by major Soviet or Chinese Communist Forces."[73] Even at a much later date, once the Chinese forces had engaged the U.S. forces in North Korea, the United States continued to ignore important evidence such as prisoners of war who spoke Chinese and claimed to be from large Chinese units that, as far as the United States believed, were not then in Northeast China, let alone North Korea.[74]

Thus, while some of the estimates were lower than actual Chinese deployments, American decisionmakers did have access to estimates from a variety of sources that were approximately correct regarding the scale and pace of Chinese ground-force deployments.[75] The United States simply did not view these numbers as threatening. The CIA's summary statement of October 12, 1950, illustrates these blinders: "Despite statements by Chou En-lai, troop movements to Manchuria, and propaganda charges of atrocities and border violations, there are no convincing indications of an actual Chinese Communist intention to resort to full-scale intervention in Korea."[76]

One wonders what evidence could have convinced the CIA if statements by senior leaders, troop deployments of enormous scale, and propaganda to

---

[72] Blair, *Forgotten War,* 366–67.

[73] MacArthur made this statement on September 28, 1950. Schnabel, *United States Army in the Korean War,* 188.

[74] Wainstock, *Truman, MacArthur, and the Korean War,* 79. Prisoner-of-war reports coming later in mid-November, suggesting that the Chinese were withdrawing after their First Campaign, were given credence. In other words, reports that fit the bias of underestimating the enemy were heeded; others were ignored.

[75] Cohen makes precisely the same point: "Although FEC [the Far Eastern Command] consistently underestimated the number of troops actually in Korea…it tracked the buildup in Manchuria more accurately.…Ironically, then, FEC intelligence had a better grasp of the size and disposition of Chinese forces not in contact with UN troops in Korea, than of those who actually were." Cohen, "Only Half the Battle," 133.

[76] Central Intelligence Agency, "Document 197. ORE 58–50 Excerpt, 12 October 1950, Critical Situations in the Far East," 450. Although not distributed until the 12th, after the key order had been given, the thinking underlying this report would have been in existance in the days prior.

prepare the local populace were insufficient. A similar reaction existed within the theater. General Ridgway wrote later that "as for the intervention of the Chinese, MacArthur simply closed his ears to their threats and apparently ignored or belittled the first strong evidence that they had crossed the Yalu in force."[77]

Moreover, this wide range of evidence was circulating broadly among the American leadership. Certainly, MacArthur was highly motivated to move northward despite evidence of Chinese opposition. However, as Ridgway suggests, the biases were not confined to MacArthur; they were widespread throughout the U.S. military:

> But it was not just the High Command [MacArthur's HQ] who refused to read the clear meaning of the mounting evidence. Typical of the re-luctance of all our troops, even the lower ranks[,] to take the Chinese threat seriously was the reaction of the forces positioned in and around the village of Unsan, just north of the Chongchon River, and about sixty miles south of the Yalu, at the end of October. Reports came in from several different quarters concerning the presence of large concentra-tions of Chinese troops.... [Ridgway then chronicles seven different such reports at the tactical level].... Still the United States command was reluctant to accept this accumulating evidence.[78]

Ridgeway describes the lack of concern at army, corps, divisional, and even regimental levels. It seems a stretch to argue that MacArthur's attitude could have overridden potential concerns throughout his command structure that, evidently, did not exist anyway. The CIA reports were disseminated beyond the command structure to a wide audience in Washington and Tokyo. The reports that were trickling up through the foreign embassies undoubtedly would have reached Secretary of State Dean Acheson. A recently declassified evaluation of the entire intelligence community's analysis of this event comes to similar conclusions:

---

[77] Matthew B. Ridgway, *The Korean War: How We Met the Challenge: How All-Out Asian War Was Averted: Why MacArthur Was Dismissed: Why Today's War Objectives Must Be Limited,* 1st ed. (Garden City, N.Y.: Doubleday, 1967), 67. There is no question that Mao and the Chinese leadership did their best to minimize the signs of China's presence in Korea, particularly in November 1950. Nevertheless, as shown above, the United States did have information of substantial forces in Manchuria. Further, as discussed more fully below, the United States systematically ignored early signs from the first offensive at the end of October and early November.
[78] Ibid., 52–53.

As for the intelligence agencies, their analysts were too prone to transfer western political military presuppositions into the minds of the
planners in Beijing. Even so, they did pay attention to COMINT and
warned, however tentatively, that the Chinese would intervene.
...

MacArthur was not the only official who miscalculated. Dean Rusk
would state forty years later than "the real failure at the Wake Island
was in our assessment of Chinese intentions and our ability to handle
Chinese forces if they actually intervened. On this one MacArthur and
the rest of us were all wrong."[79]

This multitude of intelligence streams cannot be explained away by
MacArthur's incentives to ignore them. The blinders were distributed far
and wide. The next section explains why.

PEOPLE'S WAR WAS NOT SEEN AS THREATENING

If, as argued above, Panikkar's credibility cannot account for the failure
of communication (as the Weakness Hypothesis posits), and if the United
States knew of the Chinese military signals, what does account for the
catastrophic failure of Chinese deterrence? American leaders heard the
Chinese warnings, but—underpinned as those signals were with a People's
War strategy—the United States just did not find them to be particularly
threatening. Evidence from a variety of sources strongly supports the link
between differences in theories of victory and the resulting U.S. underestimation, consistent with the doctrinal-difference misperception (DDM)
hypothesis and several of its component predictions. The previous chapter
has already shown that doctrinal difference led to a shallow understanding
of the adversary. This section will emphasize that differences in theories of
victory did cause the U.S. underestimation, in accord with the Misperception
Prediction. U.S. leaders did discount their adversary's theory of victory (the
Discounting Predictions), did not have nuanced discussions of their adversary's strategy (Superficial Views Prediction), and believed that their own
view of warfare would be dominant on the battlefield (Doctrinal Confidence
Prediction). The very large difference between the theories of victory led

---

[79] Guy Vanderpool, "Comint and the PRC Intervention in the Korean War," *Cryptologic
Quarterly* 15 (1996): 19–20. Declassified and available as document 21 at http://www.gwu.
edu/~nsarchiv/NSAEBB/NSAEBB278/index.htm.

to large and frequent underestimations (Extreme Differences Prediction). The next two sections present additional, strong evidence on these points, complementing that from the previous chapter.

In a comprehensive overview assessment in early October, the CIA noted that "the Chinese Communist ground forces, currently lacking requisite air and naval support, are capable of intervening effectively, but not necessarily decisively, in the Korean conflict."[80] That report goes on to develop this point: "Open intervention [by the Chinese] would be extremely costly unless protected by powerful Soviet air cover and naval support."[81] Although the report was published after the key decisions were taken, it illustrates the assessments that were prevalent throughout the U.S. decision-making apparatus in the final weeks before war was joined.

The Daily Intelligence Summary for October 12, read by the president, explained why the United States did not expect Chinese entry:

> The Chinese Communists undoubtedly feared the consequences of war with the United States.... In the unlikely event that the Chinese entered the war without the benefit of Soviet naval and air support, they were bound to suffer costly losses.... This report agreed with many others that, from a military standpoint, the most favorable time for the intervention had passed.[82]

Again, this assessment of intent, which comes from estimations of capabilities, is predicted by doctrinal-difference escalation hypothesis and the Nature of Signaling Prediction (which suggests that each side will use its forces in ways that accord with its own theory of victory).

Similarly, the U.S. discussions of its own capability relative to the Chinese exuded overconfidence. Even well into the main Chinese intervention in late November, the Chief of Naval Operations was suggesting that "the Chinese were probably afraid of attacks on their cities and might hold off for

---

[80] Central Intelligence Agency, "Document 197. ORE 58–50 Excerpt, 12 October 1950, Critical Situations in the Far East," 450. Other instances of CIA discounting of Chinese capabilities in general can be found at Central Intelligence Agency, "Document 186. Weekly Summary Excerpt, 28 July 1950, Soviet/Satellite Intentions," in *Assessing the Soviet Threat: The Early Cold War Years*, ed. Woodrow J. Kuhns (Washington, D.C.: Central Intelligence Agency, 1997).
[81] Central Intelligence Agency, "Document 197. ORE 58–50 Excerpt, 12 October 1950, Critical Situations in the Far East."
[82] Summarized in Schnabel, *United States Army in the Korean War*, 201.

that reason."[83] Mao and the other senior Chinese leaders had, however, long been cavalier about the vulnerability of the Chinese cities.

American thinking about the utility of airpower was central to these misperceptions. Cohen makes the point that U.S. Air Force successes against the North Korean forces early in the conflict biased the later U.S. view of airpower's utility. As he notes, studies coming out of the Far East Command (FEC) on the U.S. Air Force campaigns against the North Koreans in the first phase of the war, as they attacked down the length of the peninsula, "led [the FEC] to qualified confidence":

> Beginning in early October FEC analysts published in the Daily Intelligence Summary post-mortems on the campaigns against the NKPA [North Korean People's Army]. These retrospective analyses suggested that a massive air interdiction campaign, coupled with close air support of American troops during the previous summer[,] had played a critical role in the destruction of the NKPA.... These findings— based largely on interrogation of NKPA prisoners—paved the way for MacArthur's blithe remark to President Truman at Wake Island, "if the Chinese tried to get down to Pyongyang there would be the greatest slaughter."

Cohen continues:

> This growing—and, one must say, solidly based—faith in the efficacy of close air support and air interdiction of enemy lines of communication colored not only MacArthur's command decisions, but the nature of supporting intelligence assessments.... This overconfidence in the efficacy of air power would color FEC's estimates of Chinese military effectiveness and the Chinese strategic calculus until after the launching of the second Chinese attack in November.[84]

Cohen's suggestion that the U.S. confidence in airpower affected the American assessment of Beijing's strategic calculus is precisely the argument of doctrinal-difference theory. Although tactical airpower is of great use in

[83] Philip Jessup, "Memorandum of Conversation, by the Ambassador at Large (Jessup) (December 1, 1950)," in *FRUS, 1950,* ed. United States Department of State (Washington, D.C.: U.S. GPO, 1976), 1280.
[84] Cohen, "Only Half the Battle," 138–39. See also Eliot Cohen and John Gooch, *Military Misfortunes: The Anatomy of Failure in War* (New York: Free Press, 1990), 178, passim.

**Figure 4.2.** B-29s attacking Chinese positions in North Korea.
*Source:* ARC Identifier: 542229 (ca. 01/1951); Still Picture Records LICON, Special Media Archives Services Division (NWCS-S), National Archives at College Park, Maryland.

blunting an armored offensive, like that of the Soviet-equipped North Korean mechanized divisions, it is of greatly lessened use against the lightly equipped Chinese who required a minimal logistics tail.

Not only did the United States not view People's War as threatening but it also downplayed the prospect of limited war, if it considered this at all. As recently argued by one scholar (who also served as an intelligence officer), an important cause of the massive intelligence failures leading up to the war was that the United States believed war against the Chinese in Korea to be tantamount to general war against the Soviets, and therefore unlikely:[85]

> The United States was caught by surprise because, within political and military leaderships circles in Washington, the perception existed that only the Soviets could order an invasion by a "client state" and that such an act would be a prelude to a world war. Washington was confident

[85] See P.K. Rose, "Two Strategic Intelligence Mistakes in Korea, 1950," *Studies in Intelligence* 11 (2001).

that the Soviets were not ready to take such a step, and, therefore, that no invasion would occur.[86]

This, too, is consistent with the perceptions stemming from the American theory of victory. The nearly exclusive U.S. focus on general war meant that, until after the Korean War, little consideration was given to the particular nature of limited wars that were central to Mao's approach to violence.

All of these assessments were precisely what doctrinal-difference theory predicts. Washington viewed Chinese military signals through the lens of American strategic beliefs and doctrine, leading it to underestimate their significance. The hypothesis linking the misperception of an adversary's signals to the underestimations of them that come from differing theories of victory—the doctrinal-difference escalation (DDE) hypothesis—is thus strongly supported.

## CHINA HAD ALREADY MISSED ITS CHANCE

Another major contributor to the American tendency to ignore the evidence of Chinese intent and capability to intervene was the timing of the Chinese signals.[87] Many U.S. observers at the time believed that China had already missed its best chance to intervene. This perception grew out of U.S. strategic perspectives regarding optimal strategies. In the American view, the best time to intervene would have been when the United States had its back to the wall at Pusan, and was thus most vulnerable.[88] American strategic doctrine would suggest that the adversary would attack at that point to pursue a complete victory.[89] Willoughby, MacArthur's intelligence officer, said in October: "The auspicious time for intervention has long since passed."[90] Even signals from

---

[86] Ibid., 3.

[87] Along these lines, one intelligence officer has recently argued that the United States ignored signs of the Chinese troop deployment because of its belief that Chinese intervention would be equated with general war, a situation the United States did not view as likely. Ibid. As discussed in chapter 3, the United States was heavily focused on the prospect of general war between the United States and the Communist nations. That author summarizes similar information to that presented above, but does not document a link between the neglect of that evidence (which certainly occurred) to the specific American expectation that China would intervene only in the context of general war.

[88] Foot, *Wrong War*, 80; Stueck, *Korean War*, 110–11; Chen, *China's Road*, 169–70.

[89] See Weigley's discussion of the "Grant" strategy that was prevalent at this time in U.S. Army circles, which counseled wiping out the enemy's forces by means of mass and concentration. Russell F. Weigley, *The American Way of War: A History of United States Military Strategy and Policy* (Bloomington: Indiana University Press, 1977), 312.

[90] Wainstock, *Truman, MacArthur, and the Korean War*, 77.

foreign embassies were discounted on these grounds. For instance, the U.S. ambassador to Russia, Alan G. Kirk, used this line of argument to discount the signals he had received from contacts in Moscow regarding the likelihood of Chinese entry if the United States crossed the 38th parallel:

> In commenting on this information, Kirk says he finds it difficult to accept these reports as authoritative analyses of Chinese Communist plans. He takes the line that the logical moment for Communist armed intervention came when the UN forces were desperately defending a small area in southern Korea and when the influx of an overwhelming number of Chinese ground forces would have proved a decisive factor.[91]

The CIA made a similar point in its summary analysis of October 12 under the heading "Factors Opposing Chinese Communist Intervention."[92] The official Army history of the war takes this view.[93] Viewed through the American perceptual lens, the militarily advantageous time to intervene had already passed.

To China, however, other factors seemed more important in timing their intervention. Chinese strategic thinking emphasized the value in waiting until the U.S. supply lines were long; this was precisely the opposite of the American view.[94] A report written by the senior commanders of the Northeast Border Defense Army (NEBDA) in late August made clear the differences: it "suggested that the best timing for entering the war might be when the UN forces had counterattacked back across the 38th parallel, because this would put China in a politically and militarily more favorable position to defeat the enemy."[95] Other Chinese sources concurred, emphasizing long and vulnerable U.S. supply lines as its forces moved north:

> Chinese behavior should not have puzzled those familiar with Mao's strategy in previous wars. A key point in Maoist thought was the trading of space for time. The ideal moment to attack an enemy of superior firepower came when its forces advanced beyond their major supply bases

---

[91] Central Intelligence Agency, "Document 197. ORE 58–50 Excerpt, 12 October 1950, Critical Situations in the Far East."

[92] Ibid., 450. The general conclusions of this study did not predict Chinese entry.

[93] See Schnabel, *United States Army in the Korean War,* 277.

[94] Chen, *China's Road,* 152.

[95] Ibid. Also see Zhang, *Mao's Military Romanticism,* 76.

into rugged terrain lacking easily defensible lines of transportation and communication.[96]

This is solid evidence for doctrinal-difference theory. The Chinese, because of their views on warfare, thought the best time to intervene militarily would be as the United States moved north, with long supply lines: "Lure them in deep." The United States thought the best time for the Chinese to intervene had been earlier, when American forces were pinned down. These different perspectives shaped each side's policy, and through that, the American assessment of the meaning of Chinese signals and thus their intent. Each side expected its view of warfare to be borne out on the battlefield (Doctrinal Confidence Prediction). The United States displayed little inclination to undertake a nuanced evaluation of the adversary's thinking on the same issue (Superficial Views Prediction).

## DISSENTING VIEWS FROM OUTSIDE THE MILITARY LEADERSHIP

A few American analysts did better at assessing the signals from China. The senior China analyst at the Department of State, Edmund Clubb, was able to interpret many of these signals with remarkable accuracy even at a very early date.[97] Writing after the first battle in late October/early November that destroyed the Eighth Cavalry, but before the second and larger Chinese attacks of late November, he joined the debate over the true intent of the Chinese. After noting that there was now undisputable evidence that the Chinese were directly involved in fighting, he goes on to warn that Chinese intent was not likely to be limited:

> It seems unlikely that the Chinese Communists would be prepared to venture into the Korean theater in such a limited manner as would confront them with the danger of being promptly bloodied and thrown out by the force which they themselves had consistently characterized as a "a paper tiger." The recrudescence of Chinese Communist propaganda whipping up enthusiasm of the Chinese people for "resistance to aggression in Korea" would appear to indicate that a large effort may be involved.... The move of intervention would be designed, in short,

---

[96] Stueck, *Korean War*, 112.
[97] Clubb, like many other experienced observers of China, was later purged from the State Department during the McCarthy era. See Paul G. Pierpaoli, *Truman and Korea: The Political Culture of the Early Cold War* (Columbia: University of Missouri Press, 1999).

to achieve some real measure of victory. Although firm information to reach conclusions is still lacking, therefore, it would be hardly safe to assume other than that (1) the Chinese Communists, if they are intervening directly in Korea, propose to do so in considerable force.[98]

Clubb made similar points in a number of memos in early November.[99] Others at State expressed views similar to Clubb's.[100] Even midlevel officials there recommended great caution.[101] Indeed, even Acheson seemed more inclined than the military leadership to recognize the Chinese threats for what they were.[102]

While the CIA was often wrong, it was rarely as extreme as the Pentagon in disregarding the Chinese threat. Writing in early November, the Agency concluded, "The Chinese Communists...main motivation at present appears to be to establish a limited 'cordon sanitaire' south of the Yalu River."[103] On November 24, the day before the second and larger Chinese attack, the CIA was more cautious in its National Intelligence Estimate (NIE) on the prospect for Chinese intervention: "It is estimated that [the Chinese Communists] do not have the military capability of driving the UN forces from the peninsula, but that they do have the capability of forcing them to withdraw to defensive positions for prolonged and inconclusive operations."[104]

[98] "Memorandum by the Director of the Office of Chinese Affairs (Clubb) to the Assistant Secretary of State for Far Eastern Affairs (Rusk)," November 1, 1950 in *FRUS, 1950, Vol. 7*, 1023–25.

[99] See, for example, "Memorandum by the Director of the Office of Chinese Affairs (Clubb) to the Assistant Secretary of State for Far Eastern Affairs (Rusk)," November 4, 1950, in ibid., 1038–41. Cohen echoes this point regarding Clubb's views; see Cohen, "Only Half the Battle," 141.

[100] See, e.g., "Memorandum by the Assistant Secretary of State for Public Affairs (Barrett) to the Assistant Secretary of State for Far Eastern Affairs (Rusk)," November 3, 1950, in *FRUS, 1950, Vol. 7*, 1030. "Draft Memorandum by Mr. John P. Davies of the Policy Planning Staff," November 7, 1950 in *FRUS, 1950, Vol. 7*, 1078–85, esp. 1078–79.

[101] Foot points out that Livingston Merchant and U. Alexis Johnson both recommended caution. Foot, *Wrong War*, 80.

[102] Dean Acheson, "The Secretary of State to the Embassy in the United Kingdom," November 6, 1950, in *FRUS, 1950, Vol. 7*, 1052.

[103] "Memorandum by the Director of the Central Intelligence Agency (Smith) to the President," November 1, 1950, in ibid., 1025. See also "Memorandum by the Central Intelligence Agency: National Intelligence Estimate, Chinese Communist Intervention in Korea," November 8, 1950, in *FRUS, 1950, Vol. 7*, 1101–6.

[104] "Memorandum by the Central Intelligence Agency: National Intelligence Estimate, Chinese Communist Intervention in Korea," November 24, 1950, in *FRUS, 1950, Vol. 7*, 1220–22. The latter part of the quotation is substantially stronger than the language used in Pentagon discussions throughout the month of November.

The Depth of Immersion Prediction suggests that leaders who are outside the military or who are not inculcated in strategic thinking should be less vulnerable to the pernicious effects of biases from various theories of victory. And here, indeed, Clubb and others at State (and to a lesser extent, others outside the Pentagon) were far more accurate in their assessments than the military leaders at the Pentagon and in the field. Even though most of these assessments came too late to avoid the escalation of the war (although they might, if heeded, have lessened U.S. defeats), their differences with contemporary military officials are notable, and are explained by doctrinal-difference theory.

Thus, a range of military and diplomatic warnings did not lead Washington to careful consideration of the prospects of Chinese involvement. Eliot Cohen highlights a dynamic similar to that shown above:

> The failures—or more accurately, semifailures—in warning and order of battle intelligence have received a good deal of attention from students of the Chinese surprise attack in 1950. Another more serious and generally ignored type of intelligence failure occurred, however; failure to gauge the enemy's way of war, his methods, strengths, and weaknesses. It is in the picture of the enemy held by U.S. forces in the Far East that we find one of the chief sources of the failure of the winter of 1950.[105]

The United States crossed the 38th parallel not due to a lack of information about the size of the Chinese force or its intentions (as the Weakness Hypothesis would have predicted), but rather because Washington was unable to evaluate the signals due to its biases derived from its beliefs about the effective use of military power. This strongly suggests a link between the misperceptions arising from differing theories of victory (the DDM hypothesis) and the faulty interpretation of the adversary's signals, and a link between those misperceptions and assessments of the general balance of power (that is, both elements of the doctrinal-difference escalation or DDE hypothesis).

## POSTEVENT EVALUATIONS BY THE UNITED STATES

Several secondary predictions of doctrinal-difference theory center on postevent evaluations from the two sides. In particular, the Surprise Regarding

---

[105] Cohen and Gooch, *Military Misfortunes,* 176.

Intentions Prediction asks whether there was a degree of surprise regarding the enemy's intent and Startling Battlefield Outcomes Prediction asks whether there was surprise about how effective its military forces and doctrines were, once the war was joined. The following sections explore the evidence on these questions, showing, first, how American beliefs about Chinese intent were so firm that denial was the initial reaction to the PLA's entry, both on the ground in Korea and up the chain of command. Then, we examine American surprise at the effectiveness of the Chinese forces, especially through the evidence of evaluations made during the war and of postwar changes in American forces and strategies.

## INITIAL REACTIONS: DENIAL

The effect of the blinders worn by the U.S. decisionmakers is illustrated by widespread initial reactions to the Chinese intervention, with evidence from both tactical and strategic levels, along with some dissenting voices. This material supports the doctrinal-difference theory in many areas. First, it further bolsters the case for the doctrinal-difference misperception (DDM) hypothesis that links differences in theories of victory to underestimation. It also supports several of the specific predictions set forth in chapter 2 that link this underestimation of the adversary to perceptions of the overall balance of power, the discounting of the adversary's capacity, and simplistic discussions of the opponent's strategies (the Misperception, Discounting, and Superficial Views Predictions). We should see some evidence that the large difference between the two countries' theories of victory led to frequent and extensive misperceptions (the Depth of Immersion Prediction). Beyond that, the evidence presented here links the flawed U.S. interpretation of the Chinese signals to the underestimations of capability that the theory predicts (and thus supports the doctrinal-difference escalation [DDE] hypothesis and the associated Downplaying Prediction). Even in the face of hard evidence, American leaders continued to believe that the Chinese would not intervene. Lastly, just as the Doctrinal Confidence Prediction suggests, there is significant evidence that the Air Force in particular assumed that the tactics and doctrines associated with its own theory of victory would be key to winning battles on the ground.

*Tactical Level Overconfidence*
Tactically, the United States made many miscalculations. Even after the Chinese first offensive in late October and early November destroyed a South Korean division and severely damaged several other South Korean regiments,

Eighth Army intelligence was estimating that its sector held only two thousand Chinese soldiers, grouped in two regiments.[106] (In fact the Thirteenth Army Group of some 180,000 troops was arrayed against that particular U.S. force.)[107] As POW reports accumulated after the beginning of that offensive, the U.S. commanders received disturbing information: prisoners claimed to be from a very high number of different units. Rather than conclude from this that the Chinese had a sizable force in country, the intelligence staff of the Eighth Army offered this novel interpretation (via a November 1 cable as passed on to the Secretary of State by an American diplomat stationed in Korea):

> 8th Army Intelligence considers there now [to be] two Sino regiments, possibl[y] a third...Appears these units were formed by taking one battalion each of six divisions said to constitute [the] Sino 39th and 40th Armies, deployed along Manchurian-North Korean border.
>
> ...
>
> 8th Army Intelligence is of [the] view, with which Embassy [is] inclined to concur, [that the] Sino Communists will avoid overt intervention.[108]

A more straightforward and, in retrospect, accurate conclusion would have been that all three armies—some one hundred thousand troops—were present in the sector.[109]

The first significant engagement between the U.S. forces and the PLA came in early November in the first Chinese offensive.[110] An American general on a fact-finding mission in Korea concluded that "the Chinese had destroyed the 8th Cavalry Regimental Combat Team."[111] Ridgway notes that the regiment "lost more than half its authorized strength at Unsan, and a great share of its equipment, including twelve 105-mm. howitzers, nine tanks, more than 125 trucks, and a dozen recoilless rifles."[112]

---

[106] Blair, *Forgotten War,* 378. These reports were from October 30 and 31, 1950.

[107] Ibid., 391.

[108] "The Chargé in Korea (Drumright) to the Secretary of State (November 1, 1950)," reprinted in *FRUS, 1950, Vol. 7,* 1022.

[109] The command and control difficulties of reconstituting selected battalions from different divisions under new regimental leadership would have been severe. The whole point of having divisional headquarters units reflects the recognition that it is not so easy to plug battalions into different command structures.

[110] The offensive began a few days earlier, on October 25, although initially only South Korean units were hit. See Blair, *Forgotten War,* 371.

[111] Quoted at Schnabel, *United States Army in the Korean War,* 257.

[112] Ridgway, *Korean War,* 59.

Still, even after Chinese forces became heavily involved with the U.S. forces, American confidence was hard to shake. The story of the destruction of the Eighth Cavalry Regiment unfolded as a series of U.S. underestimations of the enemy. The regiment had deployed wearing summer uniforms, "believing [their] assigned task would be a simple power punch through a thin NKPA line, followed by a one- or two-day dash to the Yalu, then a return to the home base in Japan by Thanksgiving Day."[113] In the days before the Chinese attacked, the U.S. regiment's Third Battalion, deployed on point, was deployed vulnerably in a valley, and the battalion commander ignored suggestions to move toward a safer position on the surrounding high ground.[114] Only after the regiment was completely cut off was it ordered to withdraw, and by that time, withdrawal "had no chance of succeeding."[115] An attempt to use another heavily reinforced regiment to open a corridor to Unsan, where the 8th Regiment was holed up, was ordered almost casually: "Other elements of the 5th RCT [Regimental Combat Team] are enroute to assist the 8th U.S. Cavalry RCT."[116] However, this effort too failed in the face of unexpectedly strong Chinese opposition. The very next day the tone of the Situation Report (SITREP) is more pessimistic: "Heavy resistance from strong enemy forces prevented the 5th and elements of the 7th U.S. Cavalry RCT's from reaching the 8th U.S. Cavalry RCT...which was isolated by a hostile envelopment in the Unsan area."[117] Only then was it clear that the Eighth Cavalry Regiment had been destroyed as a functioning formation.

The confusion was not limited to the Eighth Cavalry: corps commanders across North Korea were "profoundly puzzled" by the situation they faced.[118] Chinese troop formations were not even shown on operational maps until November 6, 1950.[119] On November 12, the intelligence chief of the U.S. X Corps, Colonel William Quinn, reviewed the recent battles and the reports

---

[113] Blair, *Forgotten War,* 380.

[114] Ibid., 381.

[115] Ibid., 383.

[116] "Joint Daily SITREP, No. 128 (November 2, 1950)," in *Joint Daily Sitrep Collection.*

[117] "Joint Daily SITREP, No. 129 (November 3, 1950)," in ibid. See also Blair, *Forgotten War,* 384.

[118] Blair, *Forgotten War,* 450.

[119] See *Joint Daily Sitrep Collection.* The first time Chinese units show up is in "Joint Daily SITREP, No. 128 (November 6, 1950)." At that point three units are listed: the 55th, 56th, and 124th divisions representing some ten to fifteen thousand troops when in fact there were hundreds of thousands.

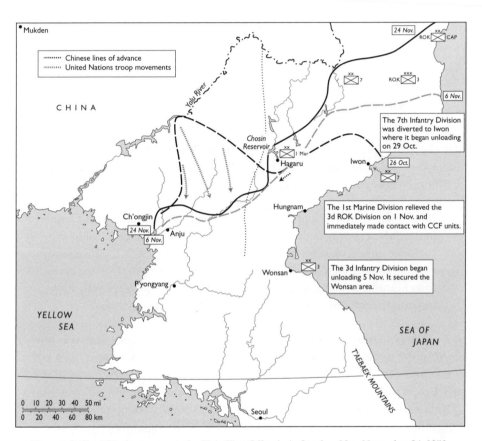

**Figure 4.3.** The UN advance meets the PLA (First Offensive), October 26 to November 24, 1950.

of significant Chinese forces to his north and northwest; even so, he was confident of his unit's ability to remain on the offensive and victorious:

> Three unconfirmed reports from different sources have indicated the buildup of enemy strength in the northeastern section of Korea, in the vicinity of Hoeryong and Ch'ongjin. The reports claim that large Chinese Communist units are present in this area. Should this information be true, it would indicate a significant increase in the enemy's capabilities on the east coast avenue of approach to the Korean border....
>
> Conclusions:
>
> a. The enemy will, if strongly attacked, continue his retreat to the north.[120]

By November 25, on the eve of the second Chinese offensive, Quinn shows an awareness of the buildup of the Chinese, but retains an unwarranted and almost Panglossian confidence:

> Additional indications of a CCF buildup on the west flank of X Corps in the Sachang-ni Yongdong-ni sector have been received.... All of this evidence tends to substantiate the statements of civilians, refugees, PWs [prisoners of war], deserters and other sources that strong reinforcements, including large numbers of CCF have been recently moving into the area between Sachang-ni and Choshin Reservoir.[121]

A brief mention of the offensive potential of the Chinese force is buried in the analysis section of his report, but his final conclusions omit any mention of risk: "Conclusions: a. Enemy forces in the western sector of the X Corps zone will attempt to defend generally along the line Chagangjin-Yudam-ni-Sachang-ni. If forced to withdraw, they will take up new defensive positions in the Chiang-no redoubt area."[122] While suggesting the Chinese capability to defend (although even here he suggests that they would not

---

[120] G-2 (Colonel William Quinn), "Headquarters X Corps, Periodic Intelligence Report #47 (November 12, 1950)," in Military History Institute Library, U.S. Army War College, Carlisle, Penn. In the next day's report, Quinn discounts as spurious reports of Chinese soldiers in rear areas.

[121] G-2 (Colonel William Quinn), "Headquarters X Corps, Periodic Intelligence Report #60 (November 25, 1950)," in Military History Institute Library, U.S. Army War College, Carlisle, Penn.

[122] Ibid.

be able to hold the line again the X Corps), he does not emphasize that they also have a dangerous offensive capability.

Quinn's boss, General Edward Almond, shared that optimism. On the morning of November 28, after the Chosin Reservoir battle had begun, he blustered to his commanders: "The enemy who is delaying you for the moment is nothing more than remnants of Chinese divisions fleeing north.... We're still attacking and we're going all the way to the Yalu. Don't let a bunch of Chinese laundrymen stop you."[123] Almond ordered an offensive into the teeth of the waiting Chinese. In the Chosin Reservoir battle that followed, two Marine regiments (approximately six thousand troops) were cut off and a "rescue" task force of brigade strength (another five thousand troops) suffered 40 percent casualties.[124] During the flight of the Eighth Army along the western side of the Korean Peninsula, there was a real danger that its line of retreat might be cut, a danger realized only belatedly. As a result, the Second Division suffered over 30 percent casualties over just less than two weeks in late November.[125] As the Chinese offensive continued, it would push the Eighth Army into the longest retreat in American military history.

*Strategic Level Overoptimism*

Even after the Eighth Cavalry was mauled in the first days of November, both MacArthur's headquarters in Tokyo and the civilian and military leadership in Washington persisted in their gross underestimations of the threat posed by the Chinese.

MacArthur was initially unruffled by the early defeat. In fact, "the eventual response from Tokyo was...irritation and impatience at [Eighth Army commander General Jonnie] Walker's failure to move forward on schedule." Blair continues, "No matter how thoroughly convinced the 1st Cavalry Division might have become that the Chinese had entered the war in force, the Commander in Chief [MacArthur] persisted in a mood of renewed optimism."[126]

Even on November 4, MacArthur exuded confident assurance that the Chinese would be unlikely to intervene, in spite of the mauling one of his regiments had just received.[127] By November 6, however, he was pleading for permission to bomb bridges and supply lines near the Chinese border.[128] By November 9, he had stopped debating Chinese intent; he now assumed

---

[123] Quoted in Blair, *Forgotten War,* 462.
[124] Ibid., 508 and 520.
[125] Ibid.
[126] Ridgway, *Korean War,* 59.
[127] Wainstock, *Truman, MacArthur, and the Korean War,* 82.
[128] Schnabel, *United States Army in the Korean War,* 243–44.

they would intervene in force, but he continued to believe in his own robust capabilities, particularly in the ability of airpower to "interdict Chinese reinforcements from Manchuria and to destroy those already in Korea."[129] As soon as the Chinese pulled back, however, in the tactical (and intentionally deceptive) lull between their first and second offensives, MacArthur's confidence returned.[130]

The intelligence reports reaching MacArthur were, indeed, ambiguous. Chinese units are not listed on the Daily Joint SITREP maps until November 6, and even then these reports describe only as generic "enemy forces" the attackers against the Eighth Cavalry and the ROK units.[131] Some reports suggested only a minimal Chinese presence in North Korea of many thousands.[132] Others implied a larger force of nearly one hundred thousand.[133] MacArthur put more credence in the former, concluding in mid-November that he was facing "certainly no more than 30,000." He insisted that the Chinese "could not possibly have got more over with the surreptitiously covert means used. If they had moved in the open, they would have been detected by our Air Forces and our Intelligence."[134]

In fact, however, MacArthur's own intelligence at the time stated the "accepted" Chinese strength in North Korea to be 51,600 and the "probable total" to be 76,800.[135] Despite the early defeat of the Eighth Cavalry and Second Division and the ambiguous evidence, MacArthur eagerly anticipated

[129] Wainstock, *Truman, MacArthur, and the Korean War,* 84.

[130] See Schnabel, *United States Army in the Korean War,* 251. This tactical lull was intended to create precisely that sense. Again see 陶、《中美关系史》 [Tao, *History of Sino-American Relations,* 32]; Yu Bin, "What China Learned from Its 'Forgotten War' in Korea," in *Mao's Generals Remember Korea,* ed. Li Xiaobing, Allan Reed Millett, and Yu Bin (Lawrence: University Press of Kansas, 2001), 15. As predicted by doctrinal-difference theory, the United States readily fell into the trap.

[131] "Joint Daily SITREP, No. 128 (November 6, 1950)," in *Joint Daily Sitrep Collection.* A similar phenomenon in a different set of daily reports is identified by Posen. The "United Nations Command, GHQ, G-3 Operations Reports" are available from British archival sources; Posen's sources have a slightly different correlation between date and numbering, suggesting that they are a different set of reports although their content overlaps heavily. See Barry R. Posen, "The Chinese Intervention in Korea: A Case of Inadvertent Escalation," draft manuscript, MIT, 1989, 58, note 73.

[132] "The Consul General at Hong Kong (Wilkinson) to the Secretary of State," October 27, 1950 and "The Chargé in Korea (Drumright) to the Secretary of State," October 31, 1950, in *FRUS, 1950, Vol. 7,* 1003–04 and 1018–19.

[133] "The Chargé in Korea (Drumright) to the Secretary of State," October 30, 1950, in ibid., 1014.

[134] "Memorandum of Conversation, by the Ambassador in Korea (Muccio)," November 17, 1950, in ibid., 1175.

[135] See "Joint Daily SITREP, No. 133 (November 13, 1950)," in *Joint Daily Sitrep Collection.*

the beginning of his offensive; "this should for all practical purposes end the war," he declared.[136] "Seldom in any war," writes Blair, "had a commanding general so foolishly revealed his hand."[137]

Both MacArthur and his intelligence officer attributed their apparent success at forestalling further attacks during November to UN airpower, precisely the sort of doctrinally laden conclusion this book argues is likely.[138] MacArthur's pronouncement on November 24, just one day before the second and much larger Chinese attack, exudes such false optimism: "My air force for the past three weeks, in a sustained attack of model coordination and effectiveness, successfully interdicted enemy lines of support from the north so that further reinforcement therefrom has been sharply curtailed and essential supplies markedly limited."[139] This passage illustrates elements such as airpower, coordination, and interdiction that were central to the U.S. doctrine but absent from that of the Chinese.

Air Force commanders displayed similarly biased views. The official Air Force history asserts that "Red China's Fourth Field Army was suffering frightful losses from Fifth Air Force attacks and from Eighth Army ground fire." However, China's force went on to retake the South Korean capital, so the official history was forced to concede that, somehow, "it had enough strength to rout American ground forces defending Seoul."[140] The writer's surprise at the Chinese capabilities is almost palpable.

Intelligence was a persistent problem for MacArthur's command. As late as December 26, the United States had no clear idea how many Chinese troops it was facing:

No one yet had a good idea of how many CCF troops had been committed to Korea or if the CCF had crossed the 38th Parallel in full force to invade South Korea. On the Eighth Army situation maps, Ridgeway remembered, the CCF was depicted merely by a large red "goose egg" with "174,000" scrawled on its center. The true figure was closer to 300,000.[141]

---

[136] Schnabel, *United States Army in the Korean War,* 273.

[137] Blair, *Forgotten War,* 435.

[138] Schnabel, *United States Army in the Korean War,* 275.

[139] Ibid., 277–78. It is likely that MacArthur was basing this conclusion on the tactical lull between the Chinese First and Second Offensives, intended to create precisely this sort of overconfidence.

[140] Robert Frank Futrell, *The United States Air Force in Korea, 1950–1953,* rev. ed. (Washington, D.C.: Office of Air Force History United States Air Force, 1983), 279.

[141] Blair, *Forgotten War,* 569.

This miscalculation persisted even though a vast intelligence-gathering effort had amassed some 27,643 photographs from aerial reconnaissance.[142] The American overconfidence in U.S. reconnaissance technology led it to underestimate its adversary.

Just as repeated underestimations of the enemy had resulted in the destruction of the Eighth Cavalry in late October and early November, the strategic retreats of the Eighth Army and X Corps also reflected repeated miscalculations. Following the renewed Chinese attacks in late November, the Eighth Army was initially tasked to hold a line running east from Sinanju, some seventy miles from the Yalu River and the border with China. Days later, it was ordered to hold another line fifty miles further south at P'yongyang. It fell back again nearly to the 38th parallel, and then surrendered Seoul for the second time in the war.[143]

Similarly, X Corps was first ordered on November 27 to counterattack to relieve pressure on the Eighth Army near the North Korean–Chinese border, then on November 30 to defend a defensive line scores of miles further south in the Hamhung-Wonsan sector, and on Christmas Eve, December 24, to withdraw completely from North Korea.[144]

Blair, in the definitive military history of the United States in the Korean War, summarizes the distorted lenses that inhibited MacArthur's vision:

> By November 28 it must have been clear to Douglas MacArthur that he had blundered badly in Korea. The wine of victory had turned to vinegar. In a broad sense, Inchon had become another Anzio. He had been outsmarted and outgeneraled by a "bunch of Chinese laundrymen" who had no close air support, no tanks, and very little artillery, modern communications, or logistical infrastructure. His reckless, egotistical strategy after Inchon, undertaken in defiance of war warnings from Peking and a massive CCF buildup in Manchuria, had been an arrogant, blind march to disaster. What must have been even more galling and humiliating was that MacArthur was on record with everyone from the president on down as unequivocally assuring that the CCF would not intervene in Korea in force, and if it did he would "slaughter" it with his air power. His considerable intelligence-gathering apparatus had

---

[142] Futrell, *United States Air Force in Korea, 1950–1953,* 273

[143] For the detailed narrative of the retreat, see Blair, *Forgotten War,* part 8, "Disaster and Retreat." Also see Futrell, *United States Air Force in Korea, 1950–1953,* chapter 8, "Two Months of Defeat and Retreat."

[144] Blair, *Forgotten War.* The JCS, at least, was less overly optimistic regarding X Corps than MacArthur's command by the end of November.

scandalously failed to detect or interpret the massive scope of the CCF intervention. His air power had abjectly failed to "slaughter" any appreciable number of CCF or even to knock out all the Yalu bridges.[145]

The American defeat in November and December can, to some extent, also be blamed on the specific operational strategies that MacArthur chose. Two decisions were particularly ill-chosen: first, the withdrawal of X Corps from Inchon and its reinsertion on the opposite side of the peninsula at Wonsan had the effect of slowing the pursuit of the retreating North Korean forces; as a result, a large American force had to chase them all the way to the Yalu. It also divided the U.S. force dangerously. Second, once X Corps was redeployed, MacArthur did not demand that it make contact with the Eighth Army to its west, but rather expected that the rugged mountain terrain would serve as a defensive obstacle to protect his force. As a result of these two decisions, when the Chinese pressed their Second Offensive the rout was dramatically worse.[146]

These two mistakes were deeply rooted in the American doctrine of the time. The U.S. Army's standard operating procedure (discussed in chapter 3) for an offensive in peninsular terrain focused on a series of flanking amphibious landings. The United States had pursued this strategy in Italy, the Philippines, and elsewhere in World War II, and MacArthur attempted to use X Corps in a textbook application of it. Reliance on mountainous terrain as an obstacle also came straight out of American doctrinal thinking: there was no major supply route through this area, and the tactical mobility of mechanized forces would have been highly constrained. The United States did not adequately consider that the far less mechanized Chinese forces might view the terrain as much less forbidding. Thus, American doctrine informed even the mistakes the Americans made in Korea; the doctrinal differences between China and the United States amplified their scale.

Much of the evidence presented above focuses on MacArthur, but the views of other leaders in the theater, and from outside his command entirely, cannot be blamed on MacArthur's extreme views. Eliot Cohen comes to similar conclusions in his analysis of misperceptions in the Korean War: "Attempts to pin the blame for the intelligence failure (which was only part of a large operational failure) on one individual vastly oversimplify, and in some respects distort, the nature of the intelligence failure in Korea."[147] A

[145]  Ibid., 464.
[146]  See ibid.
[147]  Cohen, "Only Half the Battle," 129.

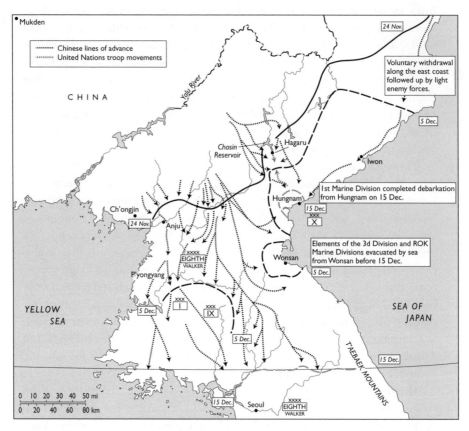

Legend:
- ········ Chinese lines of advance
- ········ United Nations troop movements

Map labels: Mukden, CHINA, Yolu River, 24 Nov., Voluntary withdrawal along the east coast followed up by light enemy forces., 5 Dec., Chosin Reservoir, Hagaru, Iwon, 1st Marine Division completed debarkation from Hungnam on 15 Dec., Hungnam, Ch'ongjin, 24 Nov., Anju, 15 Dec. XXX X, EIGHTH WALKER, Wonsan, Elements of the 3d Division and ROK Marine Divisions evacuated by sea from Wonsan before 15 Dec., P'yongyang, 5 Dec., YELLOW SEA, XXX I, XXX IX, 5 Dec., SEA OF JAPAN, 5 Dec., TAEBAEK MOUNTAINS, 15 Dec., 0 10 20 30 40 50 mi, 0 20 40 60 80 km, 15 Dec., Seoul, XXXX EIGHTH WALKER

**Figure 4.4.** The rout in North Korea (the Chinese Second Offensive), November 26 to December 5, 1950.

range of commanders in the Far East found it very difficult to change their prior beliefs about the likelihood of China's intervention and about its capabilities if it did intervene. The Chinese were able to take advantage of these blinders as they prepared their surprise attack in late November. For the Americans, escaping the distorting lens of their theory of victory proved to be very difficult.

The situation back in Washington was little better throughout this period as the conflict began. The bewilderment is explicit in Army chief of staff Lawton Collins's note of October 31: "the intervention was conforming to none of the patterns envisaged by the Joint Chiefs in their studies and in their directives to General MacArthur."[148] Other examples of difficulties in adjusting to the new situation abound.

Ten days later, and in spite of the mounting evidence of trouble, the Joint Chiefs of Staff (JCS) continued to express some confidence. Even after the loss of the Eighth Cavalry, a JCS memorandum to the secretary of defense on November 9 suggested that, absent Soviet action, the United States could not be pushed out of Korea by China.[149] The JCS memorandum claimed that a defensive line short of the Chinese-Korean border could be held without any reinforcements. However, they also conceded that "the Chinese Communists are presently in Korea in such strength and in a sufficiently organized manner to indicate that unless withdrawn they can be defeated only by a determined military operation."[150] Elsewhere they refer to the need for "some augmentation of military strength" in order to "force the action to a successful conclusion in Korea."[151] However, these top-level officers did not suggest any change in the standing orders under which MacArthur was operating. This implies that little had changed in their minds and that their overall military confidence remained, despite substantial uncertainty in the conditions.[152] Cohen writes that, after the first offensive, "the Defense Department was more sanguine [than Edmund Clubb at State], acknowledging that a limited intervention was underway but denying evidence of 'indications of psychological preparation for war in Korea" [by the Chinese].'"

Washington authorities, notably the JCS, seemed to believe that as long as direct clashes along the Yalu could be avoided, so too could war with

---

[148] Schnabel, *United States Army in the Korean War,* 234.
[149] "Memorandum by the Joint Chiefs of Staff to the Secretary of Defense (Marshall)," November 9, 1950, in *FRUS, 1950, Vol. 7,* 1117–21.
[150] Ibid., 1120.
[151] Ibid.
[152] Ibid., 1121.

China—hence proposals by the Army chief of staff, General J. Lawton Collins, that MacArthur stop five miles from the border.[153]

A series of meetings took place beginning in late November between senior representatives from the Departments of State and Defense, generally including both secretaries, all the Joint Chiefs, and sometimes several service secretaries. These provide an excellent window into the thinking of the top leadership in Washington. On November 21, days before the main Chinese attack but well after the sting of the first offensive, several of the Joint Chiefs were optimistically discussing the positioning of a line to be held just short of the Yalu River:

> [Army chief of staff] General Collins suggested that General MacArthur, after the attack is well launched and is succeeding, could announce that it was his intention only to go forward to destroy the North Korean units and that he intended to hold the high ground overlooking the Yalu with ROK forces, assigning the rest of the UN forces to rear areas.[154]

At the same meeting, Secretary of Defense George Marshall expressed continued support for MacArthur's planned offensive.[155] Others rejected any consideration of a cease-fire as suggesting U.S. weakness.[156] One of the clearest examples of the American inability to acknowledge the possibility of Chinese involvement, despite China's warnings, came in the November 21 meeting of the joint State-Defense group: it was already quite clear that the Chinese had a large force deployed in Manchuria, had at least some forces inside of North Korea, and had already dealt a large American unit a severe defeat. This meeting was one of the few opportunities for all the senior leaders in charge of U.S. security policy to get together in the same room. Nevertheless, throughout the entire meeting, no one even mentioned the possibility that China might increase its forces and initiate a massive attack on the U.S. force.[157] This cannot be chalked up to ignorance: leaders in Washington were getting timely copies of MacArthur's Daily Intelligence

---

[153] Cohen, "Only Half the Battle," 140–43. He cites a telegram from the Army Chief of Staff to MacArthur in the first passage.

[154] Philip Jessup, "Memorandum of Conversation, by the Ambassador at Large (Jessup) (November 21, 1950)," in *Foreign Relations of the United States, 1950*, ed. United States Department of State (Washington, D.C.: U.S. GPO, 1976), 1206–7. Also optimistically discussing the details of this proposal were General Omar Bradley and General Hoyt Vandenberg.

[155] Ibid., 1204–7.

[156] Ibid.

[157] Ibid., 1204–8.

Summaries.[158] When the joint State-Defense group met again a few days later on December 3, after receiving news of the full-scale Chinese attack, an apparently chagrined Acheson pointed out that previous discussions had failed to raise the prospect of the situation that they now faced: "Referring to the desire to resume the very useful session which had previously been held...[he noted that] it was now necessary to consider the contingency which had not been covered in the previous discussion; namely, what to do in case the [American] offensive failed."[159]

Either Acheson or the note taker (Ambassador Philip Jessup) was, in this case, engaging in understatement: previous sessions of the most senior foreign and military policymakers of the U.S. government had managed to ignore, despite significant evidence, the possibility of a Chinese attack. The thought that such a prospect was imminent at the time of the previous meeting must have been, quite literally, unthinkable.

## EVENTUAL ACCEPTANCE OF A LONG WAR

By the end of November, the signs of a Chinese intervention in force were too large even for MacArthur to ignore. After dithering at the beginning of the month, by mid-November he had settled into a confident frame of mind, but the PLA's second campaign begun at the end of the month prompted nearly hysterical demands for more troops.[160] At home in Washington, senior Army officials began to consider the implications of a complete withdrawal from the peninsula.[161] On December 1, rather than rejecting consideration of a cease-fire out of hand as they had just days earlier, the State-Defense group discussed in detail what provisions would make a ceasefire agreement acceptable.[162]

---

[158] In addition to the official reporting channel described above, the State Department staff on the ground in South Korea had access to Eighth Army and X Corps intelligence reports as they were produced. They often cabled summaries of these to Acheson in Washington. See, for instance, "The Charge in Korea (Drumright) to the Secretary of State (November 1, 1950)," reprinted in *FRUS, 1950, Vol. 7,* 1022. At the latest, the DIS would arrive by courier some three to five days after being published. Cohen, "Only Half the Battle," 146, note 7.

[159] Jessup, "Memorandum of Conversation (Jessup) 12/3/50," 1276.

[160] Schnabel, *United States Army in the Korean War,* 274–75.

[161] Ibid., 298.

[162] "Memorandum of Conversation, by the Ambassador at Large (Jessup)," December 1, 1950, in *FRUS, 1950, Vol. 7,* 1223–34. It was the center of attention again at a subsequent meeting on December 3. See Philip Jessup, "Memorandum of Conversation, by the Ambassador at Large (Jessup) (December 3, 1950)," in *FRUS, 1950,* ed. United States Department of State (Washington, D.C.: U.S. GPO, 1976).

By early January 1951, General Ridgway would be forced to abandon Seoul.[163] As the Chinese intervention capabilities became too clear to deny, the JCS again contradicted their earlier assessment, concluding that "the Chinese Communists had enough strength to drive MacArthur out of Korea."[164]

## SURPRISING DIFFICULTIES IN IMPLEMENTING STRATEGIES

The United States found that even the missions it expected to face were more difficult than anticipated. "The B-29 attacks on the key bridges in North Korea demonstrated both the difficulty of hitting such point targets and the enemy's growing ability to bypass and repair damaged bridges."[165] Hitting troops on the move also proved problematic: "Each day at dawn the Chinese concealed their mobile equipment in ravines, under bridges, and in other carefully hidden positions along the main supply routes. Such targets were exceedingly difficult to locate and harder to destroy."[166] Because of these difficulties, the Air Force shifted its emphasis to hitting supply centers (otherwise known as cities).[167] Yet, this strategy, too, failed to prove as effective as the Air Force had expected.[168]

More generally, the Air Force found its doctrine poorly designed to combat a light-infantry-based army.[169] Hastily innovated close air support missions were plagued with problems, particularly those strikes conducted by the Air Force.[170] One scholar of strategic bombing concludes that, by the end of October, the Air Force bombers had "achieved no perceptible effect on the course of the war."[171] MacArthur's assessment of the utility of

---

[163] Schnabel, *United States Army in the Korean War*, 309. For a less negative view, see Jonathan D. Pollack, "The Korean War and Sino-American Relations," in *Sino-American Relations, 1945–1955: A Joint Reassessment of a Critical Decade*, ed. Harry Harding and Ming Yuan (Wilmington, Del.: SR Books, 1989), 225n; Christensen, *Useful Adversaries*, 173n.

[164] Schnabel, *United States Army in the Korean War*, 310.

[165] Futrell, *United States Air Force in Korea, 1950–1953*, 224.

[166] Ibid., 263, 703. It is surprising that the U.S. forces had not learned this lesson during World War II.

[167] Ibid., 226.

[168] Conrad C. Crane, *American Airpower Strategy in Korea, 1950–1953* (Lawrence: University Press of Kansas, 2000), 79.

[169] The Air Force was pushed into relying on the tactic of bombing of villages that it "knew" to be inhabited by enemy fighters. Ibid., 67.

[170] Dennis E. Showalter, "The First Jet War," *Military History Quarterly* 8, no. 3 (1996): 71. On the Marines' relative advantage with regard to CAS, see Crane, *American Airpower Strategy*, 62.

[171] Pape, *Bombing to Win*, 145. That said, the Chinese certainly believed that American airpower was imposing heavy costs. See the discussion below in chapter 5 .

airpower declined dramatically over time. According to General Wright, one of MacArthur's planning officers, a "belief in the effectiveness of air power was one of General MacArthur's greatest weaknesses in dealing with the Chinese."[172] By December 3, a mere week after he had expressed such confidence about airpower cutting off Chinese logistics, MacArthur changed his tune dramatically. He now argued that the terrain did not favor American predominance in the air and on the sea; he seemed to have a new respect for Chinese mobility on foot across rough terrain, and expressed new concern that his forces were at risk.[173] The Chinese tactical mobility on foot would continue to surprise the United States well into the summer of 1951.[174]

## CHINESE REACTIONS MADE U.S. MISSIONS EVEN TOUGHER

Not only were anticipated missions more difficult than expected but the Chinese tactics also created problems for the United States. American planes, particularly the vaunted B-29, were ill-suited for night-strike operations.[175] The Chinese therefore quickly developed a preference for night movements, which meant that U.S. air strikes became fairly ineffective, even with the use of flares.[176] By May 1951, these problems were becoming even more pronounced as the Chinese further adapted to the Americans. "It was becoming increasingly difficult to locate and strike enemy interdiction targets in daylight. The CCF and NKPA were beginning to implement even more effective camouflage discipline and habitually moved their men and vehicles into cover and concealment during the daytime and moved only at night."[177] The tenacity of the Chinese response to the American campaign was impressive:

> The Navy, Marines, and Fifth Air Force were all assigned separate sectors to bomb. Roads were cratered, tetrahedral tacks were dispersed to puncture tires, and delayed-action and butterfly bombs were dropped to discourage repairs. Results again were disappointing. Enemy repair crews exploded the harassing charges with rifle fire or accepted the casualties necessary to fill the craters. Sometimes they just bypassed blockages on secondary roads. . . . Enemy countermeasures soon turned

---

[172] Schnabel, *United States Army in the Korean War,* 278.

[173] Ibid., 281.

[174] Ibid., 389.

[175] Crane, *American Airpower Strategy,* 42.

[176] Malcolm W. Cagle and Frank Albert Manson, *The Sea War in Korea* (Annapolis, Md.: Naval Institute Press, 1957), 380–83.

[177] Shrader, *Communist Logistics in the Korean War,* 180.

the tide. The communists built duplicate highway bridges across key waterways and cached whole bridge sections near important crossings so repairs could be completed quickly.[178]

Thus American offensive airpower strategy failed to live up to expectations against the vastly different Chinese forces.

## LIMITED WAR

As the war unfolded, it became clear that the U.S. military leaders were chafing against the requirement of limited war. As noted in chapter 3, prior to the Korean War the United States had been preparing for general war: another world war that would demand the full attention of the nation. Instead, however, they found themselves in a war that required that they limit their actions in order to avoid being dragged into a wider conflict.[179] One example of this friction was the concern over hot pursuit of enemy fighters across the Chinese-Korean border.[180] The Air Force resented restrictions on its ability to defend its vulnerable bombers, but national political leaders recognized the importance of preventing the war from spreading. The Air Force also expressed its enthusiasm for a variety of proposed uses for nuclear weapons.[181] MacArthur frequently called for additional divisions to be deployed to the peninsula from the strategic reserve.[182] Thorough anticipation of the risks of limited war would have prepared the military for the war they were actually to fight, and might have decreased their unwarranted optimism regarding their prospects.

## CHANGE IN U.S. STRATEGIES

The difficulties faced by the United States against the Chinese led to many proposed changes in the American approach to war. When Ridgway took over from MacArthur as commander in chief in the Far East in 1951, he began to implement some of these proposals. He even pushed the United States to become more like the PLA in certain regards:

---

[178] Crane, *American Airpower Strategy*, 83. Sadly, the U.S. military had the same problem in Vietnam twenty years later.

[179] Discussion this point is Jessup, "Memorandum of Conversation (Jessup) 12/3/50," 1276–82. Present at that meeting were the secretaries of State and Defense, the Joint Chiefs, the service secretaries, and senior advisers from State and Defense.

[180] Futrell, *United States Air Force in Korea, 1950–1953*, 223.

[181] E.g., John W. Dower, *War without Mercy* (New York: Pantheon Books, 1986), 701.

[182] Blair, *Forgotten War*.

The enemy, it is true, traveled light, traveled at night, and knew the terrain better than we did. He was inured to the weather and to all kinds of deprivation and could feed himself and carry what weapons and supplies he needed by whatever means the land offered—by oxcart, by pony, even by camel, a number of which had been brought in by the Chinese, or on the backs of native workmen, even on the backs of the troops themselves. There was nothing but our own love of comfort that bound us to the road. We too could get off into the hills, I reminded them, to find the enemy and fix him in position.[183]

At other times, he counseled a reinvigorated focus on firepower, while again noting the issue of off-road mobility.[184] By the end of the war, Ridgway was increasingly relying on the use of fortifications to deal with the human-wave tactics of the Chinese.[185] This was a considerable shift away from the U.S. tactics that, before the war, had emphasized mobility.[186]

After the war, the U.S. military undertook a number of broad reforms that suggested it had learned important lessons from the Chinese. One effect of the war was to immunize the Navy and Marines from some of the prewar interservice competition with the Army and Air Force: "In the Korean War naval air and the Marine Corps played such conspicuous and valuable roles that their future as part of the Navy was never again challenged, and the conceptual and operations value of sea power in a limited, protracted war confirmed."[187] More specifically, the Navy was able to restart its long-cherished plans for a supercarrier that would provide it with the ability to combine surface-control missions with substantial strike capabilities.[188] Furthermore, limited war became an explicit part of American thinking about the use of force.[189]

---

[183] Ridgway, *Korean War*, 89.

[184] Ibid., 111.

[185] See, for instance, the discussion of the defense of the Kansas Line in the summer of 1951 at ibid., 180–83.

[186] Chapter 3 discusses the American reliance on mobile armor formations in general before the Korean War. On the use of integrated combined-arms formations in the early stages of the Korean War utilizing the few M-24 Chaffee tanks available to the Eighth Army, see Roy Edgar Appleman, *South to the Naktong, North to the Yalu: June–November 1950* (Washington, D.C.: Office of the Chief of Military History Dept. of the Army, 1961), chapters 9–15.

[187] George W. Baer, *One Hundred Years of Sea Power: The U.S. Navy, 1890–1990* (Standford: Stanford University Press, 1994), 315–16.

[188] Ibid., 335.

[189] See Christopher M. Gacek, *The Logic of Force: The Dilemma of Limited War in American Foreign Policy* (New York: Columbia University Press, 1994).

## SUMMARY OF THE U.S. REACTIONS

Combat in Korea presented the United States with many unexpected challenges. Most important, before the war, it had vastly overestimated the utility of airpower against the Chinese.[190] But the United States was also forced to reassess its disrespect for the mobility and combat-effectiveness of poorly armed and nonmechanized infantry forces. All of this evidence strongly supports the predictions of doctrinal-difference theory regarding surprise, once the war begins, at the adversary's capabilities and intent (the Startling Battlefield Outcomes Prediction and Surprise Regarding Intentions Prediction). Thus, the evidence presented in this section illustrates the link between different theories of victory and underestimation of the enemy (DDM, the doctrinal-difference misperception hypothesis). Differences in theories of victory here directly contributed to U.S. misperception of its adversary's relative capabilities. This suggests that American assessments of the balance of power and of Chinese signals before the war were adversely affected by the misperceptions that this book has outlined with regard to the variants of the doctrinal-difference escalation (DDE) hypothesis.

In this case, both the ways in which the Chinese sent military signals and the ways in which the United States evaluated those signals and the overall situation strongly support the theory. The military signals that China sent were in a "language" based on its own theory of victory: large-scale infantry deployments, as anticipated by the Nature of Signaling Prediction. The United States viewed these through its own lens of understanding of military effectiveness, and therefore downplayed the likelihood that the Chinese would get involved in the war (consistent with the DDE hypothesis and Assessing Intent Prediction and Downplaying Prediction); they also discounted the effectiveness of the Chinese forces if they did get involved (confirming the DDE hypothesis and Misperception, Discounting, Superficial Views, and Doctrinal Confidence predictions). Both of these miscalculations were tragically wrong. The Chinese did intervene in force, and when they did so, American forces were repeatedly taken by surprise at the Chinese forces' effectiveness and their willingness to join in battle (Startling Battlefield Outcomes and Surprise Regarding Intentions Predictions).

This theory is, of course, not the only explanation for this American misperception. However, the Weakness Hypothesis—the primary approach to strategic coercion in the existing literature—is far less effective as an

---

[190] In particular, the emphasis on interdiction was misplaced. However, as the quotes above discuss, CAS against hard-to-find light infantry targets was also problematic.

explanation. In this case, the strength of the "objective" signal that the Chinese sent was indeed substantial, involving numerous diplomatic warnings and the redeployment of a large portion of the Chinese army.

Three other traditional arguments both depend on the dynamics highlighted in this chapter and are less compelling than doctrinal-difference theory overall. One important explanation for the crossing of the 38th parallel is the shift in overall U.S. grand strategy to favor "rollback." Although this is an accurate characterization of that particular decision, it cannot explain why the decision was taken. NSC-68, the controlling document outlining policy at that level, does not emphasize rollback.[191] The political debate both internally and publicly about the appropriate response to Communist aggression was vigorous.[192] It is precisely the resolution of that debate in favor of rollback that doctrinal differences help to explain.

Other arguments emphasize American beliefs that China would not attack because either the Soviets would never allow it given the potential for the conflict to expand to general war or because Beijing would have known the United States was not going to attack. First, these explanations work in conjunction with the Weakness Hypothesis; that is, they assume that the signals sent by Beijing were relatively weak. This is less valid than traditionally thought. Furthermore, these explanations have some consistency with the overall strategic surprise the United States experienced, but not with the failure to appreciate the tactical-level prowess of the Chinese forces. This tactical confidence was integrally involved with assessments of Chinese intent. The United States thought that the Chinese would not want to intervene because the cost of that intervention was viewed differently in Washington and Beijing.

In such complex cases, many factors contribute to explaining outcomes. In this case, weak signals and other reasons to expect Chinese acquiescence contribute to a complete understanding of the escalation. But without an appreciation for the misperceptions that doctrinal-difference theory predicts, it seems unlikely that the case would have developed as catastrophically as it did. For the reasons doctrinal-difference theory predicts, the United States failed to anticipate the Chinese reaction and its deadly effects. Doctrinal differences are a deep cause that enables other mistakes that in turn derive from misunderstandings of the adversary. Thus, Chinese attempts at deterrence failed, and a long and bloody war was the result. In the next chapter, we see how these doctrinal differences also resulted in a failure of U.S. attempts at deterring China.

---

[191] Christensen, *Useful Adversaries,* 127.
[192] Halberstam, *Coldest Winter,* chapter 22.

# 5

# CHINA CROSSES THE YALU

ONCE THE UNITED STATES CROSSED the 38th parallel, the next key escalation in the war was the Chinese decision to move south across the Yalu River into North Korea, countering the American military might that moved rapidly northward. The evidence available during the early Cold War appeared to support the argument that war might have been avoided even after the United States crossed the 38th parallel, if only MacArthur had kept his forces from approaching the Yalu River.[1] Evidence available since then, however, makes it increasingly clear that, once the United States crossed the existing border between North and South Korea at the 38th parallel, there were few opportunities to avoid war.[2] Even the November lull in fighting between the first and second Chinese offensives is now understood to have been a tactical military trap rather than a diplomatic signal by China.[3] The

---

[1] Most famously, this is the argument of Allen S. Whiting, *China Crosses the Yalu: The Decision to Enter the Korean War* (New York: Macmillan, 1960).

[2] The earliest advocate of this point in English is Thomas J. Christensen, "Threats, Assurances, and the Last Chance for Peace: The Lessons of Mao's Korean War Telegrams," *International Security* 17, no. 1 (1992). See also Sergei Goncharov, John Lewis, and Xue Litai, *Uncertain Partners: Stalin, Mao, and the Korean War* (Stanford: Stanford University Press, 1993), 159, 181, and 194; Andrew Scobell, *China's Use of Military Force: Beyond the Great Wall and the Long March* (New York: Cambridge University Press, 2003).

[3] 陶文钊、《中美关系史(1949–1972)》 (上海:上海人民出版社、1999) [Tao Wenzhao, *History of Sino-American Relations, 1949–1972* (Shanghai: Shanghai People's Press, 1999), 32]; Yu Bin, "What China Learned from Its 'Forgotten War' in Korea," in *Mao's Generals Remember Korea*, ed. Li Xiaobing, Allan Reed Millett, and Yu Bin (Lawrence: University Press of Kansas, 2001), 15.

presence of American forces in North Korea, not just on the Yalu, sparked the Chinese sense of insecurity.[4] The crossing of the 38th seemed to suggest a shift toward rollback as a touchstone for American policy, possibly calling into question other Communist victories since World War II. The security dilemma was extremely severe at this point, and it is hard to imagine how the Chinese could have escaped its grasp.

Nevertheless, the effects of the differing American and Chinese theories of victory can be seen throughout the vigorous military signaling in this period, shaping the tacit and explicit signals between the countries and how they were interpreted. Without denying the important role of the security dilemma and other causes, this chapter shows how doctrinal differences exacerbated those factors and further suggests their role in explaining the course of the war and some of the broader decisions leading to its outbreak. Furthermore, the optimism that came from doctrinal difference increased the scope of China's war aims, exacerbating the severity of the war over its three-year duration.

Chinese fears of U.S. designs were strong, but factors central to doctrinal-difference theory shaped the policy chosen to respond to them. Mao and the other senior leaders in Beijing downplayed the challenges posed by the conflict itself—most insouciantly with regard to potential nuclear dangers—as well as the prospects that it could escalate beyond the peninsula. They also laid out expansive war aims, hoping to push the United States off the Korean Peninsula. More broadly, had Mao been fearful enough of the threats of American military power, he could have slowed the drumbeat of war among the Communists in Northeast Asia early in the summer of 1950. This case contributes to the understanding of why Mao was not fearful but instead moderately optimistic regarding China's prospects in a war with the United States.

## HISTORICAL BACKGROUND

Soon after the outbreak of the war in Korea, China began to take preventive measures in case the situation called for Chinese action. A meeting of the Chinese leadership established the Northeast Border Defense Army

---

[4] For a contentious and not widely held argument that the U.S. entry into South Korea in June and July of 1950 was, by itself, enough to make war between China and the United States almost unavoidable, see Chen Jian, *China's Road to the Korean War: The Making of the Sino-American Confrontation* (New York: Columbia University Press, 1994), 128, 139, 143, 148, and 173.

(NEBDA) in early July 1950.[5] Over the next two months, Chinese military preparations stepped up, as described in Chapter 4.

By early October, after MacArthur's dramatic Inchon landings, the situation had worsened appreciably from the Chinese perspective. On October 1, the UN demanded that the North Koreans capitulate. Chinese intelligence reports from the front painted increasingly bleak pictures: "on October 1, an intelligence report reached Beijing indicating that U.S./UN vanguard units had begun crossing the 38th parallel. Twenty-four hours later, another report confirmed that American troops were moving into North Korea in large numbers."

In a secret report given to the Chinese Peoples Consultative Conference, Zhou Enlai echoed this point: "New dispatches of October 1 and 2 indicated that U.S. troops had already crossed the 38th Parallel and that the South Korean army had penetrated far north of it."[6] According to the American records discussed in chapter 4, these reports were false, but what matters here is what China believed at the time.

In response, the Chinese leaders undertook their fateful decision. Mao's leadership was paramount in October. Although Lin Biao and others opposed intervention,[7] the aggressive U.S. policy made it easier for Mao to secure wide support for his preferred policy:

> Mao might not need to yield to the different opinions held by his colleagues, but it would have been foolish for him not to take them into consideration. In fact, unless China's territorial safety were directly threatened by the Americans, Mao would have had difficulty in convincing the party and the Chinese people of the necessity to intervene in Korea.[8]

Mao was thus constrained by the views of his fellow leaders in Beijing, and he also had to consider the attitudes of allied leaders in North Korea and the Soviet Union.[9]

Nevertheless, by October 2, an enlarged session of the Politburo Standing Committee met to discuss Chinese policy. Contentious and inconclusive

[5] Ibid., 136.
[6] Zhou Enlai, "Resisting U.S. Aggression, Aiding Korea and Defending Peace," October 24, 1950, reprinted in Zhou Enlai, *Selected Works of Zhou Enlai,* 1st ed. (Beijing: Foreign Languages Press: Distributed by Guoji Shudian, 1981), 61.
[7] Chen, *China's Road,* 153. See more on the dissenters in China later in this chapter.
[8] Ibid., 155.
[9] Ibid., 160.

debate elevated the discussions to China's full Politburo on October 4.[10] That body reconvened the next day and, at Mao's instructions, Peng Dehuai spoke forcefully in support of intervention: "[His] speech transformed the mood of the meeting, and the discussion now centered on the advantages of sending troops to Korea."[11] The key factor in this conclusion to three days of deliberations that hardened Chinese policy was that the United States had crossed the 38th parallel.[12]

Subsequent to this Politburo meeting, the pace of Chinese action quickened. There were further negotiations with the Soviets over the nature and scale of Soviet support. (These negotiations became somewhat contentious. The Chinese demanded commitment of Soviet airpower at an early date, and when the Soviets declined, Mao hesitated, deliberating further before pursuing his original plan.) On October 18 Mao gave the final order, and Chinese troops crossed the Yalu River into North Korea the following day.[13] Mao's goals were anything but modest: "We shall aim at resolving the conflict, that is, to eliminate the U.S. troops within Korea and to drive them and other countries' aggressive forces out."[14]

Thus, although China's decision to enter the war was not final until late October, key choices were made in late September and early October. The following sections evaluate U.S. signals during this preparation period, as well as available evidence as to how they were interpreted in Beijing.

## SIGNALING BY THE UNITED STATES

Shifts in U.S. military posture, both nuclear and conventional, and the broad tenor of relations between the two Cold War blocs, hinted at U.S. intent toward China and toward the situation on the Korean Peninsula. These would have constituted important "general deterrent" threats to China. Several specific signals reflected U.S. "immediate deterrence" messages. This multifaceted set of signals should have sent a very strong deterrent message to the Chinese. However, their reception was complicated by features based on an American conception of military strategy that would have been difficult for the Chinese to interpret.

---

[10] Odd Arne Westad, *Decisive Encounters: The Chinese Civil War, 1946–1950* (Stanford: Stanford University Press, 2003), 322. Also, see the discussion later in this chapter on this point.
[11] Chen, *China's Road,* 184.
[12] Christensen, "Threats, Assurances, and the Last Chance for Peace."
[13] Chen, *China's Road,* chapter 7.
[14] Zhang, *Mao's Military Romanticism,* 78.

## CHANGES IN GRAND STRATEGY

At the broadest level, U.S. grand strategy should have communicated cred-
ibly the U.S. threat to engage in high-intensity warfare with the Chinese.
There had been some hardening of U.S. policy even before the outbreak of
the Korean War. The highest level of America grand strategy at this time was
the Truman Doctrine, or containment,[15] first announced to a specially called
joint session of Congress on March 12, 1947. President Truman declared
that "I believe that it must be the policy of the United States to support free
peoples who are resisting attempted subjugation by armed minorities or by
outside pressures."[16] Even at that time, it was clear to the world that the shift
in American policy involved more than simply an aid package to Greece and
Turkey. By late 1949, it was clear to audiences at home and abroad that U.S.
containment policy was to be both universal and firm.[17] There had been a
shift away from George Kennan's "strongpoint" strategy of the late 1940s to a
more comprehensive "defensive perimeter" or "containment" strategy aimed
at preventing the expansion of communism. NATO was created in July 1949.
Truman signed NSC-48 in December 1949, which focused on the security
situation in Asia, making explicit the intention of the United States to apply
containment principles more broadly in Asia than before.

However, it was NSC-68 that most pointedly epitomized this changed emphasis in policy. It had been drafted a few months before the outbreak of
the Korean War, but fear of opposition from within the Budget Bureau and
from others concerned with the domestic tax burden had prevented Truman
from implementing NSC-68 at the time. Once the war broke out, however,
NSC-68 was formally signed, and it would guide American foreign policy for
a generation or more. Its effects on the U.S. defense budget were significant,

---

[15] The concepts laid out in the President's Truman Doctrine speech and containment (as laid
out in George Kennan's "X article") are closely related and historically intertwined and are
treated as such here. John Lewis Gaddis, *Strategies of Containment: A Critical Appraisal of Postwar American National Security Policy* (New York: Oxford University Press, 1982), chapter 3,
"Implementing Containment"; Warren I. Cohen, *The Cambridge History of American Foreign
Relations*, vol. 4 (New York: Cambridge University Press, 1993), 38–41.

[16] President Harry Truman, address of the "President of the United States: Recommendation
for Assistance to Greece and Turkey," March 12, 1947, available at the Truman Library's online
collection at http://www.trumanlibrary.org/whistlestop/study_collections/doctrine/large/
folder5/tde02–1.htm.

[17] For similar characterizations, see William Whitney Stueck Jr., *The Road to Confrontation:
American Policy toward China and Korea, 1947–1950* (Chapel Hill: University of North Carolina
Press, 1981), 146–52; Rosemary Foot, *The Wrong War: American Policy and the Dimensions of the
Korean Conflict, 1950–1953* (Ithaca: Cornell University Press, 1985), 47–54.

providing a global context that justified a more than doubling of the U.S. defense budget in the first year of the Korean War.[18]

Aside from the issues raised by its financial demands, NSC-68 spelled out the Truman administration's declaratory foreign policy in detail.[19] It embodied a shift toward a much more assertive American policy, which was now "imbued with an offensive spirit."[20] It emphasized enhancing American military capabilities to provide for robust deterrence of threats. It argued that, in order to "prevent disaster," U.S. military forces must be able "to conduct offensive operations to destroy vital elements of the Soviet war-making capacity, and to keep the enemy off balance until the full offensive strength of the United States and its allies can be brought to bear."[21]

Thus, soon after the outbreak of the Korean War, American deterrent policy—particularly declaratory policy, so critical to deterrence—explicitly hardened against Communist aggression.

### GENERAL NUCLEAR WEAPONS POLICY

Several aspects of the new American policy toward Communist nations—in general and in Asia—had implications for nuclear deterrence policy. In this period, American decisionmakers were extremely confident that implicit military moves could send signals, particularly if they involved atomic weapons. Relatively small deployments of B-29 bombers had been used to send deterrent signals to the Soviet Union in the past: in 1948, for example, two squadrons had been deployed to Britain during the first Berlin Crisis to send a warning signal to Moscow.[22] Roger Dingman describes the legacy of that crisis:

> Democratic and Republican statesmen looked back to the dispatch of
> two squadrons of B-29s to Western Europe during the Berlin Blockade

---

[18] In 1950, half of which was spent at war in Korea, saw a defense budget of $15 billion. The next year, the budget rose to $33 billion. J. David Singer and Melvin Small, "National Material Capabilities (Version 2.1)," 1990 (updated April 1999), in Correlates of War Project, University of Michigan.

[19] Gaddis, *Strategies of Containment*, 107–8. On its centrality as a source of declaratory policy, see Thomas J. Christensen, *Useful Adversaries: Grand Strategy, Domestic Mobilization, and Sino-American Conflict, 1947–1958* (Princeton: Princeton University Press, 1996), 125–26.

[20] Melvyn P. Leffler, *A Preponderance of Power: National Security, the Truman Administration, and the Cold War* (Stanford: Stanford University Press, 1992), 357.

[21] Quoted from NSC-68 in *FRUS, 1950*, vol. 1: *National Security Affairs; Foreign Economic Policy* (Washington, D.C.: U.S. GPO, 1977), 283.

[22] Scott Douglas Sagan, *Moving Targets: Nuclear Strategy and National Security* (Princeton: Princeton University Press, 1989), 15.

of 1948–49 for guidance on how best to use American nuclear superiority. . . . In the summer of 1948, American statesmen doubted that the B-29 deployment contributed directly to settlement of the Berlin Blockade crisis. But as time hazed over the particulars of this episode, they came to believe that atomic arms could be instruments of "force without war." Their credibility might even exceed their actual capability if they were used, without overt threats, for the purposes of deterrence rather than compellence. Thus American statesmen and soldiers brought to the Korean War the conviction that atomic arms, if properly employed, could be extremely valuable tools for conflict management.

Similarly, Richard Betts describes a series of crises in which nuclear deterrence was attempted tacitly, without explicit atomic or nuclear threats, even in private.[23] Thus, nuclear signaling was part of the U.S. modus operandi and was thought to be effective.

Further, the United States had recently developed the capacity to launch nuclear strikes from the continental United States. The first operational B-36 "Peacemaker" aircraft had entered the inventory of the Strategic Air Command in 1948; by 1950, SAC could call on three squadrons of such planes for strikes.[24] Several long-range operational test flights displayed their capabilities in the late 1940s:

SAC celebrated the success of the program by staging a long-range navigation and bombing mission that extended from taking off at Carswell [AFB in Texas] through dropping a 10,000-pound "dummy" bomb in the Pacific Ocean near the Hawaiian Islands and returning to Carswell. The unrefueled mission covered 8,100 miles in 35–1/2 hours. The mission was, in a way, a "LeMay triumph" in that the bomber made an approach over Honolulu undetected by the local air defense system—on 7 December 1948! Early in 1949, another B-36 crew set a long-distance record of 9,600 miles. The B-36 covered the distance in 43 hours, 37 minutes. . . . There was little doubt that the vast

---

[23] See pre-1958 cases in Richard K. Betts, *Nuclear Blackmail and Nuclear Balance* (Washington, D.C.: Brookings Institution, 1987).

[24] Chris Adams, *Inside the Cold War: A Cold Warrior's Reflections* (Maxwell Air Force Base, Alabama: Air University Press, September 1999); Marc Trachtenberg, "A 'Wasting Asset': American Strategy and the Shifting Nuclear Balance, 1949–54," in *Nuclear Diplomacy and Crisis Management: An International Security Reader,* ed. Sean Lynn-Jones, Steven Miller, and Stephen Van Evera (Cambridge: MIT Press, 1990), 86.

Soviet communications monitoring system was taking note of these and other similar demonstrations of long-range strategic "reach."[25]

This brandishing of intercontinental bombers capable of delivering weapons at exceptional range should also have sent a general warning signal to both the Soviets and the Chinese.

Still, through the early 1950s, most of the American nuclear deterrent would have been launched from overseas bases if war came.[26] Just as in the 1948 Berlin crisis, similar tacit signals were also sent in Asia; from October 1949 to June 1950, for example, Guam hosted B-29 training missions.[27] By familiarizing staff at Andersen Air Force Base on Guam with the maintenance and deployment needs of the B-29 platform, the U.S. military facilitated future immediate deterrent steps, such as the deployment of nuclear-capable B-29s.

These policies were aimed at deterring Communist aggression globally and were components of a general deterrence posture. However, the way that they conveyed a general-deterrence message would not have appeared as threatening to the Chinese as the United States thought. China would have feared neither destruction of its industrial base nor the prospect of the "full offensive strength" of the United States being directed against it. In light of Beijing's theory of victory, those elements did not seem particularly threatening compared, for example, to forward deployment of very large numbers of American troops.

## DIPLOMATIC SIGNALS

There was only limited direct U.S. diplomatic signaling toward the Chinese in this period. In one of the few instances of explicit diplomacy, the United States attempted to warn China of the costs of entry into the Korean War using the usual channel, Indian ambassador Panikkar. In the wake of the successful Inchon landings, the United States sought to convey the following message:

In the US opinion it is of [the] utmost importance for [the] Chi Commies themselves that they avoid intervention in Korean hostilities.

---

[25] Adams, *Inside the Cold War,* 39.

[26] The classic analysis of these plans (and their implications for stability) is Albert J. Wohlstetter et al., *Selection and Use of Strategic Air Bases,* R-266 (Santa Monica, Calif.: RAND, April 1954), 3–8ff.

[27] It appears these were conventional B-29s, although that would not have been apparent to anyone other than the highest-ranking Americans. The same B-29s would later fly missions in Korea.

Present change [in] mil[itary] situation indicates UN may be able restore peace quickly in Korea and, on the record of UN debate and action, it [could] be expected that UN patently [would] view with grave
concern Chi Commie intervention.[28]

Although the Chinese carefully monitored such signals,[29] it is unclear
whether Panikkar actually passed on exactly that message.[30]

## MILITARY SIGNALS

If the diplomatic signals were sparse, the military ones were not. The so-
lidification of military lines around the Pusan Perimeter in late July and the
U.S. offensive successes in September were driven by battlefield necessity, but
they should also have emphasized the credibility of American intentions, as
should have several additional steps. All should have sent loud messages to
the Chinese.

By mid-July, the U.S. situation on the ground in South Korea had improved, and the Pusan Perimeter had essentially been formed, as MacArthur
informed President Truman in an optimistic strategic appraisal on July 19.[31]
U.S. capabilities to expand or escalate the war were then stepped up: ten
nuclear-capable B-29s—the premier delivery platform of the day—were deployed very publicly to the [Asian] region in late July.[32] After an intentional
leak, the *New York Times* reported this deployment, so it would have been well
known to the Chinese. Again, it was believed in Washington that such tacit
signals would be heard: "The decisions of late July 1950 demonstrated the

[28] "Secretary of State to Embassy in India," September 16, 1950, in *FRUS, 1950,* vol. VII: *Korea* (Washington, D.C.: U.S. GPO, 1976), 733.
[29] In addition to the previous chapter's discussion of Panikkar, see for instance, 裴坚章、《中华人民共和国外交史:1949–1956》(北京:世界知识出版社、1994) [Pei Jianzhang, *Foreign Relations History of the People's Republic of China: 1949–56* (Beijing: World Knowledge Press, 1994), 328–29].
[30] The reply from the Indian representatives is discussed in "The Ambassador in India (Henderson) to the Secretary of State," September 20, 1950 in *FRUS, 1950, Vol. 7,* 742.
[31] James F. Schnabel, *United States Army in the Korean War,* vol. 3, *Policy and Direction: The First Year* (Washington, D.C.: Office of the Chief of Military History United States Army/GPO, 1972), 112.
[32] Roger Dingman, "Atomic Diplomacy during the Korean War," in *Nuclear Diplomacy and Crisis Management,* ed. Stephen Van Evera (Cambridge: MIT Press, 1990), 126–27. See also Conrad C. Crane, *American Airpower Strategy in Korea, 1950–1953* (Lawrence: University Press of Kansas, 2000), 27; Mark A. Ryan, *Chinese Attitudes toward Nuclear Weapons: China and the United States during the Korean War* (Armonk, N.Y.: M. E. Sharpe, 1989), 26.

strength of Washington's belief that such weapons, even if deployed without explicit statements of intent, could serve as deterrents."[33]

Other strategic air assets were moved: the Fifth Air Force was relocated to Korea in late September after the first phase of conflict had essentially been won.[34] General George Stratemeyer, commander of the air forces in the Far East, ordered use of B-29s in early September against a wide range of targets such as roads and allowed their use at night.[35] There was military utility in these steps, but they were also intended to send messages about the might of U.S. airpower to the Communist bloc.

Third, plans were in place as late as October for the Eighth Army to return from Korea to Japan as a four-division theater reserve.[36] These would constitute full-strength divisions, not the downsized version that had been stationed in Japan prior to the Korean War. The U.S. success in two multi-division amphibious operations in Korea (Inchon and Wonson) would have demonstrated the threat that such a force could pose in Korea or beyond.

## SUMMARY

American signaling thus came in several forms. General deterrent signals aimed at preventing Communist aggression worldwide were complemented by immediate deterrent threats and signals aimed at preventing escalation of the Korean conflict. These policies should have conveyed a strong deterrent signal to the Chinese. Thus, the Weakness Hypothesis (the conventional wisdom emphasizing the "objective" quality of the signal) cannot contribute substantially to explaining the deterrence failure.

This was, in fact, a challenging case for achieving deterrence success, because the Chinese perceived an urgent threat from the U.S. presence in Korea. However, this problem was exacerbated by the military and grand-strategic elements of the signals sent by the Americans. Most of the signals sent were dependent on airpower, not regarded as efficacious by the Chinese leadership. Thus, Washington's own theory of victory shaped these signals (supporting the Nature of Signaling Prediction), which made them difficult for the Chinese to interpret.

[33] Christopher M. Gacek, *The Logic of Force: The Dilemma of Limited War in American Foreign Policy* (New York: Columbia University Press, 1994), 55.

[34] Robert Frank Futrell, *The United States Air Force in Korea, 1950–1953*, rev. ed. (Washington, D.C.: Office of Air Force History United States Air Force, 1983), 176.

[35] Ibid., 165–68.

[36] Schnabel, *United States Army in the Korean War*, 222.

## INTERPRETATION BY CHINA

Because of the closed nature of the Chinese state, there is only limited evidence on the intricacies of Chinese decision making. Thus, little information is available that could help us understand the thought processes of Chinese leaders in developing their policy toward the United States in September and October of 1950. Nevertheless, the evidence that is available shows that the doctrinal blinders predicted by doctrinal-difference theory were in place. For instance, there is substantial evidence that the Chinese had a deep confidence in the capability of their tactics against the American forces. This confidence is repeatedly expressed, as China made its decision to intervene in the Korean War, and it seems to have contributed to their decisions and shaped their expansive goals for the conflict. (Related evidence was presented in the final section of chapter 3.) Similarly, there is substantial evidence that the Chinese quite cavalierly discounted the dangers posed by the American atomic arsenal. Furthermore Mao, like Stalin, downplayed the overall threat of American involvement in Asia; this appears to be related to Mao's firm belief in Chinese military superiority.

That said, other factors also entered into Chinese decision making in this case. As we now know, China viewed an American presence in North Korea as a grave threat to its own strategic interests. This perception does much to explain why the Chinese entered the war. However, there is substantial evidence, presented below, of misperceptions held by Chinese leaders as they weighed their options in the early fall of 1950, which led to false optimism. This false optimism certainly facilitated the security-dilemma dynamics that drove Chinese entry, but also shaped the nature of China's policy and its expectations for the war in ways that had substantial consequences for all involved. Issues such as war aims, negotiating posture, and decisions to continue the final few massive (ineffectual) offensives were all shaped by these views.

### CONFIDENCE ABOUT CONVENTIONAL BATTLES

As they faced the prospect of war with the United States, the Chinese felt they had grounds for optimism regarding a number of tactical issues. The evidence presented in this section strongly supports the link between differences in theories of victory and underestimation (the doctrinal-difference misperception [DDM] hypothesis) and several of the theory's component predictions. The Misperception Prediction expects correlation between differences in theories of victory and underestimation. The Discounting Prediction warns that states with different theories of victory will discount the capabilities of their adversary. The Extreme Differences Prediction says that more extreme differences between the two states' theories of victory should correlate with more extreme underestimation of the adversary's capability. The evidence presented in this section supports all three of these predictions.

The optimism of Chinese leaders was widespread as conflict with the United States became increasingly likely. Evidence of Chinese confidence abounds. One of Mao's generals later wrote of the perceptions at the time:

> During the past several decades, our army had always defeated well-equipped enemies with our poor arms. Our troops were skillful in close fighting, night combat, mountain operations, and bayonet charges. Even though the American army had modern weapons and advanced equipment, its commanders and soldiers were not familiar with [such tactics].[37]

The Chinese expected bayonet charges to play a large role in the hypothetical next war; the United States thought that strategic bombing and nuclear exchanges would be central. This is precisely what doctrinal-difference theory would predict, as stated in the Doctrinal Confidence Prediction: states believe that battles will be dominated by factors emphasized by its own theory of victory.[38]

On October 24, 1950, in a speech to the People's Consultative Congress, Zhou Enlai said, "Our Army is capable of resolving the problem. The Air Force and Navy will not go because only next year will we establish them. But should we wait until our strength has grown before intervening? No!"[39] And when it did intervene, writes one Chinese scholar and military historian, "the CPV [Chinese People's Volunteers] employed all of these familiar tactics: numerical superiority, mobile operations, and surprise."[40]

Another Chinese source quotes the *Current Events Bulletin* of the Central Committee of the CCP of October 26, 1950, an internally circulated, classified

---

[37] Xuezhi Hong, "The CPVF's Combat and Logistics," in *Mao's Generals Remember Korea*, ed. Li Xiaobing, Allan Reed Millett, and Yu Bin (Lawrence: University Press of Kansas, 2001), 115.
[38] It is irrelevant to the theory which side was correct in its expectations: the wide disparity of views shaped their divergent threat assessments.
[39] 周恩来、《周恩来军事文选》第四卷(北京:人民出版社、1997) [Zhou Enlai, *Zhou Enlai's Selected Military Writings* (Beijing: People's Publishers, 1997), 76].
[40] Yu Bin, "What China Learned from Its 'Forgotten War' In Korea," in *Chinese Warfighting: The PLA Experience since 1949*, ed. Mark A. Ryan, David M. Finkelstein, and Michael A. McDevitt (Armonk, N.Y.: M. E. Sharpe, Inc., 2003), 127.

bulletin that would have been available only to senior Chinese decisionmakers. This report also expresses confidence in any conventional battle:

> [The United States] has economic strength and superiority of weapons and equipment, but its invasion actions toward the five continents [i.e., a CCP trope against U.S. foreign policy at the time] has received the opposition of the people of the world and led to its political isolation. Militarily speaking, it also has many weak spots: its front line is long, its rear areas are far away, its troops are not numerous, its morale is not high. Its allied friends—England, France, etc.—are no longer great powers. Japan and West Germany have yet to arm. Atomic weapons are now held by others, and furthermore do not determine victory or defeat. The final victory will certainly belong to the Chinese and Korean people.[41]

Thus, it is evident that Chinese confidence based on conventional strength was widespread.

### CHINESE CONFIDENCE IN THE FACE OF ATOMIC WEAPONS

A second element of Chinese confidence in their forces' ability to fight the Americans came on the issue of nuclear weapons. After the Korean War broke out, a wide range of China's leaders continued to express confidence in their ability to address a potential atomic threat. Some of the evidence presented below is drawn from Mao's later thinking about potential American atomic weapon use, after the key decision for war. However, if the Chinese leadership did not find American atomic weapons threatening in December, it is unlikely that they felt differently two months earlier when they decided to cross the Yalu.

As the two sides were edging toward conflict and the United States sent a number of nuclear signals, the Chinese remained uncowed, with the Chinese press declaring that nuclear weapons lacked tactical utility.[42] Ryan's study of Chinese views of nuclear weapons summarizes the "systematic, integrated party line dealing with nuclear weapons" of the Chinese policymakers once they had decided to intervene in the Korean War: "The United States had

---

[41] 沈、孟、等、《抗美援朝战史》 [Shen, Meng, and others, *The History of the War to Resist America and Support Korea*, 10].

[42] Melvin Gurtov and Byong-Moo Hwang, *China under Threat: The Politics of Strategy and Diplomacy* (Baltimore: Johns Hopkins University Press, 1980), 54.

certain glaring weaknesses in its military posture in Korea....It was futile to try to use nuclear weapons to compensate for these weaknesses. Bombing per se, including nuclear bombing, could not be a decisive military tactic."[43]

As direct war loomed in November, internal briefing papers reiterated points made months earlier:

> The atomic bomb itself cannot be the decisive factor in a war. The atomic bomb has many drawbacks as a military weapon. It can only be used against a big and concentrated object like a big armament industry center or huge concentrations of troops. Therefore, the more extensive the opponents' territory is and the more scattered the opponents' population is, the less effective will the atomic bomb be.[44]

Mao, in particular, dismissed the value of nuclear weapons for the United States in Korea. At the ninth meeting of the Central Committee on September 5, 1950, he declared: "We will not let you [the United States] attack us. If you absolutely want to do so, then go ahead. You attack us your way, we will attack you ours. You attack using atomic weapons, we will attack using hand grenades; we will grab on to your weaknesses, and after this, in the end, defeat you."[45] As a sign of his confidence about this issue, Mao's telegram to Stalin conveying his decision to enter into war makes no mention of nuclear weapons.[46]

Certainly some of the Chinese confidence stemmed from a belief that the United States was simply unlikely to use nuclear weapons.[47] Nevertheless, even this judgment contains some assessment of the likely utility of atomic weapons for the United States. The Chinese cost-benefit analysis substantially discounted any benefits that would accrue to the United States, compared to U.S. expectations on that score. This imputation of intent from perceived capability is just as predicted in the doctrinal-difference escalation (DDE) hypothesis.

---

[43] Ryan, *Chinese Attitudes toward Nuclear Weapons*, 39–40. Ryan suggests that this view applied "during the period from late October 1950 through January 1951."

[44] This is from the internal circulation (*neibu*) Current Affairs Handbook (时事资料手册) of November 5, 1950, quoted in ibid., 42. Although some U.S. observers would make similar points at the time, the overall tenor of discussion in the United States would have been quite the opposite.

[45] 沈、孟、等、《抗美援朝战史》[Shen, Meng, and others, *History of the War*, 5].

[46] For a work that emphasizes this point as significant and relates it to Mao's dismissal of such weapons, see Chen, *China's Road*, 179. For a view that places less emphasis on this, see Christensen, "Threats, Assurances, and the Last Chance for Peace," 137, note 43.

[47] Chen, *China's Road*, 178.

At times Mao explicitly discussed the possibility of American strategic bombing against China.[48] However, as in a telegram dated November 22, 1950, although he is cognizant that the United States might bomb Chinese cities, he is simply not worried about it. He notes it might happen, but is optimistic so long as the PLA can deliver a sharp blow against the U.S. ground forces in Korea.

At various times during the war,[49] and particularly during the long-drawn-out negotiations over ending the Korean War, the United States made atomic threats—more and less oblique—to influence the Chinese negotiating position. In early 1951, for example, Truman deployed to the region bombers that were not just atomic-capable but actually loaded with atomic weapons.[50] However, as one scholar familiar with Chinese sources concluded,

> There is no evidence to show that the Beijing leadership, while forming this tough [negotiating position at Panmunjom], paid any significant attention to whether or not the Americans would use nuclear weapons in Korea. Although military planners in Beijing probably considered the possibility that the Americans would use nuclear weapons for tactical targets in Korea, Mao and the other Chinese leaders firmly believed that the outcome of the Korean conflict would be determined by ground operations. Not surprising at all, then, when Mao and the other CCP leaders analyzed the means Washington might use to put pressure on the Communists, they did not even bother to mention the atomic bomb.[51]

Could this blithe attitude toward the dangers of nuclear attack by Chinese leaders have stemmed from a sense of reassurance due to an extended deterrent guarantee from the Sino-Soviet alliance? This is unlikely. China had only limited confidence in their Soviet ally. The Soviets had expressed great reluctance to include such phrases as "with all means at its disposal" in the key

---

[48] See Christensen, "Threats, Assurances, and the Last Chance for Peace," 137.
[49] There appear to have been quiet U.S. attempts to threaten the Chinese in May 1951, although precisely what was being demanded of the Chinese is unclear from the available historical record: perhaps it was simply not to expand the war further, although such a threat would more sensibly have been conveyed to the Soviets rather than the Chinese. See Dingman, "Atomic Diplomacy during the Korean War," 140–41.
[50] Robert Pape, *Bombing to Win: Air Power and Coercion in War* (Ithaca: Cornell University Press, 1996), 146.
[51] Chen Jian, *Mao's China and the Cold War* (Chapel Hill: University of North Carolina Press, 2001), 111.

provision of the Sino-Soviet treaty. Only after much diplomatic wrangling was the provision inserted, which could not have inspired confidence in Beijing. (Even then, the Soviets limited the scope of the alliance to conditions that were formally "in a state of war," providing Stalin with some leeway should Chinese behavior appear to put the Soviets in a corner.[52]) Stalin's reluctance would have limited Mao's faith in the reliability of the extended Soviet nuclear deterrent.[53] Similarly, as Goldstein's study of Chinese nuclear deterrent thought points out, "Even before a formal treaty of alliance was signed, Soviet behavior under Stalin had provided reason for China to worry about the possibility of abandonment."[54] Goldstein argues that these concerns remained unanswered throughout the 1950s.[55]

Thus, this evidence strongly supports the doctrinal-difference misperception (DDM) hypothesis and is as anticipated by the Misperception Prediction regarding the perceptions of the adversary's strategies, the Discounting Prediction about the overall balance of power, Superficial Views Prediction about the nature of war, and Extreme Differences Prediction about the effect of extreme values on the independent variable. The evidence of considerable Chinese confidence regarding both conventional and atomic warfare shows how different theories of victory can lead to underestimation of the adversary, as spelled out in the doctrinal-difference misperception (DDM) hypothesis. Regardless of whether the weapons were used or not, the two sides had vastly different views about the power of the weapons and therefore the coercive power threats to use them would have. This confidence contributed to China's views about the overall balance of power, supporting the Misperception and Extreme Difference Predictions associated with the doctrinal-difference escalation (DDE) hypothesis.

## BELIEFS REGARDING AMERICAN INTENT

There was a general tendency in China to discount any American intention to get involved in a significant war in either Korea or the region more

---

[52] Goncharov, Lewis, and Xue Litai, *Uncertain Partners,* 118. See also Avery Goldstein, *Deterrence and Security in the 21st Century: China, Britain, France, and the Enduring Legacy of the Nuclear Revolution* (Stanford: Stanford University Press, 2000), 66.

[53] Noting that Stalin downplayed the utility of the Soviet arsenal at the time is Goncharov, Lewis, and Xue, *Uncertain Partners,* 108. Interestingly, the Soviets—subsequent to their acquisition of nuclear weapons—did incorporate nuclear weapons into their evaluations of the overall balance of power. 沈志華、《毛澤東、斯大林與韓戰:中蘇最高機密檔案》 [Shen Zhihua, *Mao, Stalin, and the Korean War: The Highest Top Secret Archives*] (Hong Kong: Cosmos Books, Ltd., 1998), 204.

[54] Goldstein, *Deterrence and Security in the 21st Century,* 65.

[55] Ibid., chapter 3.

broadly. The evidence presented here supports the Downplaying Prediction robustly. The strength of these views before the war is apparent in the historical record.

The Chinese had not originally expected that the United States would commit to large-scale war in Korea. Khrushchev's memoirs state that, as Mao approved the invasion in May, the Chinese leader "put forward the opinion that the USA would not intervene since the war would be an internal matter which the Korean people would decide for themselves."[56] Evidence from Russian archives also shows that Mao convinced the North Koreans that the United States would not oppose them.[57] After the Korean War broke out, Zhou Enlai expressed a similar optimism about American behavior in the face of Chinese People's War strategies: "The unity of our nation and our people is so important and so powerful that any imperialist attempt to invade China would be frightened away by it."[58] The consensus among scholars working on this period, whether Chinese, American, or European, all point to Chinese expectations of American passivity.[59]

This is consistent with a broader evaluation of American intentions. In December 1949, Mao summarized a conversation with Stalin on the general situation in Asia: "Stalin said that the Americans are afraid to fight a war. Americans order others to fight, but they are too afraid. According to this thinking, it would be very hard for war to arise. *We agree with this estimate.*"[60] Just a fortnight later, on January 5, 1950, senior military leaders in Beijing

[56] Nikita Sergeevich Khrushchev, *Khrushchev Remembers* (Boston: Little, Brown, 1970), 368.

[57] "Document #13: 12 May 1950, ciphered telegram, Shtykov to Vyshinsky re meeting with Kim Il Sung" in Kathryn Weathersby, "New Russian Documents on the Korean War," *Bulletin of the Cold War International History Project* 6–7 (1995–96): 38–39.

[58] Zhou was speaking on October 1, 1950. Zhang Shuguang, *Deterrence and Strategic Culture: Chinese-American Confrontations, 1949–1958* (Ithaca: Cornell University Press, 1992), 94.

[59] Zhang Shuguang, "Command, Control, and the PLA's Offensive Campaigns in Korea, 1950–51," in *Chinese Warfighting: The PLA Experience since 1949*, ed. Mark A. Ryan, David M. Finkelstein, and Michael A. McDevitt (Armonk, N.Y.: M. E. Sharpe, 2003), 91; Chen, *China's Road*, 126, see also 134–35. Westad, *Decisive Encounters*, 321; Zhang Xiaoming, *Red Wings over the Yalu: China, the Soviet Union, and the Air War in Korea* (College Station: Texas A&M University Press, 2002), 56–57. Shen suggests that China had concerns that Japan, not the United States, might enter the conflict. Shen Zhihua, "China Sends Troops to Korea: Beijing's Policy-Making Process," in *China and the United States: A New Cold War History*, ed. Xiaobing Li and Hongshan Li (Lanham, Md.: University Press of America, 1998), 15.

[60] Emphasis added; Mao's summary in a telegram to Liu Shaoqi of a conversation with Stalin held two days earlier, on December 16, 1950. See 裴、《中华人民共和国外交史》 [Pei, *Foreign Relations History*, 17]. For a comparison of this source to two other reports of the same meeting, see Chen Jian, "Commentaries: Comparing Russian and Chinese Sources: A New Point of Departure for Cold War History," *Bulletin of the Cold War International History Project* 6–7 (1995–96): 20.

were downplaying the possibility that the United States might send troops to defend Taiwan in the event of a PRC invasion there.[61] Su Yu, the leader in charge of preparations for the proposed invasion of Taiwan, spoke at a military conference:

> From a military perspective, Su saw a vulnerable America. He believed that the United States needed at least five years to mobilize enough troops to enter a major military confrontation in the Far East. Su's conclusion was that "in terms of their attitude toward Taiwan, the Americans would not send troops to Taiwan but might send in planes, artillery, and tanks."[62]

Each of these examples suggests that, at a very broad level, the Chinese were inclined to downplay the likelihood of American intervention.

Often these views are attributed primarily to Secretary of State Dean Acheson's "Press Club Speech," excoriated by political opponents for seeming to exclude Korea from the interests of the United States. However, this particular signal's role is overstated. The official history of the Korean War published by the PLA press makes no mention of Acheson's speech.[63] Indeed, most discussion of that speech among Chinese leaders focused on the sovereign status of Mongolia and Manchuria and American accusations of Soviet designs on them.[64] (Indeed, that concern resonated with related Chinese concerns at the time.[65]) Furthermore, *even before the speech was given,* Chinese leaders were already downplaying the likelihood of U.S. intervention elsewhere in Asia (as shown in the paragraph above and below, and in chapter 3).

The doctrinal-difference escalation hypothesis (DDE) suggests that underestimation of an adversary's capabilities can lead to failure of deterrence and coercion, and to escalation and conflict, because it complicates both

[61] Summarized by Chen, *China's Road,* 102.
[62] Ibid.
[63] 国防大学战史简编写组、《中国人民志愿军战史简便》 (北京:解放军出版社、1992) [National Defense University Concise Military History Group, *A Brief War Fighting History of the Chinese People's Volunteers* (Beijing: People's Liberation Army Press, 1992), 2–3].
[64] 师哲、《在历史巨人身边:师哲回忆录》 (北京:中央文献出版社、1991) [Shi Zhe, *Beside the Great Men of History* (Beijing: Central Documents Press, 1991), 456]. 沈、《毛澤東、斯大林與韓戰》 [Shen, *Mao, Stalin, and the Korean War,* 179–82].
[65] See, for instance, 刘少奇、"为发外交部发言人关于西藏问题的谈话给毛泽东的电报"、1950年一月十七日《建国以来刘少奇文稿》、第一册:7/1949–3/1950(北京:中央文献出版社、1998) [Liu Shaoqi, "Telegram to Mao Zedong Regarding the Foriegn Ministry's Spokesman's Tibet Issue Statement (January 17, 1950)," in *Liu Shaoqi's Manuscripts since the Founding of the State* (Beijing: Central Party Documents Publishers, 1998)].

assessments of the balance of power and interpretations of military signals. Since Mao thought that U.S. intervention would be costly to the Americans, and because he thought the United States cared about such costs, he did not expect the United States to get involved in a broader war. This grew out of his view that contradictions among the capitalist forces would keep them from unifying to oppose Communist gains.[66] These logics had shaped Chinese interpretation in other cases, as had the belief that Communist forces had deterred the United States from intervening in the Chinese civil war. Mao claimed that "the United States refrained from dispatching large forces to attack China, not because the [U.S.] government didn't want to, but because it had worries. The first worry: the Chinese people would oppose it and the U.S. government was afraid of getting hopelessly bogged down in a quagmire."[67]

Late in the civil war the Chinese Communists deployed a large force along China's northeastern coastlines, purely for the purposes of signaling to the United States the dangers of large-scale intervention. The lack of a U.S. response convinced Mao that he had deterred the United States from intervening.[68] (In fact, there is little evidence that the United States was strongly considering intervention at that point, and it had already reduced its forces on Chinese territory, which had numbered several thousand in 1948.) Again, this is strong evidence of China signaling consistent with its theory of victory, and of that signal not being interpreted as intended by the United States.

When the Indian ambassador carried out backdoor U.S. diplomacy with the Chinese, the response from a senior PLA general discounted the likelihood of American involvement, expressing a disdain for the American style of warfare: "When Panikkar warned him of the tremendous damage from bombing which involvement in war would bring to China, General Nie [Rongzhen, at that time chief of staff of the PLA] stated that he did not believe the United States could spare combat troops to fight in China and that no war could be won by air bombardment alone."[69]

---

[66] William Whitney Stueck Jr., *The Korean War: An International History* (Princeton: Princeton University Press, 1995), 79. Describing the role of communist ideology in shaping Mao's evaluations of international relations in general is Michael M. Sheng, *Battling Western Imperialism: Mao, Stalin, and the United States* (Princeton: Princeton University Press, 1997).

[67] Mao Tsetung, "Farewell, Leighton Stuart [August 18, 1949]," in *Mao Tsetung and Lin Piao: Post Revolutionary Writings*, ed. K. Fan (New York: Anchor Books, 1972), 54. See also Zhang Shuguang, *Mao's Military Romanticism*, 35–36.

[68] See Chen, *China's Road*, 98; Chen Xiaolu, "China's Policy toward the United States, 1949–55," in *Sino-American Relations, 1945–1955: A Joint Reassessment of a Critical Decade*, ed. Harry Harding and Ming Yuan (Wilmington, Del.: Scholarly Resources, 1989), 186.

[69] "Memorandum of Conversation by the Deputy Assistant Secretary of State for Far Eastern Affairs (Merchant)," September 27, 1950 in *FRUS, 1950, Vol. 7*, 793–94. Although it is clear the

There is no evidence that the Chinese took seriously any of the U.S. saber rattling noted at the outset of this chapter. This evidence all supports the hypothesis linking underestimation to faulty assessment of the balance of power and coercive failure (the DDE hypothesis) and the prediction that leaders will downplay the likelihood of their adversary's involvement (Downplaying Prediction). Mao's December 1949 assessment and the report of the military conference in January 1950 (both discussed above, and prior to Acheson's speech) explicitly link the Chinese assessment of American intent to a pejorative view of American capabilities based on the Chinese theory of victory.

## DISSENT IN CHINA

Chinese optimism was not unchecked: China entered the war with trepidation. Even Mao is reputed to have paced the floor for days as the final moves were made, and to some extent Stalin manipulated Mao on this issue by withholding some military aid at the last minute.[70] Unquestioningly, this was a hard decision for the Chinese leader. Still, it was one enlightened by the overconfidence outlined above. The depth of these debates has been emphasized by back and forth telegrams from Mao to Stalin; however, it is important to recognize that much of this communication in early October was aimed at eliciting Soviet air support (which did not materialize until much later). The shrillest of China's communications seem to have been its attempts to get the best possible bargain from its Soviet patrons,[71] including air support and mechanized weapons. But after the Soviets rebuffed Zhou Enlai's personal request for air support—Zhou had flown to Moscow on short notice in early October—the Chinese nevertheless went ahead with their decision to intervene. Air support would have been a welcome addition, but in the end, it was not necessary. This is, again, consistent with the book's argument.

Beyond the debates in Mao's mind, there were some prominent dissenters. Although the dominant view in China was optimism regarding its own capabilities compared to the Americans, there were pessimists—often military leaders who had been exposed to Western training.

---

United States heard this message (the report was read and commented upon the secretary of state), no attempts to address this fundamental failure of military signaling were taken.

[70] For the best description of Mao's decision-making process here, see Chen, *China's Road*, 171–209.

[71] Ibid., 199. See also Richard C. Thornton, *Odd Man Out: Truman, Stalin, Mao, and the Origins of the Korean War* (Washington, D.C.: Brassey's, 2000).

Zhu De in particular repeatedly insisted that additional resources should be dedicated to artillery, air defense, logistics, and air support.[72] One of the most senior military leaders in China and commander-in-chief of the PLA at the time, Zhu De had been trained at the Yunnan Military Academy and later taught at Whampoa Military Academy. There he would have been exposed to German military operational arts.[73] Zhu De also served under Chiang Kai-shek in a number of capacities. Thus, he had reason to view warfare somewhat differently than did Mao.

Similarly, Ye Jianying had argued with Mao in early August 1950 over the merits of sending troops to Korea and the speed with which they could be deployed.[74] Ye was a senior Chinese military leader who had been trained at the Yunnan Military Academy, and who also served as an instructor at Whampoa. There is also evidence that some line officers within the NEBDA recognized problems with their units' equipment and training.[75]

Lin Biao, too, is often cited as one who had a more conventional view of military operations compared to Maoist doctrine.[76] He, too, began his career at Whampoa and was a protégé of Zhu De.[77] Later, during the late 1950s and early 1960s, Lin Biao's contributions towards modernization and professionalization of the PLA would be substantial: "On 29 September 1959, in his first major policy speech, Lin set the tone for much of what was to follow....A subtle but significant modification was...made to Mao's doctrine that 'men are superior to material.' Lin's new formulation was that 'men and material form a unity with man as the leading factor.'"[78]

---

[72] Yu, "What China Learned (2003)," 129. On Zhu De, see also Scobell, *China's Use of Military Force*, 86.

[73] Donald W. Klein and Anne B. Clark, *Biographic Dictionary of Chinese Communism, 1921–1965* (Cambridge: Harvard University Press, 1971), 245. See also Dick Wilson, *China's Revolutionary War* (New York: St. Martin's Press, 1991).

[74] Ryan, *Chinese Attitudes toward Nuclear Weapons,* 27. Ryan cites the memoirs of one of Peng Dehuai's assistants. See also Scobell, *China's Use of Military Force,* 89.

[75] Zhang, *Mao's Military Romanticism,* 62.

[76] Frederick C. Teiwes and Warren Sun, *The Tragedy of Lin Biao: Riding the Tiger during the Cultural Revolution, 1966–1971* (Honolulu: University of Hawaii Press, 1996), 17. His later turn toward extreme Maoist rhetoric is often explained with reference to another aspect of his character: "a shrewd and increasingly cynical Lin began to tailor his advocacy to the prevailing wind." See also Roderick MacFarquhar, *The Origins of the Cultural Revolution* (London: Oxford University Press, 1974), vol. 3, 449.

[77] William W. Whitson and Zhenxia Huang, *The Chinese High Command: A History of Communist Military Politics, 1927–71* (New York: Praeger, 1973), 37.

[78] Harlan W. Jencks, *From Muskets to Missiles: Politics and Professionalism in the Chinese Army, 1945–1981* (Boulder, Colo.: Westview Press, 1982), 55–56. Later in the year, Lin also reinstated Su Yu as vice-minister of defense; Su had been fired in October 1958 for advocating all-out priority to PLA modernization.

Lin's emphasis on preserving professionalism and enhancing modernization within the military would remain strong even during the tumultuous
Cultural Revolution.[79]

Thus, it is not surprising that Lin was deeply skeptical about the merits
of Chinese involvement in Korea.[80] In October 1950, Lin would have been
the obvious choice to command the Chinese forces in Korea. He was a well-
respected military leader who commanded the seasoned Fourth Route Army,
already deployed in the Northeast, which was later to serve as the core of the
intervention force. Furthermore, he was quite close to Mao. However, he
refused Mao's offer. Publicly, this was said to be because of his poor health.
However, there is little doubt among close observers of Chinese politics that
this was a polite fiction.[81] For instance, in his autobiography, Nie Rongzhen,
at that time chief of staff of the PLA, said explicitly that

> Lin Biao opposed sending our troops to Korea. At first, Mao had cho-
> sen Lin to command the CPVF [Chinese People's Volunteer Force, also
> known as the CPV] in Korea, but Lin was so fearful of this task that he
> gave the excuse of illness and obstinately refused to go to Korea. It was
> strange to me because I had never seen him so timid in the past when
> we worked together.[82]

Thus, there clearly was some difference of opinion regarding the utility of
People's War against the American forces: some leaders opposed the war early
in the fall.[83] The dissent seems centered on leaders who were least identified
with a People's War doctrine or who had been exposed to Western thinking
about military affairs. Their theory of victory would have been closer to that

---

[79] Harry Harding, "The Chinese State in Crisis, 1966–1969," in *The Politics of China: The Eras of Mao and Deng,* ed. Roderick MacFarquhar (Cambridge: Cambridge University Press, 1993), 156.

[80] Again see Scobell, *China's Use of Military Force,* 87–89.

[81] Peng Dehuai, "My Story of the Korean War," in *Mao's Generals Remember Korea,* ed. Li Xiaobing, Allan Reed Millett, and Yu Bin (Lawrence: University Press of Kansas, 2001), 32. Chen, *China's Road,* 152, 185. See also associated notes.

[82] Nie Rongzhen, "Beijing's Decision to Intervene," in *Mao's Generals Remember Korea,* ed. Li Xiaobing, Allan R. Millett, and Yu Bin (Lawrence: University Press of Kansas, 2001).

[83] Peng Dehuai is also sometimes regarded as a dissenter. See Scobell, *China's Use of Military Force,* 84–86. However, the evidence for this is debatable. Within twenty-four hours of being apprised of the plan to send Chinese troops to Korea in October 1950, he moved from believing that "troops should be sent to rescue Korea" to believing this was "essential." Neither of these statements seems fundamentally opposed to intervention. Further, Peng's statements at the time reveal little sense of particular concern regarding the power of American weaponry or its air force.

of the United States or at least they understood the U.S. theory of victory, and so their assessments of the Chinese prospects would understandably have been much more pessimistic. Unfortunately, Mao and the other dominant leaders held less realistic views.

Thus, as the doctrinal-difference theory predicts, leaders less wrapped up in their side's theory of victory were less prone to make the underestimating errors associated with doctrinal differences (Depth of Immersion Prediction).

More generally, this section has shown that China's interpretation of signals from and assessment of the balance of power with the United States was heavily influenced by doctrinal-difference theory: differences in theories of victory correlated with underestimation (Misperception Prediction). China's leaders denigrated their adversary's theory of victory (Discounting Prediction). They did not have nuanced discussions of their adversary's strategy; rather, the evidence shows a lack of sophistication in considering American strategies and capabilities, as suggested by Superficial Views Prediction. The very large difference in the theories of victory led to large and frequent underestimations (Extreme Differences Prediction). The false optimism that comes from the difference between the two sides' theories of victory supports the doctrinal-difference misperception (DDM) hypothesis and seems to have influenced China's conclusions regarding the dangers of war with the United States. It suggests that mistaken assessments of the balance of power that come from the underestimation of the adversary contributed to the escalation of the conflict and to choices about China's goals in it, both consistent with the doctrinal-difference escalation hypothesis.

Evidence of Chinese perceptions of its prospects in a war with the United States illustrates the Chinese disregard of atomic bombs, airpower, and mechanization, both before and after the key decision was taken. Although it is certainly true that other factors played a role as well, these perceptions would have informed Chinese decisionmakers and shaped their decisions about whether and how to intervene in the Korean War.

## POSTEVENT EVALUATIONS BY THE CHINESE

In addition to direct evidence through process tracing, other related predictions can be used to test the theory. The theory makes predictions about Chinese assessments of both its own and U.S. doctrines after some experience of war. Chinese leaders at all levels—tactical, operational, and strategic—displayed shock. The surprising effectiveness of American airpower comes up repeatedly in their discussions. This evidence strongly supports the Startling Battlefield Outcomes Prediction. These assessments led to significant changes in the PLA both in organizational structure and modernization. This evidence strongly supports the doctrinal-difference misperception hypothesis.

### CHINESE CASUALTIES WERE MUCH HIGHER THAN EXPECTED

Before the war, Chinese expectations on casualties were optimistic. In August 1950, addressing the question of how to replace casualties within the NEBDA, Zhou Enlai spoke of "selecting 10,000 men from all other PLA forces for the NEBDA replacements."[84] At a meeting of China Central Military Commission (CMC), the members "estimated that casualties of around 200,000 (60,000 deaths and 140,000 wound[ed]) would occur in the first year of the war and that proper medical support should be prepared."[85] In January 1951, a mere six weeks after beginning his main offensive, Peng Dehuai reported that he had already lost half his men, or at least 200,000 casualties.[86] The UN estimated by June 1951 that the PLA had suffered some 577,000 casualties.[87] That was only months after the war started. American estimates would later put total Chinese casualties for the whole war at 1 million, with the vast majority of those coming before the end of 1951.[88]

This evidence strongly suggests that Beijing's cost-benefit analysis was far too optimistic when it decided to take steps toward war.

### TACTICAL LEVEL EVIDENCE FOR GROUND COMBAT

The Chinese were shocked at their own ineffectiveness against the UN forces. The two great powers fought their initial battles in November 1950. The Chinese soon encountered pronounced difficulties in surrounding and wiping out large enemy units, the PLA's primary operational strategy. Tactical mobility and the substantial firepower available even to small American units caused these problems for the Chinese. Beyond that, the PLA found the

---

[84] Quoted in Zhang, *Mao's Military Romanticism,* 64.

[85] Chen, *China's Road,* 151.

[86] Peng, "My Story of the Korean War," 34. For the quantification, see the editors' footnote at ibid., 253, note 13.

[87] John Wilson Lewis and Xue Litai, *China Builds the Bomb* (Palo Alto: Stanford University Press, 1988), 8.

[88] Clay Blair, *The Forgotten War: America in Korea* (New York: Times Books, 1988), 975.

logistics demands of a foreign war to be much more taxing than anticipated, and the American air force also caused significant problems.

The Chinese had not expected the U.S. tactic of undertaking rapid withdrawal before unit collapse (a tactic planned by the U.S. military even before hostilities broke out).[89] The United States would simply retreat in order to stretch the Chinese lines of communication and would often do so even when not under direct pressure.[90] This led to problems for the Chinese, as Segal describes:

> There were signs that the [Chinese] strategy of ambush and luring in deep had its limits against a more modern and mobile force than Chiang Kai-shek's forces. U.S. troops soon found that Chinese forces could not fight lengthy continuous battles without having to stop for supplies and new instructions to get to the front. The swift U.S. withdrawal to the 38th parallel far outstripped the pace that the less flexible Chinese command and logistics system was designed to handle.[91]

Peng Dehuai also noted the PLA's difficulties keeping up with the rapidly moving U.S. forces: "Because of their high level of mechanization, the U.S., British, and puppet troops were able to withdraw speedily to the Chongchon River and the Kechon Area, where they started to throw up defense works. Our troops did not pursue the enemy because the main enemy force had not been destroyed."[92] As late as the middle of 1951, Peng was complaining, "In too many opportunities to wipe out the enemy, he has again escaped. This deserves thorough discussion, self-criticism, and rectification. What important shortcomings does our military have?"[93]

Even when U.S. forces had been found and fixed, the Chinese forces had trouble destroying them (despite previous successes against similarly engaged

---

[89] Dennis D. Wainstock, *Truman, Macarthur, and the Korean War* (Westport, Conn.: Greenwood Press, 1999), 89.

[90] Schnabel, *United States Army in the Korean War,* 304.

[91] Gerald Segal, *Defending China* (New York: Oxford University Press, 1985), 101–3.

[92] Peng Dehuai, *Memoirs of a Chinese Marshal: The Autobiographical Notes of Peng Dehuai (1898–1974)* (Beijing: Foreign Language Press, 1984), 475.

[93] Emphasis added. 彭德怀、"彭德怀关于几个战术问题的讲话要点"(8/15/51),从"抗美援朝战争期间彭德怀的两次讲话"、《中共党史资料》1998年12月总第68辑 [Peng Dehuai, "Summary of Lecture on Several Tactical Problems (October 15, 1951) (Reprinted in 'Two Speeches by Peng Dehuai During the Korean War')," *Party Historical Documents* 68 (1998): 3–4]. Other scholars also note that the Chinese were surprised by the speed of American offensives and counterattacks. See Zhang, "Command, Control, and the PLA's Offensive Campaigns," 97, 105, 107–8, and 111.

Japanese or KMT forces). "Luring them in deep" was not effective when the adversary unit could rapidly set up strong defensive positions from which it could easily hold off the ill-equipped Chinese forces.[94] As Peng notes,

> If we encircled a U.S. regiment, our troops would need two days to wipe it out because they were poorly equipped and the enemy air force and mechanized units would do everything to rescue the encircled unit. Only once did our troops wipe out an entire U.S. regiment and none of its men was able to escape; this took place in the Second Campaign [November and December 1950]. Otherwise our troops were able to wipe out only whole U.S. battalions. If a U.S. battalion encircled in the night were not wiped out while it was still dark, the Americans had the means to rescue it the following day.[95]

The Chinese logistics system faced substantial problems. Beyond the paucity of military equipment, the PLA troops lacked even basic supplies:

> We had a big problem feeding our soldiers in the war. Since enemy airplanes bombed us frequently, grain could be transported to the front only with difficulty. Even though some reached the front, our troops could not cook their food. Cooking needed fires, and fires caused smoke, which would surely expose our troops' position and attract enemy air raids. There was almost no way to solve this problem. During our five offensive campaigns, many CPVF troops had to allay their hunger with "one bite parched flour and one bite snow."[96]

Zhou Enlai, who was organizing supply issues for Mao during the war, recognized that the food supplies that the PLA had brought along were insufficient. "Every day he called twice" to check on the production of winter clothes.[97]

---

[94] Zhang, "Command, Control, and the PLA's Offensive Campaigns," 102. This was the case even for the first offensive in October–November 1950. Yu Bin, "What China Learned (2003)," 128 and 130.

[95] Peng, *Memoirs of a Chinese Marshal*, 481. For a similar point, see Yu, "What China Learned (2001)," 15.

[96] Nie, "Beijing's Decision to Intervene," 54. The five campaigns referred to in this passage include the first two discussed in this book (of October–November and November–December 1950, respectively) as well as three others in the phase of attritional warfare in the next two and a half years of war.

[97] 周恩来传编写组、《抗美援朝》(周恩来传选载、《党的文献》1998、第一期(总第六十一期) [Zhou Enlai Editorial Group, "Resist America, Support Korea (Zhou Enlai Biography Selected Publication)," *Party Documents* 1 (cumulative #61) (1998): 52].

Poor preparation meant difficulties for the troops in Korea: "A large number of CPV troops were severely frostbitten and unable to fight. Some had even died of exposure. The troops had virtually no protection against frostbite; they coated their faces with pork fat and wrapped their feet in straw."[98]

The general supply situation was so bad that on January 22, 1951, Zhou hurriedly called for a meeting of the senior political-military leaders (including Nie Rongzhen and others) to discuss logistics, the first formal meeting regarding the Northeast army and the forces in Korea.[99] The supply situation complicated the PLA's ability to prosecute its offensives. "The CPV's defeat in May 1951 demonstrated the Communist forces' inability to overwhelm the enemy without air cover to guarantee the delivery of supplies."[100] The demands on the domestic transportation system back in China were tremendous: the war required the use of 20 percent of all Chinese trains in the fall of 1951.[101]

The Chinese had not appreciated the full extent of the dangers that the U.S. Air Force would pose. It exacerbated all of the other problems. For instance, the U.S. bombing campaign had a significant impact on logistics. Mao reported to Stalin, with chagrin, that "the enemy has been constantly bombing transport lines. Only sixty to seventy percent of the resupply matériel for our forces are reaching the front lines, and the remaining thirty to forty percent is being destroyed."[102] Zhou Enlai's biography also emphasizes the difficulties the enemy's air force posed for logistics, particularly to the front lines.[103] The tactical effects of all UN air strikes were devastating: "The Chinese [later] admitted that for three years their ground forces were unable to carry out large military activities in the daytime because of such intensive bombing."[104]

The Chinese found themselves fighting a war that in some ways they simply did not understand. The PLA's use of artillery was rudimentary; dealing with counter-battery fire gave it problems. As late as October 1951, a full year after Chinese entry, Peng Dehuai—the top military commander of the PLA forces in Korea—was admonishing the senior leadership of the Third

---

[98] Zhang, "Command, Control, and the PLA's Offensive Campaigns," 104.

[99] 周恩来传编写组、《抗美援朝》 [Zhou Enlai Editorial Group, "Resist America, Support Korea," 53].

[100] Zhang, *Red Wings over the Yalu*, 117.

[101] Nie, "Beijing's Decision to Intervene," 56.

[102] Telegram from Mao to Stalin, March 1, 1951, reprinted in Michael H. Hunt, *Crises in U.S. Foreign Policy: An International History Reader* (New Haven: Yale University Press, 1997), 228.

[103] 周恩来传编写组、《抗美援朝》 [Zhou Enlai Editorial Group, "Resist America, Support Korea," 53].

[104] Zhang, *Red Wings over the Yalu*, 204.

Army with precepts that would have been familiar to any enlisted soldier in the artillery corps in the U.S. Army: "Under this condition of our inferiority to the enemy in terms of range, if we are unrealistic and fire our own artillery from exposed, open positions, this is not appropriate. If we do not carefully attend to camouflage and cover, we will immediately encounter unnecessary personnel losses."[105]

It is not only the problems that the PLA faced that are instructive, but the acute surprise they prompted. Few tenets of People's War were effective against the Americans. A survey of some three hundred prisoner-of-war interviews found:

> PLA military doctrine was discredited in the eyes of the Chinese soldiers by what they had experienced in Korea. It is of particular importance to note that disillusionment with Mao Tse-tung's doctrine extended to combat cadres. ... Eighteen hard core prisoners (mostly junior combat cadres at company and lower levels) were virtually unanimous in reporting that they and their fellow soldiers had come to question the applicability of PLA military doctrine to the conditions of combat and the nature of the enemy in Korea.[106]

In interviews with nearly a hundred soldiers who had entered Korea with the first wave of Chinese forces in the fall of 1950, more than 85 percent reported that their training was "totally inadequate" for the Korean War.[107] These forces, committed to the war at the outset, had been among the PLA's best trained and best equipped.[108]

Considerable evidence suggests that the PLA had not expected to face such a capable military. This is what doctrinal-difference theory predicts in the context of such differing theories of victory (Startling Battlefield Prediction). Repeated Chinese surprise at the shortcomings of its way of war is apparent. This suggests that the Chinese misperceived the overall balance of power before the war, which contributed to their decision-making errors and their mistaken assessment of the U.S. adversary.

---

[105] 彭、《彭德怀关于几个战术问题的讲话要点》 [Peng, "Summary of Lecture on Several Tactical Problems (October 15, 1951)," 2].

[106] Alexander L. George, *The Chinese Communist Army in Action: The Korean War and Its Aftermath* (New York: Columbia University Press, 1967), 171.

[107] Ibid., 168.

[108] Some former KMT troops were used, mostly later in the war. In the earlier campaigns, troops were drawn mostly from the Fourth Route Army, the most storied in PLA history from the Chinese civil war.

## CHANGES IN DOCTRINE DURING THE WAR
## AND AFTERWARD

After the Chinese had entered the Korea War and had experience engaging U.S. forces, they made a number of changes in PLA doctrine and strategy. Ellis Joffe, who has been a leading scholar in PLA studies for decades, summarizes these doctrinal and force structure changes: "In sum, the Korean War not only gave the Chinese an almost newly equipped army, but it also probably raised serious doubt in the minds of at least some leaders regarding the continuing validity of many facets of their experience."[109] These suggest that the Chinese side had failed earlier to assess the other side's capabilities accurately.

Many of these changes addressed difficulties stemming from the unexpected effectiveness of the Americans against China's People's War strategies:

> Overwhelming UN firepower...forced the CPV to change its tactics.... The CPV adopted its so-called mobile defense tactic. It would deploy its forces lightly at the front while reserving the main units at greater depth. This helped reduce casualties from UN fire and maintained some flexibility for mobile operations.[110]

The infantry increasingly used infiltration tactics with highly trained small units, in place of large, poorly trained masses as would have been called for under a People's War strategy.[111] China's logistics system was thoroughly overhauled after the bloody losses of the Fifth Campaign in spring 1951.[112] The nature of units brought to Korea also changed. As Whitson notes, the second set of units the PLA deployed to the Korean theater show increased emphasis

---

[109] Ellis Joffe, *Party and Army: Professionalism and Political Control in the Chinese Officer Corps, 1949–1964* (Cambridge: Harvard University Press, 1965), 12.

[110] Yu, "What China Learned (2003)," 133. This is a standard application of a defense-in-depth strategy against a mobile, armored adversary.

[111] 彭、《彭德怀关于几个战术问题的讲话要点》 [Peng, "Summary of Lecture on Several Tactical Problems (October 15, 1951)," 3]. Peng's mid-1951 lecture to the senior leadership of the Third Army emphasized the importance of company and battalion infiltration by highly trained "crack" troops who would aim to destroy command and control targets, as well as the importance of artillery. In contrast with traditional People's War tactics that would aim to wipe out entire units, these tactics were similar to Germany's doctrinal innovations late in World War I when it faced a similar strategic terrain: static front lines well supported with substantial firepower.

[112] Evan A. Feigenbaum, *China's Techno-Warriors: National Security and Strategic Competition from the Nuclear to the Information Age* (Stanford: Stanford University Press, 2003), 17.

on the technical branches: "artillery, anti-tank, engineer, railway-guard, and eighteen out of twenty-two new air divisions were committed in an apparent process of modernization under fire."[113] After the war, Peng proposed increasing the relative weight of the artillery, air defense, armored, engineers, and other technical branches still further, deemphasizing the infantry.[114]

Of the largest long-term importance, after the war the PLA began to emphasize modernization. "The impact of the Korean War on the modernization of the Chinese army can hardly be overestimated."[115] When Peng presented a ten-point report to the senior military leadership of the PLA in early 1954, less than six months after the war, most of the discussion focused on military modernization and military technology development.[116] Peng Dehuai's biography suggests that these lessons reverberated far beyond the military. It points to the emphasis on military technology in the 1952 Five-Year Plan: "That was the plan made during the period while the war was still continuing, [calling for] large scale development of technology in all branches of the armed services."[117]

Doctrinal changes were also pervasive. The PLA's Academy of Military Science (AMS) reoriented its military education:

> PLA training for conventional warfare was [now] to employ combined arms operations in the Soviet model. AMS recommendations indicate that future training was to go beyond simply combining ground force arms to include all three services in addition to the infantry, artillery, and tank and air defense units of the ground forces. The PLA was taking its first steps toward joint warfare.[118]

A comprehensive study of the evolution of China's military science and technology research programs highlights the extent of this change:

> Doctrinal differences erupted full-force within the PLA, although the precise tenor and scale of the disputes remain difficult to gauge even

---

[113] Whitson and Huang, *Chinese High Command*, 95.

[114] 王焰、等、《彭德怀传》 (北京:当代中国出版社、1993) [Wang Yan et al., *Biography of Peng Dehuai* (Beijing: Modern China Press, 1993), 505].

[115] Joffe, *Party and Army*.

[116] 王,等、《彭德怀传》 [Wang, *Biography of Peng Dehuai*, 510–13].

[117] 王,等、《彭德怀传》 [Ibid., 502].

[118] Paul H. B. Godwin, "Change and Continuity in Chinese Military Doctrine: 1949–99," in *Chinese Warfighting: The PLA Experience since 1949*, ed. Mark A. Ryan, David M. Finkelstein, and Michael A. McDevitt (Armonk, N.Y.: M. E. Sharpe, 2003), 34.

five decades later. As early as 1952, Liu Bocheng, a hero of the civil war, began to deliver a series of now-famous lectures to division-level officers at the PLA's new Military Academy in Nanjing that offered a theoretical rationale to undermine Mao's doctrine of "man over weapons." After the Korean armistice, the practical impact of American firepower combined with Liu's theoretical insights to establish what Lewis and Xue have termed a "new baseline of knowledge" for military professionals. The academy began to teach the "lessons" of Korea in the classroom and nurtured an entire generation of Chinese senior officers on the notions of "modern," mechanized, technologically oriented warfare that had emerged from the PLA's brutal encounter with American technology in Korea.[119]

Liu Shaoqi, later to serve as China's defense minister, served as commandant of the Nanjing Military Academy during this time of debate and change. There he disputed the established Maoist ideology.[120] Peng Dehuai, who would be minister of defense through much of the later 1950s, tried to implement these changes in the middle and late 1950s as a senior military leader.[121] The Chinese high command was "united by a nearly universal sense that the PLA's guerrilla heritage had lost relevance in the face of enemy firepower."[122]

Peng Dehuai's biography suggests that these lessons reverberated far beyond the military. It points to the emphasis on military technology in the 1952 Five-Year Plan that guided the entire economy: "That was the plan made during the period while the war was still continuing, [calling for] large scale development of technology in all branches of the armed services."[123]

These shifts suggest that the Chinese found their previous doctrine lacking when tested against that of their adversaries, and this called into question the assessments of power and intent that sprang from them. This is precisely as the theory predicts: that a nation will be surprised at its relative weakness on the battlefield (the Startling Battlefield Outcomes Prediction), strongly suggesting that its original estimation of the adversary was mistaken. Thus, the doctrinal-difference misperception hypothesis is supported by the evidence of China's postwar doctrinal adaptations.

---

[119] Feigenbaum, *China's Techno-Warriors*, 18.
[120] Ibid., 22. Discussing the Nanjing School in similar terms is Whitson and Huang, *Chinese High Command*, 462.
[121] Yu, "What China Learned (2003)," 138.
[122] Feigenbaum, *China's Techno-Warriors*, 27.
[123] 王、等、《彭德怀传》[Wang, *Biography of Peng Dehuai*, 502].

## SLOWLY BUDDING INTEREST IN AIRPOWER
## AND NUCLEAR WEAPONS

Even after the war began, Mao continued to downplay the role of airpower. His persistent reluctance to appreciate fully the impact of U.S. airpower on his ground forces was a constant source of tension with the operational commander on the ground, Peng Dehuai. Mao repeatedly pushed Peng to move faster and to push harder, while Peng would point out the severe damage American airpower was imposing.[124] Mao expressed skepticism about the effects of airpower to line commanders who, having been on the receiving end, knew better.

> Zhu Guang, commander of the Second Artillery Division, later recalled that when he returned to Beijing several months later, Mao invited him to his office and asked for Zhu's opinion about how serious a threat UN airpower was to ground operations, and how many casualties were actually inflicted upon Chinese forces by aircraft. The chairman appeared displeased with those he thought exaggerated the role of enemy airpower.[125]

Only after the war was over did the air force receive substantial attention. Rather than demobilizing, as might be expected following the conclusion of a large war, the Chinese made plans to more than double the size of the air force within a mere five years.[126] Peng emphasized the importance of the air force for the postwar security of the PLA.[127]

Chinese thinking regarding nuclear weapons was changed by the Korean War and even more by the 1954–55 Taiwan Strait Crisis.[128] Early inklings of change were apparent during the final stages of the Korean War.

> The Chinese Peoples' Volunteers launched an urgent campaign to construct fortifications, including, "in the frontline battlefield, Anti-Atom

---

[124] Zhang, *Red Wings over the Yalu,* 114.

[125] Ibid., 115. Although Zhu Guang may have been exaggerating the role of American airpower, this is inconsistent with Zhang's line of reasoning when he uses this evidence. Zhang presents this data to bolster a point he made regarding Mao's "reservations about the effect of the enemy's airpower in Korea."

[126] Ibid., 209.

[127] 王、等、《彭德怀传》 [Wang, *Biography of Peng Dehuai,* 506].

[128] On the role of the Korean War in particular, see Pape, *Bombing to Win,* 170–71. More generally see Lewis and Xue Litai, *China Builds the Bomb,* chapter 2, "American Power and Chinese Strategy, 1953–55."

shelters…built deep in the middle of the mountains." And then too there were the deliberate leaks: "We purposefully let the spies of the other side…get some intelligence of the preparations we were waging."[129]

Parallel to these military defense measures for their forces in the field, the Chinese engaged in a significant civil defense program at home.[130] By 1953, the Chinese were carefully monitoring changes in the U.S. nuclear posture under President Eisenhower.[131] By 1958, Mao's conversion on the issue of nuclear weapons was complete: "without atomic and hydrogen bombs, 'others don't think what we say carries weight.'"[132] Chinese scholars, too, place Mao's conversion on this issue to the mid-to-late 1950s.[133]

These shifts emphasize that, when faced with incentives to consider atomic weapons more carefully, Mao changed his views. This highlights the facile way in which China had considered nuclear weapons in the past, thus supporting the Superficial Views Prediction, which predicts an absence of nuanced discussion regarding the adversary. It also suggests that Mao had underestimated the utility of nuclear weapons in the prewar period, as this theory would predict. This supports the main hypothesis linking differences in theories of victory to underestimation of the adversary (doctrinal-difference misperception hypothesis). A lack of understanding of nuclear weapons led Mao to misperceive American military power.

## SUMMARY OF CHINA'S INTERPRETATIONS AND EVALUATIONS

Thus, in nearly every relevant area, the U.S. intervention surprised the Chinese. They had misjudged American intent about involvement in Korea, underestimated their own casualties, overestimated their ability to push the U.S. forces off the peninsula, and were deeply mistaken regarding the dangers posed by airpower and mechanized combined-arms formations.[134] After the war, the PLA made numerous doctrinal and strategic changes in response.

---

[129] Lewis and Xue, *China Builds the Bomb,* 15. The sources are interviews conducted with Chinese nationals with access to such information in the mid-1980s.

[130] Ryan, *Chinese Attitudes toward Nuclear Weapons,* 109.

[131] Lewis and Xue, *China Builds the Bomb,* 18, 195, and 256 note 35.

[132] Ibid., 36.

[133] He Di, "Paper Tiger or Real Tiger: America's Nuclear Deterrence and Mao Zedong's Response," *American Studies in China* 1 (1994): 17.

[134] Some of these misjudgments may have come from ignorance about American doctrine and the PLA's limited study of American doctrine and tactics from World War II. However, such ignorance is clearly related to the fact that the American doctrine was so different from that

This all suggests that when deciding whether to support Kim's invasion plan in May and shaping their own plans for intervention in the early fall, the Chinese based their thinking on a flawed cost-benefit analysis. U.S. signals were not given significant consideration in China. The costs of potential conflict with the United States were much higher than China expected. Had they known, they might have made different choices about intervention and strategy. The Startling Battlefield Outcomes and Surprise Regarding Intentions Predictions receive robust support from the historical record, and the role of doctrinal differences is clear. All this bolsters the linkage of differences in theory of victory to underestimation (the DDM hypothesis).

China was highly motivated by security-dilemma dynamics to enter the Korean War. However, any such momentous decision depends on an assessment of the likelihood of success. In this case, it is clear that false optimism pervaded the Chinese assessment in ways that provide strong support for doctrinal-difference theory. The effects of the two sides' theories of victory certainly shaped China's perception of its capabilities relative to the United States, supporting the doctrinal-difference misperception hypothesis. Although China was likely to intervene for many reasons, Beijing's expectations that it could achieve victory would have shaped this choice by creating false optimism. Further, important elements of signaling were not heard, as the doctrinal-difference escalation hypothesis expects. These points are clearly apparent in the way that the United States used threats and force to send deterrent signals. There is also circumstantial evidence that the Chinese did not understand these U.S. signals. Given the doctrinal differences, this is precisely what doctrinal-difference theory predicts. The effects of doctrinal difference also shaped Chinese thinking about its goals in the war, leading to massive Chinese casualties and a prolonged war. Absent the doctrinally driven optimism, China might not have crossed the 38th parallel itself or attempted to drive the United States from the peninsula. The dramatic postwar reevaluation of People's War strategies by the PLA suggests that its leaders felt their prior theory of victory had been incorrect in many ways, also supporting the theory (the misperception hypothesis, in particular).

The explanation suggested by the Weakness Hypothesis, focusing on the objective strength and clarity of the signal in accounting for this failure of deterrence, receives only mixed support from the case. The U.S. signaling was neither focused nor clear. Furthermore, the Chinese were highly

---

of the Chinese: had they been more similar, such ignorance would have been dramatically easier to overcome.

motivated to intervene. Nevertheless, there were some robust military signals sent by the United States, and these should have caused the Chinese to be more cautious in October 1950.

Thus, although this escalation has many explanations, doctrinal-difference theory enriches our understanding of the outcome. Chinese insecurity after the United States crossed the 38th parallel was high. This book's argument also complements that explanation and helps us to understand the nature of some of the choices taken by the Chinese.

The next case turns to a different theater of the Sino-American conflict to see how the proposed theory works there.

# 6

# CHINA POSTPONES THE INVASION OF TAIWAN

IN 1950, THE UNITED STATES DETERRED CHINA from invading Taiwan as China sought to conclude its civil war. Doctrinal-difference theory predicts that when two adversaries practice similar doctrines, deterrence is facilitated because signals are more likely to be clearly understood and assessments of the balance of power are more likely to be consistent. Both of these elements are seen in the U.S.-Chinese confrontation over the Taiwan Strait in 1950. There, a primarily symbolic deterrent threat was sufficiently clear to both sides to forestall Beijing's plans.

## HISTORICAL BACKGROUND

In April 1949, Communist forces crossed the Yangtze River, the critical strategic geography in continental China that divides the north from the south. The resistance from their opponents, the Kuomintang (KMT), rapidly crumbled in the south. Immediately thereafter, Mao began to turn his attention to the KMT's last redoubt on the island of Taiwan.

Taiwan was the central Communist Chinese concern for both offensive and defensive reasons. The KMT military on Taiwan was regularly attacking Shanghai from the air at the time, and Chinese air defense forces were having only limited success checking these attacks.[1]

---

[1] 刘少奇、"转呈华东局关于敌机狂炸上海情况电报的批语"、1950年二月七日《建国以来刘少奇文稿》、第一册:7/1949–3/1950(北京:中央文献出版社、1998) [Liu Shaoqi, "Telegram to

Plans were gathering momentum to take Taiwan by mid-1950; most analysts, then and since, viewed the KMT's situations as hopeless. More than thirty thousand soldiers had been transferred to reinforce the Chinese Communist navy.[2] The Chinese Communists' military preparations had advanced quite substantially:

By spring 1950, the Communists had assembled a motley armada of 5,000 vessels for the invasion by commandeering freighters, motorized junks, and sampans and [by] refloating [naval warships] that had been sunk in the Yangtze River. Further, they gathered and trained over 30,000 fishermen and other sailors to man the flotilla.[3]

The 1950 Chinese New Year's proclamation by the official Xinhua news agency asserted that Taiwan would be attacked that year.[4]

American sources also thought the invasion was imminent. The CIA predicted in March that Mao's forces "are estimated to possess the capability of carrying out their frequently expressed intention of seizing Taiwan during 1950, and will probably do so during the period June–December."[5] According to American weekly intelligence digests prepared by the Far East Command in July and August 1950, the Chinese planned to start probing operations in July; the main assault was expected to follow in early August.[6] While the status of the actual Chinese timetable for invasion during late June 1950 was

Mao Presenting Notes on the East China Bureau's Report on the Situation Surrounding the Unrestrained Bombing of Shanghai (February 7, 1950)," in *Liu Shaoqi's Manuscripts since the Founding of the State* (Beijing: Central Party Documents Publishers, 1998)].

[2] 刘少奇、"关于调四个师到倾倒演习海军的电报"、1950年二月十日《建国以来刘少奇文稿》、第一册:7/1949–3/1950(北京:中央文献出版社、1998)    [Liu    Shaoqi,    "Telegram Regarding the Transfer of 4 Divisions to Qingdao for Naval Training (February 10, 1950)," in *Liu Shaoqi's Manuscripts since the Founding of the State* (Beijing: Central Party Documents Publishers, 1998)].

[3] Edward John Marolda, "The U.S. Navy and the Chinese Civil War, 1945–52" (PhD diss., George Washington University, 1990), 139.

[4] The Chinese New Year in 1950 fell on February 17 on the Western calendar. Later in the year, Mao chastised the head of *Xinhua* for this broadcast. See 毛泽东、"关于在宣传中不说打台湾,西藏的时间给胡乔木的信"、1950年九月二十九日《建国以来毛泽东文稿》、第一册: 9/1949–12/1950 (北京:中央文献出版社、1987) [Mao Zedong, "Letter to Hu Qiaomu Regarding Not Mentioning the Time for the Attacks on Taiwan and Tibet in Propaganda Broadcasts (September 29, 1950)," in *Mao Zedong's Manuscripts since the Founding of the State* (Beijing: Central Party Documents Publishers, 1987)].

[5] "Memorandum by the Assistant Secretary of State for Far Eastern Affairs (Rusk) to the Secretary of State (April 17, 1950)," in *FRUS, 1950*, vol. VI: *East Asia and the Pacific* (Washington, DC: U.S. GPO, 1976), 330.

[6] David G. Muller, *China as a Maritime Power* (Epping, U.K.: Bowker, 1983), 16–7.

**Figure 6.1.** The Taiwan Strait area.

unclear, scholars today generally all agree that it was imminent. Attack was expected to start any time from just weeks to at most nine months away.[7]

Once the Korean War broke out, concerns about Chinese goals in Taiwan were paramount in Washington. On June 25 the secretary of defense recommended immediately assessing Taiwanese security needs, and viewed the North Korean attack as a Communist feint, presaging a broader offensive.[8] Therefore, two days after the outbreak of the Korean War, the United States signaled its intent to defend Taiwan against any Chinese offensive by ordering the "neutralization" of the Taiwan Strait by the Navy's Seventh Fleet.[9] Initially, this was a symbolic deployment only; the Seventh Fleet never deployed en masse, and indeed only token patrols were made for months. Nevertheless, for more than fifty years since then, there has been no invasion: deterrence succeeded.

This case evaluates how the two sides' theories of victory in the naval sphere contributed to the success of deterrence in this case.

## THEORIES OF VICTORY AT SEA

Although the previous two chapters centered on warfare in the Korean Peninsula (and potentially in China itself), this case demands consideration of a different military environment. Thus, we must go beyond chapter 3's characterization of the two sides' theories of victory: for the Taiwan Strait theater, the relevant military forces were naval forces. In particular, we are interested here in amphibious doctrine rather than general naval doctrine.

Although Chinese naval doctrine for high seas combat was quite a contrast with that of the United States,[10] in the case of U.S. deterrence of China's invasion of Taiwan the key comparison is in U.S. and Chinese doctrine for

---

[7] He Di's article is widely acknowledged as the best on the topic: He Di, "The Last Campaign to Unify China: The CCP's Unmaterialized Plan to Liberate Taiwan," *Chinese Historians* 5, no. 1 (1992): 10–12; Chen Jian, *China's Road to the Korean War: The Making of the Sino-American Confrontation* (New York: Columbia University Press, 1994), 101. See also 宋连生、《抗美援朝再回首》(昆明:云南人民出版社、2002) [Song Liansheng, *Recollections on the Korean War* (Kunming: Yunnan People's Press, 2002), 194].

[8] Clay Blair, *The Forgotten War: America in Korea* (New York: Times Books, 1988), 71.

[9] See ibid., 75. This decision was cast as an attempt to neutralize Taiwan; accordingly, Chiang was directed to cease bombing and raiding of commerce. However, MacArthur's military orders as of June 29 still did not mention restraining Chiang. (Glenn D. Paige, *The Korean Decision, June 24–30, 1950* [New York: Free Press, 1968], 183–84 and 251, respectively).

[10] For an excellent discussion of the Soviet roots of China's naval doctrine, see Muller, *China as a Maritime Power*, 48.

amphibious operations. The coercive attempt here is one of deterring a Chinese amphibious invasion of Taiwan. Thus, the question for doctrinal-difference theory is whether the Chinese had difficulty understanding the threat posed to their invasion plans by the Americans due to differences in the two nation's amphibious operations doctrine. In particular, would the Chinese be likely to underestimate the threat posed to their plans by the American Seventh Fleet?

## AMERICAN AMPHIBIOUS OPERATIONS DOCTRINE

In 1950, the primary objective of the U.S. Navy focused on sea control; the World War II experience still influenced the more peripheral issue of future amphibious operations. In any amphibious operation, the United States recognized that "the principal danger in such an operation is an attack on the invading force by an opposing navy."[11] If an opponent's navy can attack the landing force's vessels, particularly vulnerable shallow-draft landing craft and tank-landing ships, the landing is likely to be defeated. Thus, American thinking focused on the challenges of *opposed* amphibious landings in contrast to many other nations' emphasis on the less challenging goal of *unopposed* landings.[12]

This was not the only difficulty for an attacker, however. The difficulties in moving across challenging terrain with no rear area to assemble logistics and reinforcements are tremendous. Allan Millett summarizes these key doctrinal concerns in the United States regarding amphibious operations:

> The amphibious force would have to isolate the objective area, then pound the defenders into a stupor with naval gunfire and close air support. The landing itself would require a violent assault by a combined arms team, probably over a broad front, perhaps a beach of a thousand yards' width or more. To secure the beachhead, the landing force would need rapid reinforcement, complete with artillery and tanks. The greatest threat to a landing was disruptive air and naval attack, which might pull critical fleet units from the objective area, but a combined air and ground counterattack was the most immediate concern.

---

[11] Allan R. Millett, "Assault from the Sea: The Development of Amphibious Warfare between the Wars—the American, British, and Japanese Experiences," in *Military Innovation in the Interwar Period,* ed. Williamson Murray and Allan R. Millett (Cambridge: Cambridge University Press, 1996), 51.

[12] For example, British and Japanese doctrine before World War II focused on unopposed landings; see ibid.

A counterlanding might give the enemy a striking advantage because it would be difficult for a landing force to protect its supply line and logistics support areas as well as defend the perimeter of its own enclave. An amphibious expeditionary force could not rely on guile for success, but would require local superiority in every element of air, naval, and ground combat power.[13]

The U.S. experience in World War II covered a great many campaigns: Patton's unopposed landing in North Africa, MacArthur's island-hopping in the Pacific, the landings in Italy, and the largest amphibious operation ever conducted, the Normandy landings.[14] In the Pacific theater, where nearby airfields were generally not available, carrier-based air was critical. In the Sicily and Normandy landings, carriers were absent, and land-based craft provided both defensive and offensive air support.[15]

Another important element in American doctrine centered on reliance on a mix of dedicated military amphibious craft and ships alongside the use of commercial shipping: "The navy followed the prewar assumption that it could create an amphibious transport force by converting merchantmen and liners to military service, including the installation of davits and cranes capable of handling landing craft."[16]

Rapid securing of a port was central for follow-on logistics (the absence of such a facility necessitated an expensive artificial dock in the Normandy landings). By 1950, U.S. amphibious capabilities, tested in demanding battle conditions during World War II, were deeply rooted in American military thinking.

## CHINESE AMPHIBIOUS OPERATIONS DOCTRINE

There would have been considerable shared understanding between Beijing and Washington on the issue of amphibious operations. China faced broadly the same strategic situation that the U.S. military had in World War II: it needed a doctrine for *opposed* amphibious landings. Several factors affecting the Chinese navy merit discussion. First, in contrast to the backward PLA

---

[13] Ibid., 77.

[14] See John Keegan, *Six Armies in Normandy: From D-Day to the Liberation of Paris, June 6th–August 25th, 1944* (New York: Viking Press, 1982), chapters 1–3; Cornelius Ryan, *The Longest Day: June 6, 1944* (New York: Simon and Schuster, 1959).

[15] George W. Baer, *One Hundred Years of Sea Power: The U.S. Navy, 1890–1990* (Palo Alto: Stanford University Press, 1994), 311.

[16] Millett, "Assault from the Sea," 83–84.

ground force, the Chinese navy was relatively modern (for idiosyncratic reasons, as discussed below). Second, China's naval doctrine regarding amphibious warfare drew lessons from a series of failures at the end of the civil war. Third, a successful attack on Hainan displayed many of these improvements, and China's navy continued to improve after that point with an eye toward the imminent invasion of Taiwan.

*The Roots of the PLAN: The Nationalist Navy*

China's People's Liberation Army Navy or PLAN, as it was officially known, was relatively professionalized and technically advanced compared to the PLA ground force. Leaders in this service were mainly either graduates of Soviet training academies or KMT defectors, many of whom had Western naval training. By 1949, over four hundred Chinese students were in the Soviet Union receiving naval training.[17] Even more numerous in the PLAN were recent defectors from the KMT: "While the Soviet naval advisors and instructors played an important role in the beginnings of the Communist naval force, the core of the new navy was formed by the 2,000-odd former R.O.C. naval personnel who defected in 1949, most of them with their ships."[18]

Some analysts go even further in emphasizing the role of the KMT turncoats, noting that the PLAN's very organization was imported from the losing side of the civil war:

> General Chang's [an early PLA leader] "navy" was the forerunner of Red China's present navy; yet it was Communist in name only. Most of the officers and men were Nationalist deserters, while the naval craft were captured or brought over from the enemy. With the exception of the highest command echelon and the ever-watchful political commissars, Red China's first navy was made up almost *in toto* of the enemy.[19]

This would have substantial effects on organizational culture in the PLAN, which differed from the other branches of the Communist forces. Communist leaders struggled to indoctrinate these former KMT sailors and officers with

---

[17] Muller, *China as a Maritime Power,* 19.

[18] Ibid., 13.

[19] Gene Z. Hanrahan, "Report on Red China's New Navy," *United States Naval Institute Proceedings* 79, no. 8 (1953): 847. In 1950, the PLAN's "only naval personnel were those who had defected from various segments of the Nationalist Navy." Captain E. J. Cummings Jr., "The Chinese Communist Navy," *United States Naval Institute Proceedings* 90, no. 9 (1964): 66.

Maoist ideology.[20] Many of the defectors had been trained in the West, so they were familiar with the American way of war: "The officers and sailors from the KMT were a special new type of serviceman. Most had received relatively high levels of education and they were politically quite sensitive. Many had gone to England or the United States to receive training or take delivery of a warship."[21]

In general, intellectuals were more welcome in this service than they were in the army.[22] As the official naval history notes:

> People recruited from the ground forces [to the PLAN] normally were required to have achieved more than an elementary school degree. In order to supply the navy with people having technical ability, the Central Military Committee [CMC] required each field army to comprehensively assess their people. As many as possible of the following were to be provided to the navy: anyone who has previously served in the navy, worked on board a ship, studied shipping, and has even a little bit of knowledge regarding machinery or has driven tanks or cars. The CMC was very diligent in attracting intellectuals to the navy.[23]

The defecting troops, and in many cases their ships, formed the core of the new navy. Indeed, the very first naval vessel that the PLA obtained was a KMT vessel—a tank landing ship it captured in 1947—and the tactics learned from that ship's crew were put to use in later river crossings by the PLA in the civil war.[24] The Nationalist flagship—the *Chongqing*, formerly the *HMS Aurora*, a 7,400-ton cruiser—defected on February 24, 1949, and would eventually serve as the PLAN's flagship. In April 1949, another twenty-six craft, from destroyers to amphibious landing craft to gunboats, also defected:[25] "Zhang Aiping, who had been deputy commander of the central China military, was appointed commander and commissar. He accepted the task of organizing

---

[20] See 卢如春、江吉泰、等、《海军史》中国人民解放军军兵种历史丛书(北京:解放军出版社、1989) [Lu Ruchun, Jiang Jitai, and et al., *History of the Navy* (Beijing: People's Liberation Army Press, 1989), chapter 2, "Emergence, Part III: Competing for and Reforming the Sailors Originally from the KMT," 22–25].

[21] 卢、江、等、《海军史》[Ibid., 23].

[22] For an explanation for this phenomenon, see Eric Heginbotham, "The Fall and Rise of Navies in East Asia: Military Organizations, Domestic Politics, and Grand Strategy," *International Security* 27, no. 2 (2002).

[23] 卢、江、等、《海军史》[Lu, Jiang, et al., *History of the Navy*, 21].

[24] 卢、江、等、《海军史》[Ibid.].

[25] Muller, *China as a Maritime Power.* Also see Hanrahan, "Report on Red China's New Navy," 847.

the foundation of the navy around the naval vessels that had defected and joined our side from the KMT."[26]

This first naval unit in the PLAN was made up entirely of ships that had defected from the KMT's Second Fleet.[27] By 1950, "the PRC Navy found itself in possession of some 30 landing ships of U.S. World War II construction, all left behind by or defected from the ROC navy."[28] This was enough to move twenty thousand amphibious assault troops at a time. In addition to these captured ships, the PLAN also relied on salvage operations and some foreign purchases: "Between late 1949 and early 1950, China bought forty-eight used warships totaling 25,470 tons."[29]

The former KMT officers were well versed in Western-style amphibious operations, and provided a core of expertise for the PLAN to refine. The Nationalist navy had conducted unopposed amphibious landings numerous times, including a major operation in August 1947.[30] As the civil war turned against the Nationalists, their navy conducted a series of amphibious extractions, often while the ground element was under attack, a particularly challenging tactical situation.[31] Further, they had experience using naval gunfire support in many of these battles.[32]

As a result of this legacy of ties to the KMT's navy, in particular the advantage of professionalization relative to the army, exposure to Western training, and experience with amphibious operations, the PLAN's understanding of amphibious warfare was from the start relatively similar to that of the U.S. Navy.

*Hard Lessons: The PLAN's Early Experience with Amphibious Operations*
Building upon these background conditions, the Chinese Communist leadership learned quite a bit in this area against a relatively advanced foe, including abysmal defeats of their attempts to conquer the small coastal islands of Jinmen, Zhoushan, and Dengbu in late 1949.

[26] 卢、江、等、《海军史》 [Lu, Jiang, et al., *History of the Navy*, 15].

[27] He Di, "The Last Campaign to Unify China: The CCP's Unrealized Plan to Liberate Taiwan, 1949–50," in *Chinese Warfighting: The PLA Experience since 1949*, ed. Mark A. Ryan, David M. Finkelstein, and Michael A. McDevitt (Armonk, N.Y.: M. E. Sharpe, 2003), 77.

[28] Muller, *China as a Maritime Power*, 53. Cummings, "The Chinese Communist Navy," 69. Cummings puts the figure at fifty landing ships; he emphasizes the large number of ex-U.S. vessels.

[29] Zhang Shuguang, *Mao's Military Romanticism: China and the Korean War, 1950–53* (Lawrence: University Press of Kansas, 1995), 51.

[30] Muller, *China as a Maritime Power*, 8.

[31] Ibid.

[32] Ibid.

Mao assessed the October 1949 attack against Jinmen as "our biggest loss of the war."[33] A KMT navy–led counterattack inflicted tremendous losses, totaling nearly ten thousand men, on the Chinese Communist forces.[34] One Western analyst noted that the PLAN was poorly prepared for that attack: "landing in scantily-armed junks and on rafts, with no support from artillery or aircraft, the PLA forces were mauled, losing thousands of men without ever gaining a beachhead."[35]

The subsequent attack on Dengbu also incurred a "heavy price":

On October 3, 1949, the PLA 21st Army, 61st Division sent a force of five battalions' strength to attack Dengbu Island in eastern Zhejiang Province. That day, troops landed smoothly and secured the capture of six hundred of the enemy. However, on the second day the enemy's second regiment reinforced from the sea. Facing the enemy on three sides, the PLA landing force had no other alternative but to fight out in retreat. Casualties reached 1,490 men.[36]

The official Chinese naval history, relating a series of examples from this period, draws a lesson with which military leaders in the Pentagon would agree: "the bloody facts show, if you want to break through an ocean blockade to liberate offshore islands, the navy, ground force, and air force must all work in cooperation."[37]

These setbacks taught the Chinese many lessons about how to conduct such landings.[38] For instance, they initiated specialized training of their

---

[33] Odd Arne Westad, *Decisive Encounters: The Chinese Civil War, 1946–1950* (Stanford: Stanford University Press, 2003), 301.

[34] Zhang, *Mao's Military Romanticism*, 53.

[35] Muller, *China as a Maritime Power*, 16.

[36] 卢、江、等、《海军史》 [Lu, Jiang, et al., *History of the Navy*, 18].

[37] 卢、江、等、《海军史》 [Ibid.].

[38] 毛泽东、"关于同意粟裕调四个师演习海战等问题给刘少奇的电报"、1950 年二月十九日《建国以来毛泽东文稿》、第一册:9/1949–12/1950(北京:中央文献出版社、1987)  第257页 [Mao Zedong, "Telegram to Liu Shaoqi Approving Li Yu's [Deputy Commander of the 3rd Field Army] Proposal for the Training of Four Division for Amphibious and Related Operations (February 10, 1950)," in *Mao Zedong's Manuscripts since the Founding of the State* (Beijing: Central Party Documents Publishers, 1987), 257]. 毛泽东、"关于同意四十三军以一个团先行渡海给林彪的电报"、1950 年二月十二日《建国以来毛泽东文稿》、第一册:9/1949–12/1950(北京:中央文献出版社、1987)第259页 [Mao Zedong, "Telegram to Lin Biao Approving the 43rd Army to Operate Jointly in Amphibious Crossings (February 12, 1950)," in *Mao Zedong's Manuscripts since the Founding of the State* (Beijing: Central Party Documents Publishers, 1987), 259]. 毛泽东、"军委转发栗裕关于占领舟山群岛后的直处置意见的电报"、1950 年四月二十九日《建国以来毛泽东文稿》、第一册:9/1949–12/1950(北京:中央文献出版社、1987)第357页 [Mao Zedong, "Telegram to Li Yu from the Central Military Committee Regarding Dealing with the Zhoushan

troops for amphibious landings. Soon they would begin using translated U.S. Marine amphibious warfare manuals.[39] They established the navy as a separate branch of the PLA on April 14, 1950.[40] Their prior defeats taught them that "without the support of regular navy ships, landing operations by small boats could be disastrous."[41] They prepared to remedy this problem. These defeats had also emphasized the importance of follow-on logistics support: "Although PLA forces eventually secured their beachheads [in Jinmen], most of their boats were left aground when the tide went out. The first wave could not be reinforced, and Ye Fei and other PLA commanders were forced to watch helplessly as the defending Nationalist forces destroyed their troops."[42]

Thus, a key lesson was the importance of controlling the sea to prevent the opposing navy from attacking or reinforcing.[43] The PLAN would have to address this problem, too.

Over time, the PLA had benefited from the lessons of these earlier campaigns, and from Soviet training of an amphibious assault group in late 1949 and early 1950.[44] By April 1950, they were ready to resume their attacks on the offshore islands.

### The Payoff of Learning: The Attack on Hainan

Their diligence following the earlier defeats led to a resounding PLAN victory on Hainan on April 22, 1950. Hainan is a large island, similar in size to Taiwan. Hainan was defended by some three hundred thousand well-equipped KMT soldiers on the ground and also by the Nationalist navy's Third Naval Squadron, consisting of three destroyer escorts and fifteen other smaller warships.[45] The squadron engaged in aggressive patrolling of the Hainan Strait on a regular basis and also patrolled the nearby coastline of the mainland, sinking Communist shipping there and preventing any large amphibious force from gathering.[46] This allowed the KMT navy to fend off

---

Islands after Their Capture (February 10, 1950)," in *Mao Zedong's Manuscripts since the Founding of the State* (Beijing: Central Party Documents Publishers, 1987), 357].

[39] Hanrahan, "Report on Red China's New Navy," 853.

[40] 卢、江、等、《海军史》[Lu, Jiang, et al., *History of the Navy*, 15].

[41] Alexander C. Huang, "The PLA Navy at War, 1949–1999: From Coastal Defense to Distant Operations," in *Chinese Warfighting: The PLA Experience since 1949*, ed. Mark A. Ryan, David M. Finkelstein, and Michael A. McDevitt (Armonk, N.Y.: M. E. Sharpe, 2003), 252.

[42] Ibid., 251.

[43] This was central to U.S. thinking as well; Millett, "Assault from the Sea," 51.

[44] Westad, *Decisive Encounters*, 304.

[45] Marolda, "U.S. Navy and the Chinese Civil War," 125.

[46] Ibid., 126.

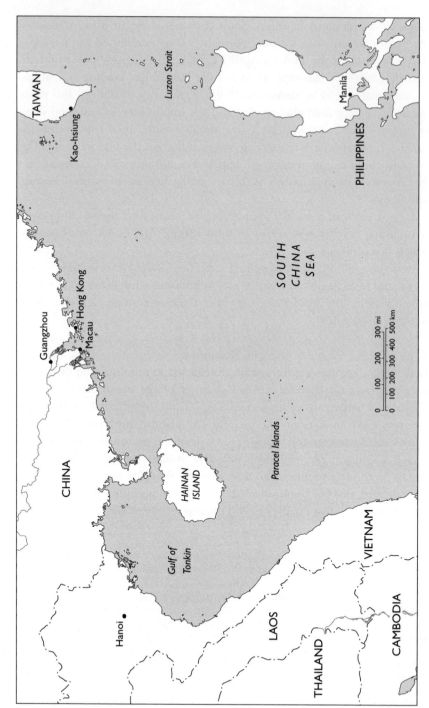

**Figure 6.2.** Map of Hainan Island region.

eleven separate probing attacks during March and early April 1950.[47] Scores of Communist boats and hundreds of Communist soldiers and sailors were lost.[48] However, "the preliminary operations revealed to the Communists that the main invasion fleet would be destroyed if the relatively lethal Nationalist Navy and Air Force patrol units were not driven from the strait."[49]

In contrast to other times in the civil war, during the Hainan battle the Nationalist military did not collapse, but rather "by most accounts fought long and hard against the invasion forces. There were no mass defections to the Communists before the island's fall."[50] American military attachés in Hong Kong reported that the Nationalist navy and air force were "doing their most effective work since the end of World War II with morale and reliability the highest in years."[51]

To achieve victory against this force, the Chinese relied on a hodgepodge landing fleet, closely coordinated timing, and some naval gunfire support. The armada used for the Hainan operation included four hundred boats of assorted types. "Many of the vessels were armed with light artillery pieces, antitank guns, mortars, and machine guns."[52] China's use of civilian shipping, reinforced with military hardware, echoed a practice the United States had relied on in several instances in World War II. Responding to the lessons of previous defeats, this motley navy, supported by significant coastal artillery and antiaircraft fire, was able to defend the strait for the initial landing and the critical resupply sorties that followed.[53] As a result, "the Nationalist Navy and Air Force [were] driven from the strait, after a hard-fought interdiction effort": "Having previously learned the hard way what Nationalist sea and air forces could do to invasion flotillas, the Communists lined either side of the strait with coastal artillery [some of it radar-directed] and antiaircraft weapons that effectively covered the entire water way."[54] The Communist forces were able to deliver adequate logistical supplies, and used advanced forces to prepare beachheads on which the main force could land.[55] The victory

[47] Ibid., 128.

[48] Ibid., 128–29.

[49] Ibid., 129.

[50] Ibid., 134. For a differing view, albeit one offering little detail to back it up, see Muller, *China as a Maritime Power*, 16.

[51] "Memorandum by the Assistant Secretary of State for Far Eastern Affairs (Rusk) to the Secretary of State (April 26, 1950)," in *FRUS, 1950, Vol. 6*, 333.

[52] Marolda, "U.S. Navy and the Chinese Civil War," 127.

[53] Ibid., 131.

[54] Ibid.

[55] Westad, *Decisive Encounters*, 304–5. The Chinese used guerrilla forces already on the ground. This seems quite similar to the American practice of using paratroopers and other special forces for such a mission.

was complete, with the KMT forces routed. Many retreated to Taiwan; others were killed or captured before they could embark.

Chinese Communist confidence after the success at Hainan rose appreciably. Senior Chinese Communist Party leaders believed that the lessons of this experience had prepared the PLA well for an invasion of Taiwan. Following this victory, Liu Shaoqi (soon to be groomed as Mao's successor) trumpeted the "PLA's mastery of the art of the sea-borne landings."[56]

### Looking toward Taiwan

As the Chinese looked forward to an invasion of Taiwan, they recognized that "victory would depend on cooperative operations of the three services."[57] They also knew that they now had units that were experienced in conducting successful amphibious assaults against opposition.[58] These units continued to train for their highly specialized amphibious assault roles, leading Beijing to repeatedly postpone the invasion of Taiwan before mid-1950.[59]

Many of the elements of advanced Chinese thinking regarding amphibious operations would have been quite familiar to the U.S. Navy. The Chinese forces were not as well equipped nor as technologically capable as the U.S. forces, but where this difference was most acute, the PLA was striving to improve on the basis of the lessons of its earlier failures. Thus, while airpower had not previously played a major role in Chinese amphibious operations,[60] the Chinese recognized the importance at least of land-based airpower in this sort of operation. For instance, Liu Shaoqi averred early in 1950 that "regarding Zhoushan, Taiwan, Jinmen, and Hainan islands... if we do not have air support as well as a certain amount of naval support, advancing across the sea for an amphibious attack cannot be done. Today's report from Hainan and Jinmen makes these points clear."[61]

---

[56] Quoted in Melvin Gurtov and Byong-Moo Hwang, *China under Threat: The Politics of Strategy and Diplomacy* (Baltimore: Johns Hopkins University Press, 1980), 33.

[57] He, "The Last Campaign to Unify China," 80.

[58] Marolda, "U.S. Navy and the Chinese Civil War," 159.

[59] See again, 毛、"关于同意粟裕调四个师演习海战等问题给刘少奇的电报"、第257页 [Mao, "Telegram to Liu Shaoqi [February 10, 1950]," 257]. See also 宋《抗美援朝再回首》[Song, *Recollections on the Korean War,* 194].

[60] 张驭涛、《新中国军事大事纪要》(北京:军事科学出版社、1998)第15–16页 [Zhang Yutao, *Summary of Important Events in the New China's Military* (Beijing: Military Science Publishers, 1998), 15–16].

[61] 刘少奇、"关于舟山等地作战需要空军协助问题给毛泽东的电报"、1950年一月十一日《建国以来刘少奇文稿》、第一册:7/1949–3/1950(北京:中央文献出版社、1998)    [Liu    Shaoqi, "Telegram to Mao Regarding the Problem of Needing Assistance from the Air Force in the Battles for Zhoushan Island and Other Similar Locations (January 11, 1950)," in *Liu Shaoqi's Manuscripts since the Founding of the State* (Beijing: Central Party Documents Publishers, 1998), 252].

Later, having the amphibious assault of Taiwan in mind, Mao implored the Soviets to provide the Chinese with an air force.[62] As mid-1950 approached, China did increasingly get the support of Soviet air assets in its conflict with Taiwan. The KMT had flown bombing strikes against the mainland with some effect throughout 1949 and 1950.[63] In March 1950, the Soviets deployed several squadrons of Soviet-piloted MiG-15s, at that time the premier jet fighter in the world, to Shanghai.[64]

Much of the Soviet aid to China provided in the wake of the signing of the Sino-Soviet Alliance on February 14, 1950, was used to improve Chinese military capabilities, with an eye toward a Taiwan invasion:

> Although Stalin cautiously did not agree [with China] to use Soviet air and naval assets to support the attack against Taiwan, in the end he did agree [that] an appropriate opportunity to liberate Taiwan required preparation. He also agreed that one half of the Soviet aid to China, a loan of $300 million (U.S.), would be used to order equipment that would be most important in order to attack Taiwan.[65]

Zhou Enlai pressed for that hardware to be delivered that same year, 1950, so that the invasion plans could be kept on track.[66] By some reports, the entire loan was used for military hardware to be aimed at Taiwan.[67] Furthermore, the Chinese had captured scores of Higgins shallow-draft landing craft from retreating KMT forces.[68] There is more to building a navy or an air force than simply obtaining the hardware, but this is evidence that China recognized the importance of both services for amphibious missions.[69]

---

[62] Zhang Xiaoming, *Red Wings over the Yalu: China, the Soviet Union, and the Air War in Korea*, 1st ed. (College Station: Texas A&M University Press, 2002), 32–33.

[63] For discussion of the costs of these KMT air attacks, see 王焰、等、《彭德怀传》(北京:当代中国出版社、1993) [Wang Yan, et al., *Biography of Peng Dehuai* (Beijing: Modern China Press, 1993), 530].

[64] Zhang, *Red Wings over the Yalu*, 61, 78–84. Although the rules of engagement nominally restricted them to the coastline, in at least one instance the Soviet fighters were prepared to attack Nationalist naval vessels. Ibid., 82.

[65] 宋、《抗美援朝再回首》 [Song, *Recollections on the Korean War*, 196].

[66] Ibid.

[67] Sergei Goncharov, John Lewis, and Xue Litai, *Uncertain Partners: Stalin, Mao, and the Korean War* (Stanford: Stanford University Press, 1993), 99–100.

[68] Bernard D. Cole, *The Great Wall at Sea: China's Navy Enters the Twenty-First Century* (Annapolis, Md.: Naval Institute Press, 2001), 18.

[69] The PLAAF was prepared to fight in Korea in the middle of 1951 after a crash course in tactics and organization. It is likely that this force would have fared better against the KMT air force than it was to do against the UN in the Korean War. See Zhang, *Red Wings over the Yalu*.

In other small-scale naval engagements after Hainan, the PLAN continued to hone its skills at sea: "The campaign near Lajiwei Island [in late May
1950] was considered the PLA Navy's first direct warfighting engagement,
and the designation of some gunboats as an attack squadron, separated from
the landing ships, may be taken as the earliest PLA Navy development of
naval tactics."[70] This battle showed increasingly sophisticated command and
control by the Chinese, including not least the coordination of multiple
forces in a single naval battle. Of particular interest was the use of the small
fleet of naval line vessels to clear the area of KMT naval vessels before the vulnerable amphibious element went to sea.[71] This lesson would become central
to the PLAN's amphibious doctrine.

*Summary*

In the case of confrontation centering on amphibious warfare, the difference between the U.S. and Chinese theories of victory was relatively small.
Both sides understood the paramount importance of defending the landing
force from attack, and of ensuring a steady supply of reinforcements and
resupply over the same waters. Whether the threat was from the opponent's
navy or its air force, it had to be neutralized for an amphibious operation
to succeed. Beyond that, the Chinese shared with the Americans a recognition of the utility of naval gunfire support, specially trained amphibious
assault troops, and specialized landing craft. The Chinese at least aspired,
if they did not yet have, to create an air force to support their fleet and the
landing force.[72]

Furthermore, both sides understood that the other's view was similar to
their own. In the U.S. case, the engagement with the military operations in
the waning days of the Chinese civil war pervades State Department reporting in this period.[73] MacArthur's headquarters in Tokyo had an even greater
interest. On the Chinese side, one strong piece of evidence emphasizes the
degree to which the Chinese understood the American view of amphibious
operations. The senior members of the PLA anticipated the Inchon landings
that the United States would later undertake during the Korean War.[74] Not

---

[70] Huang, "What China Learned," 256.

[71] Zhang, *Mao's Military Romanticism*, 53.

[72] Although China's airpower was substantially behind that of the United States, Mao and his
compatriots seemed to pay far more attention to developing an air force for the Taiwan theater than to their deliberations regarding crossing the Yalu.

[73] See the section entitled "Political and Military Situation in China" in *FRUS, 1949*, vol. IX:
*The Far East: China* (Washington, D.C.: U.S. GPO, 1974), 1–651.

[74] Chen, *China's Road*, 147.

only naming the specific location, the leadership went on to provide prescient detail about the strategic goals of such an attack:

> [The U.S. goal would be] to make a large-scale landing of its main force on our flank rear areas (near Pyongyang or Seoul) and at the same time employ a small force to pin down the [North Korean] People's Army in its present positions, enabling it to attack from the front and rear simultaneously. In that case the People's Army would be in a very difficult position.[75]

This was precisely the plan that X Corps would put into place in its first landing on the peninsula on September 15. That the PLA senior leaders were able to anticipate the likelihood and the dangers posed by MacArthur's daring plan suggests they shared the U.S. understanding of how amphibious warfare could be carried out effectively. Indeed the detail and accuracy of the Chinese understanding about the U.S. amphibious landing strategy stands in noted contrast to many of China's discussions of the American land strategy on the Korean Peninsula. The nuanced Chinese understanding of the opponent's amphibious strategies and tactics is exactly what is expected in cases of doctrinal similarity, as spelled out in the Superficial Views Prediction in chapter 2.

## SIGNALING BY THE UNITED STATES

American signaling to China about Taiwan consisted of both diplomatic and military elements. The diplomatic signals were clear and forceful. The military signals, much less strong, were conveyed through the use of forces central to the American theory of victory for amphibious operations. That is, those military signals were consistent with the predictions derived from doctrinal-difference theory, the Nature of Signaling Prediction.

### DIPLOMATIC SIGNALS

The American announcement of June 27, 1950, was very clear: at a widely reported morning press conference, President Truman announced the U.S. policies of providing air, naval, and logistics support to the South Koreans and the policy of "neutralizing" the Taiwan Strait. The president stated

---

[75] Zhang, *Mao's Military Romanticism*, 73.

that the Seventh Fleet would neutralize the Taiwan Strait because "the occupation of Formosa [Taiwan] by communist forces would be a direct threat to the security of the Pacific area and to United States forces performing their lawful and necessary functions in that area" around Korea.[76] Supplementing this diplomatic signal, in August 1950 the commander of the Seventh Fleet joined General MacArthur on a trip to Taipei.[77]

## MILITARY SIGNALS

The rapid U.S. reinforcement of South Korean positions in June and July should have sent a broad signal about the robustness of American containment policy in general, although the American performance on the battlefield may have undermined that signal to some extent.

Deployment of the Seventh Fleet in late June was the sole U.S. military signal in the Taiwan Strait itself. The American forces available in the region were limited. The vaunted Seventh Fleet at this point consisted of a single aircraft carrier (the USS *Valley Forge*), one heavy cruiser (the USS *Rochester*), and eight smaller destroyers.[78] Even this small force was not actually sent to the Strait, however:

> As a result of budgetary constraints, American naval power in the western Pacific was seriously understrength. Given the navy's tasks in Korea, few ships or planes were left to protect Chiang Kai-shek. Until late July [1950], little was done around Taiwan except reconnaissance flights with navy airplanes. A month after the Korean attack, a destroyer division traveled southward from the Yellow Sea through the Taiwanese straits, but on 1 August it headed north again. On 4 August, the Seventh Fleet formed a new task group, consisting of only three destroyers, to patrol the waters separating Taiwan from the mainland. Thus the announcement that the United States would prevent a Communist attack on the Nationalists' last stronghold was largely a bluff.[79]

[76] Quoted in James F. Schnabel, *United States Army in the Korean War,* vol. 3, *Policy and Direction: The First Year* (Washington, D.C.: Office of the Chief of Military History United States Army/ GPO, 1972), 368.

[77] James A. Field, *History of United States Naval Operations: Korea* (Washington: U. S. Government Printing Office, 1962), 139. While MacArthur was in Taipei, Chiang Kai-shek exaggerated his relationship with the United States well beyond the degree of commitment that Washington had offered. Schnabel, *United States Army in the Korean War,* 368.

[78] Paige, *Korean Decision,* 135.

[79] William Whitney Stueck Jr., *The Road to Confrontation: American Policy toward China and Korea, 1947–1950* (Chapel Hill: University of North Carolina Press, 1981), 196.

There was at least initially little permanent deployment to the Strait by U.S. surface ships. The few early passing shows of force are, however, worth discussing in detail because of their impact on Chinese decisions. A single destroyer, the *Brush,* was dispatched to Keelung on Taiwan to evaluate Taipei's defensive needs on June 28.[80] On the morning of June 29, the *Valley Forge* sent some twenty-nine planes through the Strait, although it appears that the carrier did not traverse those waters itself.[81] The bulk of the Seventh Fleet did not stop in Taiwan, but continued north, arriving in Okinawa on June 30, where it was to begin operations in support of the Korean War.[82]

While the Seventh Fleet had received orders from the Joint Chiefs of Staff to defend the Strait,[83] for the next several months most operations to "neutralize" the Taiwan Strait were carried out by patrol planes. However, the size of the air squadrons deployed was quite small. Further, the emergency nature of the 1950 patrol program was reflected in the improvisational and hasty way it was arranged and implemented.[84] While five squadrons of naval patrol planes were deployed to support operations around the Korean Peninsula (where they could also count on the surface fleet for support and information), just two patrol squadrons were deployed to the Taiwan Strait area.[85] Each of the VP-46 and VP-28 squadrons was equipped with nine patrol planes. Their missions began on July 16 and 17, to the north and south of Taiwan respectively.[86] The squadrons were initially based out of the Pescadores, islands in the middle of the Strait, and Okinawa, just to its northeast.[87] However, as the weather worsened in October, the southern squadron was moved to the Philippines, dramatically decreasing its ability to monitor the situation closely and regularly.[88]

[80] Marolda, "U.S. Navy and the Chinese Civil War," 156.

[81] Given the limited range of naval air at this time, the proximity of the *Valley Forge* to the Strait is significant.

[82] Field, *History of United States Naval Operations: Korea,* 54–55; Malcolm W. Cagle and Frank Albert Manson, *The Sea War in Korea* (Annapolis, Md.: Naval Institute Press, 1957), 34. Crane suggests that the *Valley Forge* continued to monitor the situation in the Taiwan Strait for a few days after its first strike missions on the Korean Peninsula in early July. Conrad C. Crane, *American Airpower Strategy in Korea, 1950–1953* (Lawrence: University Press of Kansas, 2000), 28.

[83] Mark A. Ryan, *Chinese Attitudes toward Nuclear Weapons: China and the United States during the Korean War* (Armonk, N.Y.: M. E. Sharpe, 1989), 206, note 3.

[84] Marolda, "U.S. Navy and the Chinese Civil War," 174.

[85] Cagle and Manson, *Sea War in Korea,* 375, 520. The squadrons would have been equipped with some offensive patrol planes such as the PB4Y-2 Privateer, derived from a B-24 bomber, that were capable both of reconnaissance and antisurface strikes against naval assets.

[86] Field, *History of United States Naval Operations: Korea,* 110.

[87] Cagle and Manson, *Sea War in Korea,* 384.

[88] Marolda, "U.S. Navy and the Chinese Civil War," 174.

The official U.S. Navy history of the Korean War suggests that the patrols were "brandished [as] a weapon of publicity against the Chinese Communists."[89] Another historian makes a similar point:

> During this first patrol, in July 1950, MacArthur approved [commander of the Seventh Fleet] Struble's recommendation that the patrols be publicized. The U.S. interest in the inviolability of Taiwan, first demonstrated by the Seventh Fleet's June 29th aircraft flyover of the strait, was to be made absolutely clear. For deterrence to work this was considered an essential measure.[90]

Thus, the Chinese would have been aware of this deployment, small though it was.

As for the capability of this initial deployment, a U.S. Naval War College history claims: "these two squadrons maintained a continuous 24-hour patrol of the Formosan Straits and the China coast....Around-the-clock coverage of the China coast was maintained with two flights of landplanes of seven to eight hours' duration during the daylight hours and one seaplane patrol during the period of darkness."[91]

It does not take much reading between the lines to note the bravado in this report: covering a coastline of several hundred miles with a single aircraft patrol at night is very thin coverage. Other evidence supports that conclusion: these patrols occasionally sounded warnings that possible invasion fleets might be massing. One report on December 7, 1950, found some 750 junks at sea in two separate fleets, far larger than the usual fishing fleet.[92] That these fishing fleets were not spotted gathering at the Chinese ports, but only after they were under way towards Taiwan, suggests how thin the American coverage was. Secretary of State Acheson recognized these concerns, "conced[ing] that the reconnaissance has been inadequate as a basis for firm conclusion" on the unusual concentrations of junks.[93] Further, it was

---

[89] Field, *History of United States Naval Operations: Korea*.

[90] Marolda, "U.S. Navy and the Chinese Civil War," 177.

[91] Cagle and Manson, *Sea War in Korea*, 384. Cagle and Manson suggest that these patrols were "supported by ready-duty destroyers from the Seventh Fleet maintained in constant readiness in Formosan waters." Cagle and Manson, *Sea War in Korea*, 384. However, there is no evidence that such arrangements existed before late July or early August, and Field directly contradicts the assertion that there were destroyers in the strait. Field, *History of United States Naval Operations: Korea*, 67.

[92] Cagle and Manson, *Sea War in Korea*, 384–85. In this particular instance, the fleet turned around within hours.

[93] "The Secretary of State to the Secretary of Defense (Johnson) (July 31, 1950)," in *FRUS, 1950, Vol. 6*, 403.

not until August 2, 1950, that the rules about what reconnaissance would be allowed were actually finalized.[94] MacArthur had attempted a unilateral decision on this issue a few days earlier, likely prompting Washington to assert control of the policy.[95] The final rules were relatively restrictive and did not allow any air or watercraft to cross into Chinese territorial waters.[96] It appears from the discussion between the Department of State and Department of Defense representatives that previous reconnaissance had been restricted to even further offshore.

It would have taken several days for ships from Korean waters to respond to any convincing report that a PLAN attempt to land on Taiwan was under way.[97] Typically, the first response was to send out additional reconnaissance planes to reconfirm the sighting the next day, adding to the potential delay that would have benefited any actual invasion force.

Eventually the U.S. air reconnaissance patrols were reinforced. They were joined on July 18 by two fleet submarines, the *Catfish* and the *Pickerel,* which conducted reconnaissance along the Chinese coast.[98] However, this deployment was not announced, thus negating any potential deterrent value, and it was temporary, with the boats returning to Japan on July 30.[99] One brief deployment of surface ships to the area—including the heavy cruiser *Helena* and four destroyers—was ordered on July 26 in response to stepped-up reports of imminent attack.[100] The Joint Chiefs clearly intended this deployment to have deterrent value; their directive to MacArthur (who had protested that Seventh Fleet assets were needed in Korea) declared that the "presence of elms [elements] of 7th Flt in Formosa Strait and [waters] of Formosa even for a short time, would be an [effective] demonstration of U.S. intentions and a deterrent to invasion."[101]

---

[94] See note 2 in "Memorandum by the Executive Secretary (Lay) to the National Security Council (August 2, 1950)," in ibid., 407.

[95] See "Joint Daily SITREP No. 34 (July 31, 1950)" in *Joint Daily Sitrep Collection,* (Carlisle, Penn.: Military History Institute Library, U.S. Army War College, 1950). This was the situation report for the entire Far Eastern Command.

[96] "The Secretary of State to the Secretary of Defense (Johnson) (July 31, 1950)," in *FRUS, 1950, Vol. 6,* 405.

[97] Marolda, "U.S. Navy and the Chinese Civil War," 117. Although some air support might have been provided by the obsolete prop-driven Twin-Mustang (F-82) fighters based in Okinawa, the jet fighters there, the F-80s, would have been out of range.

[98] Field, *History of United States Naval Operations: Korea,* 67.

[99] Marolda, "U.S. Navy and the Chinese Civil War," 178–79.

[100] Field, *History of United States Naval Operations: Korea,* 125. One source suggests that there were at most four destroyers. See Marolda, "U.S. Navy and the Chinese Civil War," 182.

[101] From a message dated July 27, 1950, cited in Marolda, "U.S. Navy and the Chinese Civil War," 181.

The *Helena* and its destroyers were soon relieved by a smaller fleet centered around the *Juneau*—a light antiaircraft cruiser—and an escort of two destroyers. This group, Task Group 77.3, was permanently tasked with the defense of the Taiwan Strait in early August.[102] Although not a trivial deployment, this fleet by itself would not have been enough to stop an invasion fleet. The PLA had successfully fought off attacks by one or two destroyers in their campaigns against the KMT.[103] Only in winter, however, was the group reinforced more significantly with another cruiser and a third destroyer.[104]

## AMERICAN INSECURITY ABOUT THE CAPABILITIES USED TO SIGNAL

The initial U.S. force deployed was relatively small; even local American commanders repeatedly expressed concerns over whether it would be sufficient to defend Taiwan. Throughout the Korean War, the dual responsibility of the Seventh Fleet—to neutralize the Taiwan Strait and to support the war in Korea—predominantly favored the Korea mission. The Joint Chiefs recommended to the secretary of defense that the capabilities for the defense of Taiwan be enhanced.[105] Indeed, there were repeated attempts to reinforce the small U.S. Navy deployment to the Taiwan Strait; however, each request was rebuffed because the requested forces were needed even more urgently in Korea.[106] The Seventh Fleet's commander "complained that he could not fight in Korea and stop a PRC invasion at the same time."[107]

The United States remained concerned about a possible Chinese Communist invasion of Taiwan throughout much of 1950. In early July, the CIA reported "an analysis of recent Chinese Communist troop movements, propaganda and press comment [that] indicates that the Peiping regime

---

[102] Field suggests the date of August 1; Field, *History of United States Naval Operations: Korea*, 128. Marolda puts it at August 4; Marolda, "U.S. Navy and the Chinese Civil War," 1183.

[103] Huang, "What China Learned."

[104] Field, *History of United States Naval Operations: Korea*, 398.

[105] "Memorandum by the Joint Chiefs of Staff to the Secretary of Defense (Johnson)," July 27, 1950, in *FRUS, 1950, Vol. 6*, 393.

[106] Field, *History of United States Naval Operations: Korea*, 58, 62–63, 67, 120, 266. On the pull of Korea for forces also tasked with the defense of Taiwan, see Robert Frank Futrell, *The United States Air Force in Korea, 1950–1953*, rev. ed. (Washington, D.C.: Office of Air Force History United States Air Force, 1983), 50.

[107] Roger Dingman, "Atomic Diplomacy during the Korean War," in *Nuclear Diplomacy and Crisis Management*, ed. Stephen Van Evera (Cambridge: MIT Press, 1990), 125.

may now be capable of launching an assault against Taiwan."[108] Later that month, the Joint Chiefs themselves expressed similar concerns:

> Current intelligence indicates that sufficient build-up of troops and water lift now exists on the China coast for launching an invasion of Taiwan. Estimates of Chinese Communist air strength indicate that moderate air support would be available for an assault. It is doubtful...that information of an imminent attack may be obtained except through photographic reconnaissance.[109]

The JCS warned that "neither the Seventh Fleet nor Chiang's troops were capable of stopping an invasion."[110] They recommended "approval for Chinese Nationalist 'offensive-defensive' preemptive actions there, despite President Truman's previous rejections of that course of action."[111] Even after the U.S. naval deployments to the region became routine, repeated "war scares" in the Taiwan Strait caused grave concern in Tokyo and Washington.[112]

Even in the spring of 1950, before the Korean War began to make demands on the Seventh Fleet's assets, the U.S. military leadership felt that it lacked enough forces in the region to defend Taiwan from mainland China.[113] Paul Nitze, head of policy planning at the State Department and the primary author of NSC-68, later recalled a discussion with the Joint Chiefs of Staff on this question: "The upshot was that the Chiefs decided that we could not prudently make the forces available to defend Taiwan despite a [hypothetical] determination that it was politically important to do so."[114] Thus, even when forces had not yet been committed to the Korean

---

[108] Central Intelligence Agency, "Document 183. Daily Summary Excerpt, 12 July 1950, Possible Assault on Taiwan," in *Assessing the Soviet Threat: The Early Cold War Years*, ed. Woodrow J. Kuhns (Washington, D.C.: Central Intelligence Agency, 1997), 418.

[109] "Memorandum by the Joint Chiefs of Staff to the Secretary of Defense (Johnson)," July 28, 1950, in *FRUS, 1950, Vol. 6*, 395.

[110] Dennis D. Wainstock, *Truman, Macarthur, and the Korean War* (Westport, Conn.: Greenwood Press, 1999), 39.

[111] Dingman, "Atomic Diplomacy during the Korean War," 126. Johnson conveyed many of these concerns to Acheson. "The Secretary of Defense (Johnson) to the Secretary of State," July 29, 1950, in *FRUS, 1950, Vol. 6*, 401.

[112] Field, *History of United States Naval Operations: Korea*, 110, 256, 274, 343.

[113] In this period, the United States was also moving away politically from support for the KMT, so the question was moot. That said, the fact that it was discussed at senior levels is interesting.

[114] Paul H. Nitze, "The Development of NSC-68," *International Security* 4, no. 4 (1980): 175. (Nitze does not specify the date.) That passage addresses both intent and ability that, as I

Peninsula, the defense of Taiwan would have been a stretch for the United States. This further emphasizes that the military signal could not have been an extremely strong one.

Additionally, U.S. pessimism indicates that the United States was not over-estimating its own capabilities, as it had done in the prior two cases. This, too, is as doctrinal-difference theory predicts: the more similar the theories of victory are, the less overoptimism we should find, according to the Misperception and Extreme Differences Predictions.

Thus, the deployment of the Seventh Fleet was less strong as a military move than it might have appeared. For a month, there was a limited show of force by one carrier and a series of air patrols. After that, only a small fleet was deployed, and it was frequently pulled away to Korean waters—days away from the Strait—to support the war effort there. U.S. military leaders repeatedly expressed concern throughout the fall that they would be unable to stop a significant Chinese attack. However, no such attack ever came. For the possible reasons, we look at how China perceived these diplomatic and military signals.

## INTERPRETATION BY CHINA

There is limited information available about the Chinese process of interpre-tation of the U.S. signals. However, Chinese response was immediate, and it displayed none of the wildly optimistic misperceptions of the cases discussed in chapters 4 and 5. This section presents evidence that strongly supports the theory. Large differences in theories of victory were absent, and there was no underestimation of U.S. capabilities by China, thus supporting the doctrinal-difference misperception (DOM) hypothesis; nor was there subsequent mis-perception of American signals or capabilities leading an avoidable military conflict in the Strait. This case thus supports both aspects of the doctrinal-difference escalation (DDE) hypothesis. Minimal differences in the theory of victory correlate with more accurate perceptions (the Misperception Prediction), and China does not appear to have questioned American intent, just as the Assessing Intent and Downplaying Predictions posit.

---

argue and as Nitze noted, are often closely interrelated. Note that the FRUS records here support only a somewhat less pessimistic view although the tenor of discussion throughout late 1949 was leaning towards abandonment of Taiwan. See, for instance, "Memorandum of Conversation, by the Secretary of State," in *FRUS, 1949, Vol. 9*, 463.

Prior to the outbreak of the Korean War, the Chinese increasingly expected the United States to avoid direct military involvement in the conflict.[115] As discussed in chapter 5, Beijing had believed that the United States had been deterred from intervening in the Chinese civil war. According to Mao's perspective prior to the Korean War, the lack of American involvement in the Chinese civil war implied that the United States would be unlikely to interfere in an invasion of Taiwan either.[116]

Additionally, even before President Truman's January 5, 1950, declaration that it would not get involved (further, in any event) in the final stage of the Chinese civil war, Chinese military leaders argued that the United States was already too overstretched to get directly involved defending Taiwan.[117] The president's speech signaled the beginnings of U.S. moves toward abandonment of Chiang Kai-shek.[118] Meanwhile, Chinese plans for the invasion of Taiwan were moving forward.

The declaration of June 27 and associated movement of a few planes and vessels caused the Chinese to change their assessment of U.S. intentions radically and abandon their invasion plans. This single new policy by the United States spelled disaster for Mao's plans for amphibious operations. The contrast with Korea is stark: there, doctrinal blinders continued to nourish China's false optimism, from the initial decision to intervene and even for several months after People's War tactics should have been thoroughly discredited.

Following the announcement of the Seventh Fleet deployment, Beijing immediately issued a number of orders to postpone the invasion of Taiwan. Just over two days after Truman's declaration, on June 30 Zhou Enlai recognized a need for additional naval vessels to challenge the U.S. ships, ordering that "the date for the invasion of Taiwan [should] be postponed. The army should continue to demobilize, [but] the establishment of the air force and

---

[115] On January 5, 1950, hours before the president's speech outlining a "hands off" policy on the Chinese civil war, senior military leaders in China were downplaying the possibility that the United States might send troops to defend Taiwan in the event of a PRC invasion there given its then-overstretched commitments. Chen, *China's Road,* 102.

[116] See ibid., 98; He, "The Last Campaign," 2; Chen Xiaolu, "China's Policy toward the United States, 1949–55," in *Sino-American Relations, 1945–1955: A Joint Reassessment of a Critical Decade,* ed. Harry Harding and Ming Yuan (Wilmington, Del.: Scholarly Resources, 1989), 186.

[117] Chen, *China's Road,* 102.

[118] For discussion of this "hands off" speech by Truman, and of the politics surrounding and resulting from it, see Thomas J. Christensen, *Useful Adversaries: Grand Strategy, Domestic Mobilization, and Sino-American Conflict, 1947–1958* (Princeton: Princeton University Press, 1996), chapter 4.

navy should be strengthened."[119] The CMC's formal order to relocate troops that had been slated for the invasion of Taiwan was issued on July 7.[120] In early August, they were shifted northeast where they would participate in the Korean intervention.[121] In early August, the CMC gave its formal approval to an extended postponement of the invasion until after 1951.[122] Troops were moved and military construction projects were discontinued. Work on six airbases in the Taiwan Strait area "ceased at the beginning of the Korean War as assets were shifted to northeastern China."[123]

There exists clear evidence that the Chinese leaders viewed the American military threat as both credible and capable. One Chinese scholar provides context for Zhou's June 30 statement postponing the invasion:

> Zhou Enlai pointed out the General Staff Headquarters and the Ministry of Foreign Affairs must watch the Korean battlefield's situation attentively and carefully. However, the demobilization work should still continue according to plan. Only *the plan to liberate Taiwan must immediately be abandoned because of the Seventh Fleet that the Americans had stationed in the Taiwan Strait.* According to the memoirs of Xiao Jinguang, on June 30, 1950, Zhou conveyed [the Central Committee's] analysis of this situation to him [Xiao], saying "the changed situation adds to the problems we face in attacking Taiwan. Because the U.S. blocks the Taiwan Strait...the ground forces should continue to demobilize, and we'll continue to establish our navy and air force. We will postpone the attack on Taiwan."[124]

Similarly, in an internal directive, the Central Committee of the CCP had to admit that China "did not have the ability to compete with the United States in a trial of modern navies."[125] Finally, a report of Beijing's reaction to the American deterrent threat comes from a Chinese Nationalist intelligence

---

[119] Quoted in  廖国良、李士顺、徐焰、《毛泽东军事思想发展史》修订版(北京:解放军出版社、2001) [Liao Guoliang, Li Shishun, and Xu Yan, *The Development of Mao Zedong's Military Thought* (Beijing: People's Liberation Army Press, 2001), 372].

[120] Zhang, *Mao's Military Romanticism,* 59.

[121] Chen, *China's Road,* 132.

[122] 宋、《抗美援朝再回首》 [Song, *Recollections on the Korean War,* 204].

[123] Muller, *China as a Maritime Power,* 55.

[124] 宋、《抗美援朝再回首》 [Song, *Recollections on the Korean War,* 204]. Emphasis added. Xiao Jinguang was a senior Chinese military leader, and a veteran of the revolutionary war; he later commanded the PLAN.

[125] Ibid., 197. The precise date of this "internal directive" is unclear from the text of Song's book, although it appears to be only a few days after June 28, 1950.

agent who reportedly attended a high-level meeting in Beijing in which senior Communist cadres concluded that the Chinese assault fleet would "last only a few [hours] against 7th Flt [Fleet] and U.S. Air Force."[126]

Thus, there is explicit evidence linking the decision to postpone the attack to the specific dangers posed by the U.S. Navy and, in at least one set of signals, the Air Force. The Chinese appear to have understood that even this minimal U.S. deployment would decimate any prospects for a successful invasion. They understood both the capability that the signal entailed and the intent that it conveyed (as suggested in the DDE). After this, China was no longer in any doubt regarding whether the United States would intervene nor what such an intervention could mean to the Chinese invasion plan.

This case suggests, first, that the Weakness Hypothesis, which focuses on the "objective" quality of the signal as critical to coercive success, is only partially supported. The successful deterrent signal was, at best, moderate in size. In terms of "objective" quality, the diplomatic signal certainly was quite clear—Truman's speech left little ambiguity—but the strength of the military signal was initially quite weak. Even over time, it grew to be at most only moderately strong.[127] Nevertheless, deterrence was achieved. The Weakness Hypothesis can take some credit for explaining this, but doctrinal-difference theory enriches the explanation.

There is evidence that neither side had an excessive or unwarranted optimism about its own capabilities. For weeks, the United States was worried about its ability to defend Taiwan; some observers in the U.S. government were not reassured until the full buildup for the Korean War was under way in early 1951. The Chinese backed down in the face of a moderate deterrent threat. Thus, this case clearly and directly supports the doctrinal-difference misperception hypothesis.

This case further supports the argument that, in instances where the two sides have similar theories of victory, international communication is easier and joint assessments of the military balance are likely to be more accurate,

---

[126] Marolda, "U.S. Navy and the Chinese Civil War," 192. Marolda cites a message sent from the U.S. air attaché in Taipei to the Chief of Naval Operations on August 25, 1950, available in the MacArthur archives.

[127] The alternate explanation cannot be rescued completely even by invoking Mearsheimer's "stopping power of water." See John J. Mearsheimer, *The Tragedy of Great Power Politics* (New York: W.W. Norton and Company, 2001), 114–28. The stopping power of water may have played a role in amplifying the clarity of the American signal to the Chinese, but it cannot explain why Mao's views on the feasibility of the attack changed in direct response to the U.S. moves.

as posited by the two elements of the doctrinal-difference escalation hypothesis. In this case, the signal was moderate, not large. However, the signal was so clear and the military "language" so straightforward under the circumstances that the signal was sufficient to deter China from continuing its path to invasion. Because both sides understood amphibious war similarly, they both instantly understood the damage even a few surface ships or a rapidly deployed air squadron could do to a Chinese landing force. In this case, there is none of the "explaining away" of the adversary's capabilities that was evident in the other cases (chapters 4 and 5). Both sides knew how to interpret this signal. No translation was needed.

# PART III

# EXTENDING THE STORY

# 7

# THE EMERGENCE OF DOCTRINAL DIFFERENCES IN THE MIDDLE EAST, 1956 TO 1973

SINCE ITS FOUNDING IN 1948, Israel has always faced adversaries on its borders, at times implacable and numerous. However, the intensity of militarized conflict between Israel and its neighbors has varied. In this chapter, doctrinal-difference theory explains, in part, that variation: during one particularly violent period in Arab-Israeli relations in the early 1970s, differences between the key players' theories of victory complicated assessments of the balance of power and interpretations of one another's military signals.

Doctrinal-difference theory can thus make an important contribution to explaining the outbreak of the 1973 Arab-Israeli War. It does less to explain other conflicts; in 1967, for example, war broke out despite the presence of factors that should have been conducive to peace. Doctrinal-difference theory does not predict all wars, but it does enrich our understanding of the processes of assessing adversaries during the years surrounding the 1967 war. This chapter begins with a brief discussion of the importance and relevance of these cases. It proceeds to an overview of the historical background and then examines two distinct periods. From 1956 to the early 1970s, Egypt and Israel relied on similar blitzkrieg-style doctrines for ground warfare. As predicted by doctrinal-difference theory, there were few underestimations of the opponent in this period. However, one major war and other significant outbreaks of conflict took place. By the early 1970s, however, Egypt had shifted its doctrine substantially; the resulting difference with its adversary's doctrine, I argue, played a major role in the misperceptions that led to the outbreak of the Yom Kippur War in 1973.

This case provides robust evidence for the doctrinal-difference theory. The conventional explanations for this case, having to do with intelligence failures, are not as broad in their context and explanation. Still, the existing literature on the 1973 case is strongly supportive of doctrinal-difference theory. One scholar of this case identifies relevant concepts in the case: "Images serve as screens for the selective reception of new messages, and they often control the perception and interpretation of those messages which are not completely ignored, rejected or suppressed."[1] The 1973 case shows this phenomenon clearly.

This chapter focuses on the Egyptian-Israeli dyad in the period starting after the 1956 war through the 1973 war. This dyad was the most important in the ongoing Arab-Israeli conflict throughout this period: Egypt was involved in every war the Israelis fought from 1948 through 1973, and it was central to most, providing more military capability than any other neighboring Arab state. Following its violent genesis in 1948, Israel and its neighbors inflicted recurring low-level violence on one another throughout the early 1950s. Central to intense wars in 1956 and 1967, the Sinai Peninsula served as a strategic territory for controlling shipping lanes and as a buffer between Israel and Egypt. In both cases, the Sinai was the locus of large and fast-moving military operations. Following the second of these, Israel occupied the Sinai Peninsula, which was traditionally Egyptian territory. A simmering low-level conflict between 1967 and 1970 became known as the War of Attrition, followed by the return of a degree of stability between the two states in 1970. It was shattered on October 6, 1973, when Egyptian president Anwar Sadat attacked Israeli forces in the Sinai at the same time that Syria attacked the Golan Heights. Sadat hoped to coerce a political solution that would allow Egypt to reassert its sovereignty on the peninsula.

This history has been intensively examined. The Egyptian surprise that is elemental to the 1973 case has usually been explained as a product of specific intelligence failures and "groupthink" affecting the entire Israeli political-military leadership.[2] Nevertheless, a critical issue remains understudied: the source of that groupthink. I argue in this chapter that it was due to differences in the adversaries' theories of victory. Thus, although this chapter does not add substantial new historical material, it outlines an important causal element that has been missing from previous explanations of the 1973 war.

---

[1] Avi Shlaim, *The Iron Wall: Israel and the Arab World* (New York: Norton, 2000), 357.

[2] The best overall study is Uri Bar-Joseph, *The Watchman Fell Asleep: The Surprise of Yom Kippur and Its Sources* (Albany: State University of New York Press, 2005). He chronicles groupthink (244–46) as well as other factors.

The remainder of this chapter focuses on two periods: since conflict is frequent, they are separated according to change in the independent variable. Thus, the first period ranges between 1956 and the early 1970s, when Egypt and Israel had essentially similar doctrines. Although there was conflict during this period, it did not display the false optimism characteristic of large doctrinal differences among antagonists. The second period addresses the lead-up to the 1973 war, highlighting the substantial shift in Egyptian doctrine and the false optimism in both Egyptian and Israeli assessments of the strategic situation.

## EGYPTIAN-ISRAELI MILITARY STATECRAFT FROM 1956 TO THE EARLY 1970s

Between the 1956 war and the final period before the 1973 war, both Israel and Egypt emphasized a blitzkrieg strategy that integrated an emphasis on armor, heavy ground forces, tactical air support, and fast-moving tactical penetration of the enemy's lines. Over this period, there was considerable continuity in Israeli armor-heavy doctrine. What is less often remembered is that this was also true of the Egyptians. Egypt built explicitly on the German model from World War II, bringing in "80 former Wehrmacht officers to reform the Egyptian Army."[3] These officers did most of the operational planning for the Egyptian military during the 1950s, and laid the basis for the organizational structure of the entire postcolonial Egyptian military.[4] In the 1956 war in which Britain, France, and Israel wrested control of the recently nationalized Suez Canal from Egypt, Cairo had made moderately good use of airpower.[5] (The contrast with their 1967 performance in the air should not be attributed to doctrinal change: the Egyptian air force was effectively demolished on the ground on the first day of the 1967 war.)

Although it had a lopsided outcome, the 1967 war was fought by two militaries with very similar doctrines. The Israeli emphasis on armored warfare is widely recognized; Egypt's tank divisions were also quite heavy, even

---

[3] Kenneth M. Pollack, *Arabs at War: Military Effectiveness, 1948–1991* (Lincoln: University of Nebraska Press, 2002), 29–31.

[4] The Soviets also played a role in shaping Egyptian doctrine in the 1960s. Theirs too was an armor-heavy approach, similar in most respects to the German model. Isabella Ginor and Gideon Remez, *Foxbats over Dimona: The Soviets' Nuclear Gamble in the Six-Day War* (New Haven: Yale University Press, 2007), 68.

[5] Pollack, *Arabs at War*, 41.

by today's standards, as were its mechanized infantry units.[6] Egypt aimed to implement a defense-in-depth strategy, relying on mobile armored forces rather than frontal defenses:[7]

> In 1966 the Egyptian General Staff had evolved a defensive and offensive plan for the defense of the Sinai, with the code-name "Kahir." The basic concept was of a mobile defense in depth, with the mass of the army to be concentrated in the center of the peninsula, with only a covering screen in the border area.[8]

The planning called for a classic double envelopment of attacking Israeli forces.[9] The failure of these plans says less about the nature of Egypt's doctrine than about the quality of its tactical military leadership.[10]

Both sides aimed for first strikes in this period. Israeli Defense Forces (IDF) leaders at the time "believed almost exclusively in preemptive attacks."[11] The Egyptians also recognized the importance of surprise; before the Israeli surprise attack, Egypt had been preparing to make a surprise attack of its own.

The period known as the War of Attrition (1967–70) showed the parallels between the Egyptian and Israeli strategies, if less violently than in the wars of 1956, 1967, and 1973. During the period from 1967 to 1970, both sides continued their parallelism, engaging in punitive attacks that were not aimed at military victory, but at political coercion. These began with artillery duels, escalating to commando raids by both sides and some strategic air sorties, mostly by Israel.[12]

Thus, from 1956 through the early 1970s, Egypt and Israel approached conflict with each other in similar ways: both relied on a tank-heavy modernization of German blitzkrieg tactics. Both viewed airpower and maneuver of armored units as the keys to victory. The next section described the effects

---

[6] For the historical table of organization and equipment (TOE) data, see Eric M. Hammel, *Six Days in June: How Israel Won the 1967 Arab-Israeli War* (New York: Maxwell Macmillan International, 1992), 142.

[7] Ibid., 145.

[8] Trevor N. Dupuy, *Elusive Victory: The Arab-Israeli Wars, 1947–1974*, 3rd ed. (Dubuque, Iowa: Kendall/Hunt Publishing, 1992), 240.

[9] Pollack, *Arabs at War*, 61.

[10] Ibid.

[11] Tom Segev, *1967: Israel, the War, and the Year That Transformed the Middle East* (New York: Metropolitan Books, 2007), 165, see also 229, 236, 262, and 325.

[12] Ahron Bregman, *Israel's Wars: A History since 1947* (New York: Routledge, 2002), 98; Jonathan Shimshoni, *Israel and Conventional Deterrence: Border Warfare from 1953 to 1970* (Ithaca: Cornell University Press, 1988), 146.

of the similar doctrines in this period; by its end, the two sides would diverge from this shared understanding, with catastrophic results for stability.

## EGYPTIAN-ISRAELI RELATIONS PRIOR TO THE EARLY 1970S

It is true that a major war took place in 1967 even though the adversaries had broadly similar doctrines. No theory can explain all cases. As a subsequent section explains, the conventional understanding of that war assigns the cause not to overestimation of the adversary, the key intermediate variable posited by doctrinal-difference theory, but to Soviet manipulation of Egyptian fears.

That explicable anomaly aside, doctrinal-difference theory otherwise holds up well between 1956 and 1973. In that period, there was an exceptional degree of security tension between nearly implacable adversaries, yet escalation to military conflict was limited. Throughout this period, there was much internal turmoil in both countries and sporadic militarized conflict, but only once did it rise to the level of war.[13] As noted by Eric Hammel, "Since late 1956, virtually all aspects of the perpetual war had been more symbolic than real."[14] That conclusion highlights both the exceptional tension and the relatively low degree of militarization, apart from the 1967 war.

Throughout this period, the potential for substantial conflict was high. The number of militarized incidents was substantial, as shown in table 7–1. Throughout this period, a series of guerrilla raids and terrorist attacks by Palestinian insurgents and other forces also provoked many of the conventional militarized incidents.[15]

Despite this pervasive military tension, full-scale violence was rare. For instance, Israel's November 1966 Samua raid was the largest Israeli attack in ten years, mobilizing a total force of several thousand with five hundred crossing the border to retaliate for an earlier attack on Israeli police forces. It led to substantial noncombatant casualties in Jordan and resulted in significant outcry by the UN and the United States. However, while it led to further military signaling and posturing, it did not escalate to larger-scale violence between Israel and its Arab neighbors.[16]

[13] Dupuy, *Elusive Victory*, 224.
[14] Hammel, *Six Days in June*, 7.
[15] See Segev, *1967*.
[16] Hammel, *Six Days in June*, 19.

TABLE 7.1
Militarized Incidents between Arab States and Israel, 1956–1973

| Date | Event |
| --- | --- |
| February 1, 1960 | Mobilization of multiple Egyptian divisions[1] |
| June 1964<br>March 1965<br>May 1965<br>August 1965<br>July 1967 | Skirmishing or border clashes between Israel and Syria[2] |
| November 1, 1966 | Israeli raid in Samua, Jordan, raid, and subsequent Egyptian mobilization[3] |
| May 12, 1967 | Israeli chief of staff engages in saber rattling against Syria, warning of military escalation[4] |
| May 1, 1973 | Israeli war scare with Egypt (known as the "Blue White mobilization" in Israel)[5] |

1. Michael B. Oren, *Six Days of War: June 1967 and the Making of the Modern Middle East* (Oxford: Oxford University Press, 2002), 14; Eric M. Hammel, *Six Days in June: How Israel Won the 1967 Arab-Israeli War* (New York: Maxwell Macmillan International, 1992), 29.

2. Ahron Bregman, *Israel's Wars: A History since 1947* (New York: Routledge, 2002), 64; Hammel, *Six Days in June*, 6 and 11.

3. Hammel, *Six Days in June*, 19–29.

4. Bregman, *Israel's Wars*, 65.

5. Uri Bar-Joseph, *The Watchman Fell Asleep: The Surprise of Yom Kippur and Its Sources* (Albany: State University of New York Press, 2005), 50.

Significant violence in the period from late 1967 to mid-1970 became known as the War of Attrition. Over a three-year period, Israel lost about 750 soldiers killed in action, with another thirty-five hundred wounded. Egyptian losses were probably three times as great.[17] This period began with somewhat sporadic artillery fire in mid-June 1967. Beginning over a year later, both sides launched commando raids. However, again, there was no further escalation. Israeli raids were meant to be punitive and coercive, not militarily effective in terms of fundamentally degrading the adversary's forces. These should thus be characterized more as political signaling than as military conflict.[18]

During this period, some obvious opportunities for escalation on both sides were not taken. By late 1968, the Egyptians began to feel that the re-building of their forces in reaction to their 1967 defeat was complete, and that the basic ground force balance relative to Israel looked positive.[19] As a noted military analyst described Egypt's prospects in this period: "Th[e] imbalance of forces must also have tempted the Egyptians to think in terms of a

[17] Richard Bordeaux Parker, *The Politics of Miscalculation in the Middle East* (Bloomington: Indiana University Press, 1993), 125.

[18] Characterizing this period in similar terms are Bregman, *Israel's Wars*, 95; Shimshoni, *Israel and Conventional Deterrence*, 139.

[19] Saad Shazly, *The Crossing of the Suez* (San Francisco: American Mideast Research, 1980), 12.

limited crossing. How could one Israeli division (in spring 1969) be expected to prevent a crossing completely on a front 200 kilometers long. Another temptation must have been the proximity of the forces."[20] Yet the Egyptians did not attack, neither in 1969 nor for more than three years thereafter.

What accounts for this degree of stability—apart from the 1967 war—during the decade and a half from 1956 to 1973? Throughout the governmental deliberations on both sides of the Egyptian-Israeli dyad, there appeared a healthy level of caution against further escalation. Both sides assessed their own prospects as limited, whatever the balance in matériel. In the immediate post-1956 period, Gamal Abdel Nasser realized that his primary geopolitical strategy had to be one of delay, given the weakness of his military.[21] The same weakness and need for delay remained true in 1966, on the eve of major war: "These factors—... [including] the absence of a viable military option against Israel—persuaded Nasser that the time was not yet right for the expulsion of the UNEF."[22] After the 1967 war, Nasser rapidly returned to an acknowledgment that the prospects for victory would not be significantly in his favor for years.[23] He explicitly counseled patience and diplomacy after the Khartoum conference, which affirmed the solidarity of the Arab countries in the wake of the 1967 war.

One result was that there was some progress on the diplomatic front between 1956 and the early 1970s, and many times a negotiated peace seemed within reach. The exception—the 1967 war—looms large, and so it is to that war that this chapter now turns.

EXPLAINING THE EXCEPTIONAL CASE OF 1967

If there was no overconfidence stemming from doctrinal difference in 1967, what explains the outbreak of this war? Doctrinal difference offers little here. Instead, this case is one of the clearest examples of the spiral model known to the political science literature.[24] Each side, rather than underestimating its adversary, was deeply worried. Rather than overestimating its prospects for victory, as in cases when doctrinal difference plays a major role, each side

---

[20] Shimshoni, *Israel and Conventional Deterrence*, 143.

[21] Michael B. Oren, *Six Days of War: June 1967 and the Making of the Modern Middle East* (Oxford: Oxford University Press, 2002), 13.

[22] Ibid., 40.

[23] Muhammad Hasanayn Haykal, *The Road to Ramadan* (New York: Ballantine Books, 1975), 57.

[24] Dan Reiter, "Exploding the Powder Keg Myth: Preemptive Wars Almost Never Happen," *International Security* 20, no. 2 (1995).

was gravely concerned that it would be defeated. This concern, coupled with a belief in the efficacy of first-strike attacks, heightened the potential for war: as tensions intensified, a desire to inflict a first strike led each side to undertake steps that seemed to confirm the other side's fears, thus deepening the crisis.

The key spark to this spiral in tension was a series of Soviet warnings to the Egyptians that an Israeli attack was imminent, although it was, in fact, not. "There could be no dismissing a warning of such specificity from so many [Soviet] sources, including the Kremlin itself."[25] The archival revelation of these warnings in recent years has forced a shift in the historiographical literature on this crisis: "This evidence provides striking proof that, contrary to popular belief, the 1967 war was not instigated by the local states—neither Egypt nor Israel—but rather by the USSR as part of its competition with the U.S. for world influence and supremacy."[26]

Egypt's belief in these warnings resulted in a genuine spiral. Nasser demanded a partial UN pullout from the Sinai to facilitate Egypt's remilitarization of the Sinai Peninsula; UN secretary-general U Thant, concerned about the safety of his observers, overreacted and withdrew all members of the UN team. This, in turn, created a security vacuum in Sharm al Sheik at the southern tip of the Sinai into which Egypt stepped, moving military units and then closing the Straits of Tiran to Israeli shipping, which—for Israel—was grounds for war.

Consistent with doctrinal-difference theory, there was not much overestimation by either side heading into this conflict. Israel was aware that the war would be extremely intense.[27] Both sides were pessimistic about the final outcome.[28] Thus, while doctrinal-difference theory does not contribute to our understanding of this case, it is not fundamentally undermined by it either. Other factors dominate outcomes in this case. As noted in the introductory chapters, doctrinal-difference theory is not an explanation for all cases.

## EVALUATING THE SITUATION IN THE PERIOD BEFORE 1973

Between 1956 and the early 1970s, it is fairly clear that the two central adversaries had doctrines that were fairly similar. Yet, the 1967 conflict does not

[25] Oren, *Six Days of War,* 55.
[26] Bregman, *Israel's Wars,* 69.
[27] Oren, *Six Days of War,* 86.
[28] Pollack, *Arabs at War,* 37, 41.

undercut the underlying logic of doctrinal-difference theory. The predicted cause of conflict is absent, and the dangerous processes that it would have warned of were also nonexistent.

Furthermore, despite severe underlying conflicts of interest between Egypt and Israel for nearly two decades, no other major wars broke out during this period. Rather, despite constant tension, there was a fairly clear understanding of the dangers if military posturing and bluster escalated to actual use of substantial combat forces.

This understanding would diminish dramatically in the early 1970s.

## THEORIES OF VICTORY IN 1973

After Israel's stunning victory in 1967, the views of the two countries regarding optimal military doctrine diverged markedly.

### THE "TOTALITY OF THE TANK" AND ISRAEL'S OBSESSION WITH AIRPOWER

The primary lesson taken by the Israelis from the 1967 war was that armored warfare dominated all other forms of ground combat. Israel took one aspect of blitzkrieg, the armored maneuver unit, and amplified it to dominate all other aspects of war. One author refers to this view as "the totality of the tank."[29] The origins of the belief in the tank above all other arms stemmed from the particularities of the Israeli victory in the 1967 war.[30] One military analyst argued that

> after the 1967 war, the Israelis drew the wrong lesson from the performance of their armored forces. They came to the conclusion that the tank-airplane team was all-powerful and needed little support from other combat arms. In particular they believed that infantry and artillery were not major contributors to modern mechanized warfare.[31]

This went beyond imbalance in military doctrine: it bordered on fetishization of the armor branch. "Veteran armor officers permitted themselves to fanta-

---

[29] Abraham Rabinovich, *The Yom Kippur War: The Epic Encounter That Transformed the Middle East* (New York: Schocken Books, 2004), 34.
[30] Dupuy, *Elusive Victory*, 346.
[31] Pollack, *Arabs at War*, 107.

size about commanding a full armored division deploying into battle—two brigades forward, one to the rear, as they swept into the attack."[32]

The reciprocal side of this obsession with armor was a neglect of combined arms. "Israel's bias in favor of armor and against infantry stemmed from a belief (almost a dogma) that infantry would find it increasingly difficult to survive and fight on the battlefield."[33] Both infantry and artillery were downplayed. The forces that Israel deployed to the field of battle were unbalanced, but those of its adversaries were not: "Israel's emphasis on armor deprived it of many of the elements of combined arms present in Arab forces both at the outset of the war and once the forces on each side were fully mobilized."[34]

Critics later charged that by focusing on the Bar-Lev Line, the Israeli defenses along the east bank of the Suez, Israel had emphasized frontal defense rather than defense-in-depth; however, that greatly overstates the case. The fortifications of the Bar-Lev line were primarily intended as shelters from artillery during the War of Attrition. By 1973, much of the emphasis in Israel's war plan was on use of the strategic reserve tank force (particularly the armored Sinai Division) and offensive options on the western side of the Suez Canal.[35] With this approach, Israeli doctrinal development diverged further from that of Egypt, described below.

The 1967 war also influenced the Israeli understanding of the role of airpower. One lesson for Israel was the importance of a devastating offensive first strike against the adversaries' air forces. Successful first strikes against the Syrian and Egyptian air forces in the first minutes of the 1967 war had paved the way for Israeli dominance in the air. The IDF also came to value the utility of airpower for close air support. Indeed, for years afterward, the idea of airpower was surrounded by the "magical aura of the Six Day War."[36]

## EGYPT'S DEVELOPING DOCTRINE

Egyptian doctrine also changed substantially in the lead-up to the 1973 Yom Kippur War. As in Israel, the experiences of the Six Days' War and of the War of Attrition prompted doctrinal changes; in Egypt, however, they pushed in rather different directions and were linked to a shift in the political goals of

---

[32] Rabinovich, *Yom Kippur War*, 7.
[33] Anthony H. Cordesman and Abraham R. Wagner, *The Lessons of Modern War* (Boulder, Colo.: Westview Press, 1990), 55.
[34] Ibid.
[35] Rabinovich, *Yom Kippur War*, 19. For a supporting view, see also Shlaim, *Iron Wall*, 297.
[36] Rabinovich, *Yom Kippur War*, 125.

conflict. Rather than destroying Israel, the goal was to show that a perpetual conflict was not viable.

After its failures of the 1960s, Egypt began serious planning for another potential conflict in September 1971.[37] The operational concept underlying the "Badr" war plan (at that time known as "High Minarets") was based on an entirely new strategic goal: Egypt would seek to achieve only a limited penetration into the Sinai. There was some debate over how far penetration should be attempted—with goals ranging from a few miles to a few dozen miles, that is, as far as capture of the strategic Mitla and Gidi passes—but retaking the whole Sinai Peninsula was off the table.

Egypt's shift to a limited-aims strategy was consequential: it diminished the need for assets such as long-range strike aircraft. Even as early as February 1968, Nasser was moving away from tactical aircraft. To some extent this represented a shift toward reliance on surface-to-surface (SCUD) missiles for the same role, but there was also the beginning of some thinking regarding the requirements for limited war in this period.[38] Key Israeli capabilities—armored units and tactical airpower—could be confronted with a mix of tactical responses. High-technology Soviet surface-to-air missiles (SAMs) could defend against IDF aircraft in a limited war. Infantry-borne antitank weaponry would blunt Israel's armored attacks. Both of these tactics, however, could be effective only in support of a limited-aims strategy.[39] The justification on the airpower side was clear: "Sadat and his generals...had already decided that the Egyptian attack would halt well short of the passes so that the army remained under the SAM umbrella."[40] In the infantry-armored competition, infantry's inherent lesser mobility also suggested that narrower—or more to the point, closer—goals would be more attainable.

Closely related to this were several other changes. First was Egypt's shift away from aspirations for a massive maneuver-based victory. Typically, the goal of armored warfare was a crucial breakthrough of a front line followed by an exploitation phase in the enemy's rear areas.[41] Instead, Egypt's goal would be a modest initial offensive success that could be quickly transformed into a defensive position. Rather than focusing its capabilities narrowly along a few specific axes to facilitate breakthrough, Egypt planned an offensive on a wide front. This broad-front attack would also reduce the vulnerability of

[37] Shazly, *Crossing of the Suez*, 29.
[38] Haykal, *Road to Ramadan*, 59.
[39] Pollack, *Arabs at War*, 108–11.
[40] Rabinovich, *Yom Kippur War*, 45.
[41] General Heinz Guderian, *Panzer Leader* (Cambridge, Mass.: DaCapo Press, 1996).

the offensive to discrete airpower attacks.[42] General Ahmad Ismail, who had commanded Egypt's field army facing the Sinai after the 1967 war, argued for a package of doctrinal changes:

> The qualitative difference [in the two sides' conduct of armored warfare] was less than the Israelis assumed, and he also believed that Egyptian soldiers were as good as or better than the Israelis on the defensive. And the Arab numerical manpower superiority—even the manpower of Egypt alone—was so great that ways should be found to trade manpower losses with the Israelis in situations of static combat where the Israelis could not employ their superior capabilities against the Arabs.... As a result, with surprising resilience, the defeated Egyptian Army began to seek ways and means of fighting the Israelis under circumstances in which the Israelis could not bring their superiority to bear.[43]

Inherent in this approach, Egypt would try to prolong the conflict.[44] Doing so would put pressure on the Israeli reliance on reserve forces and its need to mobilize the whole society for its wars, which therefore had to be abbreviated before damaging Israel's civilian economy.

Under the Egyptian limited-aims strategy, "the offensive would rely on attrition rather than maneuver to defeat the IDF": "In addition, to neutralize Israel's two great advantages in armored warfare and airpower, the Egyptians deployed enormous numbers of early generation Soviet antitank guided missiles (ATGMs), rocket-propelled grenades (RPGs), mobile AAA systems, and SAMs."[45] All of these components wedded together created a distinct approach for the Egyptians. Tactically, the most critical changes were the addition of man-portable antitank systems and modern SAMs.

At one level, the Egyptians merely returned to a more balanced approach, utilizing the "proper elements of combined arms."[46] (For instance, unarmored antitank guns were used extensively, and effectively.[47]) However, the key was equipping infantry units with new, Soviet-made Sagger antitank guided missiles (ATGMs) that could be carried by infantry teams of two or

---

[42] Jordanian Lt. General (ret.) Bassam Kakish, quoted in Richard Bordeaux Parker, *The October War: A Retrospective* (Gainesville: University Press of Florida, 2001), 94.
[43] Dupuy, *Elusive Victory*, 347.
[44] Shazly, *Crossing of the Suez*, 26.
[45] Pollack, *Arabs at War*, 102.
[46] Cordesman and Wagner, *Lessons of Modern War*, 54, and the same general point at 433.
[47] Bregman, *Israel's Wars*, 133.

three.[48] ATGMs had been recently introduced into Egypt; in preparation for the war, they were mainly given to the units that would be making the initial crossing of the Suez Canal.[49] Modern RPG systems had also been recently acquired from the Soviets and were also lethal.[50] Egypt's ground forces were equipped with night-vision goggles more advanced than most of those possessed anywhere in the Israeli forces.[51] With these weapons, Egypt's infantry could infiltrate when on the tactical offensive, and dig in when on the defensive.[52] Massive changes in the soldiers' kit—water, food, personal arms, and so forth—facilitated offensive action. Also important was a shift in the way mobilization was organized to allow for more rapid movement to attacking positions.[53]

Egypt recognized Israeli airpower to be a key threat. General Saad El Shazly believed SAMs were the way to address it.[54] Egypt's air defense had long been regarded as insufficient; the lack of an integrated air defense system in 1969 and of mobile SAMs into the early 1970s were viewed as restraints on a more assertive Egyptian posture.[55] However, by 1973 the acquisition of new systems allowed a more comprehensive solution: "The advancing forces would be covered part of the way by the fixed air defense system and for the rest by mobile SAM-6 missiles, radar-guided antiaircraft guns, and shoulder-fired SAM-7 missiles."[56]

Although Egypt's air defenses have received most of the attention from military historians, Egypt also foresaw a role for its modernized air force: medium-range bombers could use air-launched cruise missiles to attack targets well within Israel.[57] Furthermore, "the bulk of the Arab air forces would be preserved as a strategic reserve in order to impose caution on the enemy."[58]

Thus in contrast to the preceding two decades, Egypt and Israel brought to the 1973 war very different military doctrines, and indeed, different goals.

---

[48] For general description, see Rabinovich, *Yom Kippur War,* 29 and 35–36.

[49] Haykal, *Road to Ramadan,* 15.

[50] Cordesman and Wagner, *Lessons of Modern War,* 64.

[51] Lt. Commander Youssef H. Aboul-Enein (U.S. Navy), "Egyptian General Saad-Eddine El-Shazly Controversial Operational Thinker and Architect of the 1973 Yom-Kippur War," *Infantry* (2005): 22; Dupuy, *Elusive Victory,* 448.

[52] Dupuy, *Elusive Victory,* 455.

[53] Shazly, *Crossing of the Suez,* 75.

[54] Rabinovich, *Yom Kippur War,* 27.

[55] See, respectively, Dupuy, *Elusive Victory,* 364; Shazly, *Crossing of the Suez,* 21.

[56] Nadav Safran, "Trial by Ordeal: The Yom Kippur War, October 1973," *International Security* 2, no. 2 (1977): 136.

[57] Rabinovich, *Yom Kippur War,* 115.

[58] Safran, "Trial by Ordeal," 136.

The next sections address how these distinct doctrines affected the signaling and interpretation of the balance of power and thus led to war.

## EGYPTIAN STATECRAFT LEADING UP TO THE WAR

Egypt was striving for several goals in the early 1970s. Certainly it wanted to restore its wounded prestige in the wake of its 1967 military rout. More important was a restoration of the territory it had lost in the Sinai. It also sought, in conjunction with the other Arab states, to address the broader question of Israel's status in the Middle East. How to achieve these goals? Cairo viewed military power and diplomatic leverage as two sides of the same coin. Further, as doctrinal-difference theory predicts, Egyptian military doctrine affected both. Egypt's confidence in its capabilities was exaggerated by its recent military doctrinal changes. This shaped the country's assessment of the balance of power, and therefore what it expected to achieve through diplomatic negotiation. It also shaped the military signals that it tried to send.

### MILITARY BASIS OF EGYPT'S DIPLOMATIC POWER

Diplomacy and military signaling were inextricably intertwined in Cairo's understanding of international relations during this period. Numerous types of evidence show this. Describing one round of his own diplomatic proposals, Sadat said to one of his generals:

> The Americans want to distort my proposals. They agree about the Israeli withdrawal, our crossing, and the reopening of the canal. But although they say that all issues could then be settled by negotiation, they want no time limit.... *Without some sanction,* Israel could spin out negotiations for 10, 15, 20 years. We would have lost everything.[59]

He then turned directly to a discussion of the military modernization that would give Egypt the power to impose such a sanction.

This linkage between diplomacy and the military balance was Egypt's central motivation in the War of Attrition, which involved considerable diplomatic signaling aimed at various strategic goals such as convincing Israel

---

[59] Shazly, *Crossing of the Suez,* 176–77. Emphasis added. See also Parker, *October War,* 4.

of Egyptian resolve and involving the superpowers in regional politics.[60] National Security Advisor Henry Kissinger explicitly encouraged such thinking by Egypt, emphasizing that its military weakness should lead Cairo to make more concessions.[61] Sadat had fully internalized this logic, recognizing that it was critical to convince Israel that the military balance was not overwhelmingly in its favor:

> The President [Sadat] repeated his conviction that "no political solution is possible unless continued pressure is exerted on the United States and Israel and unless Israel is made to understand that the balance of military strength is not in its favor," and again emphasized the need for the speedy implementation of the agreed programs for the supply of arms and for training.[62]

As the military components of Egypt's modernization begin to take shape, Cairo found reasons to be increasingly confident. As the Soviet SAM system was moved farther and farther eastward toward the canal, the air balance in the region shifted dramatically. The Egyptians declared the week beginning June 30, 1970, as "the week of the falling of enemy aircraft" with more than five of Israel's advanced F-4s destroyed.[63] After the War of Attrition ended in 1970, Sadat continued to engage in substantial saber rattling: "The time has come for a shock. Diplomacy will continue before, during, and after the battle.... The resumption of the hostilities is the only way out. Everything is now being mobilized in concert for the resumption of a battle which is inevitable."[64]

By the outbreak of the war itself, Egypt believed that it could undertake a limited war that would be unlikely to escalate, given Egypt's strategic-escalation options, as well as the limited threats posed to Israel by such a strategy.[65]

---

[60] Kenneth W. Stein, *Heroic Diplomacy: Sadat, Kissinger, Carter, Begin, and the Quest for Arab-Israeli Peace* (New York: Routledge, 1999), 58.
[61] Ibid., 67. The importance that the Egyptians attributed to Kissinger's message is described by Ahmad Maher El-Sayed, an aide to Hafez Ismail, in Parker, *October War*, 77.
[62] Haykal, *Road to Ramadan*, 170.
[63] Shazly, *Crossing of the Suez*, 14.
[64] Quoted in Stein, *Heroic Diplomacy*, 68.
[65] Shimshoni, *Israel and Conventional Deterrence*, 144; Safran, "Trial by Ordeal," 134. One of the great puzzles of this conflict is how the Egyptian's synthesized their limited goal aspirations with the nearly existential dangers that would have been posed by a Syrian breakthrough in the north. This would have potentially raised the specter of nuclear escalation, deeply calling into question Egypt's limited war aims. This issue remains remarkably understudied. For

Thus, by 1973, Egypt believed that it faced a straightforward strategic problem, with an implementable solution. Its doctrinal change left it with a radically different approach to warfare than Israel had. Doctrinal-difference theory predicts in this case misperceptions and resulting escalations.

## DIPLOMATIC POLICY

Egypt sought to shift the balance of power through doctrinal innovation, and its military moves were closely associated with its saber rattling. This section examines Egypt's concurrent diplomatic maneuvering. Various diplomatic initiatives were meant to serve as tacit signaling: Egypt was trying to negotiate, on its own terms, an end to the Israeli occupation of the Sinai Peninsula. Although the focus of this section is on Egypt, it is clear from the historic record that the two sides were not particularly far apart. (For instance, immediately after the 1967 war, Israel's cabinet had already agreed to return all territories in the context of broad peace agreements.[66])

The point is that the Egyptians were signaling an interest to negotiate the terms of the future status of the Sinai, as their active diplomacy evidences. However, the Israelis were not willing to make substantial concessions, because of their overconfidence and false optimism that the military balance was substantially in their favor.

There were numerous major diplomatic initiatives in the period between the 1967 and 1973 wars. For several, the primary impetus came from outside, such as U.S. secretary of state William Rogers and mediation by UN envoy Gunnar Jarring. The latter in particular brought the two sides fairly close together by 1972.[67] Also promising was Kissinger's shuttle diplomacy:

> The concessions [Israeli Prime Minister Golda] Meir made at her meeting with Kissinger, on 10 December 1971, were not too little, but they were too late. Had they been made six months earlier, they would probably have produced a breakthrough in the search for an interim agreement. But Sadat's position had hardened in the meantime.[68]

---

exceptions, see Barry M. Blechman and Douglas M. Hart, "The Political Utility of Nuclear Weapons: The 1973 Middle East Crisis," *International Security* 7, no. 1 (1982); Yair Evron, *Israel's Nuclear Dilemma* (Ithaca: Cornell University Press, 1994).

[66] Shlaim, *Iron Wall*, 253.

[67] Ibid., 300.

[68] Ibid., 308.

This quotation from one of the most respected diplomatic histories of the period strongly suggests how close the two sides were in the early 1970s to resolving the fundamental issues of the international border, the militarized status of the Sinai, and the level of diplomatic status each state would accord the other.

Several other efforts were primarily Egyptian efforts. In December 1970,

> Sadat considered the possibility of arriving at some form of phased Israeli withdrawal from Sinai in exchange for something far less than a peace treaty, a military agreement but not a political document. Independently of Sadat's musings, Israeli Defense Minister Moshe Dayan also considered some form or framework for a phased Israeli withdrawal from Sinai. Each wanted a change in the status quo: Sadat wanted his land without having to go to war; Dayan too wanted an agreement without fighting a war.[69]

Sadat had also sent the diplomat who was his equivalent of a national security adviser to engage in secret meetings with Kissinger; a final meeting occurred as late as February 1973. The United States opened this channel specifically to become involved in the Israeli-Egyptian dyad in the hopes of securing some compromise from Tel Aviv.[70]

Sadat also made a proposal known as the Interim Canal Agreement initiative in early 1973.[71] This was viewed as a fairly moderate proposal, aimed at achieving partial agreement on the Suez issue alone. The United States among others viewed it as promising: "Israelis were urged by Washington to take his [Sadat's] proposals seriously."[72]

There is much debate over how much Sadat would have been willing to concede in several of these initiatives.[73] There are also ample grounds for criticizing the general quality of Israeli and American diplomacy.[74] However, the point is that there was some basis to think diplomacy might have made progress, if both sides had been more willing to make concessions at the negotiating table. Instead, as shown in subsequent sections, due to overoptimism

---

[69] Stein, *Heroic Diplomacy,* 59.

[70] On the importance of this channel, see William B. Quandt, *Peace Process: American Diplomacy and the Arab-Israeli Conflict since 1967,* 3rd ed. (Berkeley: University of California Press, 2001), 96–99.

[71] Ibid., 89–92.

[72] Ibid., 89.

[73] For an excellent discussion of these initiatives, see Parker, *October War.*

[74] Professor I. William Zartman, quoted in ibid., 21.

based on misperceptions of the balance of power, each preferred to take its grievances to the battlefield (consistent with the Misperception Prediction and Discounting Prediction). The surprise with which the Israelis encountered Egyptian military prowess strongly suggests that a more accurate assessment might have led Israel, at least, to more concessions at the negotiating table.

## ISRAELI INTERPRETATION OF THE EGYPTIAN BALANCE AND STATECRAFT

It was as common in Israel as in Egypt to view military power and diplomatic statecraft as intertwined.[75] This section looks at how Israel interpreted the mix of Egyptian diplomatic and military signals in the period leading up to the outbreak of the Yom Kippur War. Israel's perceptions regarding the efficacy of peace negotiations, its assessments of the overall balance of power, and its conclusions regarding Egyptian intentions were all shaped by its view of Egypt's military might through its own military lens. Even in the final lead-up to the war, AMAN, Israel's military intelligence, repeatedly ignored or explained away valuable last-minute intelligence. Israeli analysts routinely invoked a particular view of Egyptian doctrine that mirrored, in key elements, Israeli approaches to conflict, using it to draw conclusions about Egypt's capabilities and intentions. The section begins by analyzing this view, referred to by Israel as the "concept," before turning to its effect on Israeli assessments and statecraft.

### ISRAEL'S "CONCEPT" OF EGYPT'S MILITARY DOCTRINE

Critical to understanding the Israeli interpretation of the balance of power with Egypt, and indeed its entire relationship with Egypt, were Israeli perceptions of Egyptian strategy. Israeli intelligence services had developed an understanding of how the Egyptians would fight, which they referred to as "the concept." It was deeply flawed.

Substantively, the concept centered on the air balance.[76] Israelis believed that the Egyptians would want to be able to hit strategic Israeli targets early in the war, which would require either long-range surface-to-surface weapons or strike aircraft that were capable of penetrating Israeli airspace.[77] Indeed,

---

[75] Shimshoni, *Israel and Conventional Deterrence,* 148; Shlaim, *Iron Wall,* 293.
[76] Rabinovich, *Yom Kippur War,* 22.
[77] Ibid., 43 and 48.

this did to some extent reflect Egypt's approach: some such elements were nearly in place by late 1973.[78] Israel expected Egypt to use such an offensive strike force in part to neutralize the Israeli air force on the ground, in much the same way that the IDF had destroyed Egypt's air force at the outset of the 1967 war.[79] Israeli analysis of the Egyptian balance invariably looked to this specific aspect of the air balance in reaching conclusions about the overall balance of power. Until Egypt had created this offensive air option, Israel believed, it would not launch an attack. This was, in fact, quite inconsistent with Egypt's limited-aims strategy.

In part, this myopia was part of a broader difficulty: the Israelis gave consideration only to "all-out" or total-war scenarios, not, in any detail, to various limited-war strategies. Israeli intelligence did consider the prospects for extremely small crossings of the Suez Canal, but it never gave serious attention to any intermediate limited-war approach that would move large ground forces a few dozen miles into the Sinai.[80]

The "concept" went essentially unquestioned; it was a "combination of dogmas (which, by their nature cannot be falsified), groundless interpretation that is incoherent with available information, and an exaggerated self-assurance."[81] In this context, it is not surprising that Egyptian warnings were repeatedly ignored, despite their sheer quantity and quality. Evidence that war loomed was explained away as being inconsistent with the "concept." Overt signals were ignored in the prewar period, and so was intelligence obtained in the final few days before the war. The "concept" was based on a mistaken mirror-imaging of Israeli doctrine when, in fact, Egypt had, with Soviet assistance, innovated its approach to warfare:

> Sadat's decision under the conditions of 1973 represented a subtle combination of force and diplomacy at the service of rational and limited aims. In other words, "the concept" was simply out of date, having failed to register the important strategic and political changes that took place between 1970 and 1973.[82]

This divergence led to a variety of failings in statecraft.

---

[78] Egypt possessed cruise missiles compatible with Tu-16 bombers (which it used just once during the war). It had also recently received a brigade of Scud-B missiles, although these were not operational by the outbreak of the war. Bar-Joseph, *Watchman Fell Asleep*, 21–22 and 70.

[79] Shlaim, *Iron Wall*, 352.

[80] Bar-Joseph, *Watchman Fell Asleep*, 60.

[81] Ibid., 170–71.

[82] Shlaim, *Iron Wall*, 365.

This has been the conventional wisdom regarding the outbreak of the Yom Kippur War. Nearly all sources emphasize the distortions caused by "the concept" throughout Israeli military thinking as the cause of the degree of Israel's surprise. The added contribution of this chapter is to explain that surprise in terms of the doctrinal difference between the two adversaries and its effect on the statecraft that preceded the war.

## ASSESSING THE BALANCE OF POWER

Israel was markedly optimistic in 1973, and its views were bolstered by its expectations of the way the war would be fought. The optimism affected politicians, the army high command, and the intelligence services.[83] The IDF expected a quick collapse of the Egyptian forces if war did break out.[84] Leaders in Tel Aviv expected the model of 1967 to hold again.[85]

The failure was not merely one of overoptimism. The specific nature of the assessment was heavily influenced by the doctrinal differences between the two sides. This flaw pervaded Israel's intelligence assessments: "As for AMAN [Israeli military intelligence], its failure went deeper than the failure to warn of war. It did not prepare the IDF for the kind of war that was coming. It failed to indicate the innovative tactics the Egyptian army would employ."[86]

The difficulty was not confined to Israel's intelligence analysts. Operational leaders had similar doctrinal blinders. When war scares flared up from time to time and prompted a reassessment of plans, the Israeli response would typically reemphasize existing capabilities, enhance offensive options, flesh out additional armored units, or undertake similar approaches that simply reaffirmed existing IDF doctrine.[87] This is consistent with the Doctrinal Confidence Prediction. What Israel needed, instead, was to reinforce artillery units or develop tactics to overcome infantry armed with RPGs. This it did not do.

## ISRAELI CONFIDENCE STYMIES PEACE TALKS

This mistaken assessment of the balance of power shaped the conduct of diplomacy in the prewar period. At a number of points between the end of

[83] Ibid., 362.
[84] Bar-Joseph, *Watchman Fell Asleep*, 41.
[85] Segev, *1967*, 253 and 265.
[86] Rabinovich, *Yom Kippur War*, 126. That said, there was some limited awareness within AMAN that SAMs would pose some dangers to the IDF. Bar-Joseph, *Watchman Fell Asleep*, 75.
[87] Bar-Joseph, *Watchman Fell Asleep*, 74.

the 1967 war and the outbreak of the 1973 war, the two sides were close to diplomatic accommodation. Israeli confidence on the military front repeatedly contributed to its hard-line position at the bargaining table.

In the wake of the 1967 war, "time [had] seemed to be on Israel's side" as it contemplated negotiations over the return of the Sinai to Egypt.[88] Israeli prime minister Golda Meir argued in the early 1970s that "Israel's best policy at present is to let Egypt's President Sadat 'sweat it out,' with his range of alternatives narrowing all the time, eventually driving him to negotiations with Israel itself."[89] This view persisted until the brink of the 1973 war. Kissinger recalled that

> when I saw [Israeli foreign minister Abba] Eban on Thursday afternoon [just before the war], he explained to me at great length that there was no real need for a peace initiative, which I had urged on him, because the military situation was absolutely stable and could not be changed, and politically there was nothing to be gained by a peace offensive.[90]

A final major diplomatic initiative by Egypt in early 1973 had some chance of success: Egypt had by that time thrown out the Soviet military advisers that had been so critical to its military modernization. Its reasoning in doing so was to facilitate overtures to Washington.[91] Another element in its policy to improve relations with the United States was a round of diplomacy between Ismail, Egypt's national security adviser, and the U.S. secretary of state, Henry Kissinger. In February, an intensive round of "shuttle diplomacy" occurred, but it foundered: Israel believed, even at this late date, that the military balance heavily favored itself. Prime Minister Golda Meir argued that, "'We never had it so good' and suggested that the stalemate was safe for the time being because the Arabs had no military option."[92] Israel's assessment of the utility of diplomatic initiatives, in this case as well as the others discussed above, was predicated on a flawed and doctrinally biased assessment of the military balance. This is entirely consistent with the Assessing Intent Prediction.

---

[88] Quandt, *Peace Process*, 45.

[89] Quoted in Shlaim, *Iron Wall*, 314.

[90] National Archives and Records Agency, October 23, 1973, "Secretary's Staff Meeting," p. 4, available from William Burr, ed., *The October War and U.S. Policy*, electronic briefing book, *National Security Archive*, October 7, 2003, at http://www.gwu.edu/~nsarchiv/NSAEBB/NSAEBB98/.

[91] Parker, *October War;* Stein, *Heroic Diplomacy*, 63 and 66.

[92] Shlaim, *Iron Wall*, 315.

### ASSESSING EGYPTIAN INTENTIONS

Israeli assessments about Egyptian intentions flowed directly from the "concept" and the assessment that the ground balance overwhelmingly favored Israel. This is clear from numerous items of evidence: "Overall estimates made by Israeli intelligence sources succumbed to a general concept which said that although there 'was a possibility that Egypt and Syria would start a war against us [they would] not start a war as long as counterweight to our military advantage' did not exist."[93]

Similarly, in early August 1973, Defense Minister Moshe Dayan told senior IDF leaders that "the balance of forces is so much in our favor that it neutralizes the Arab considerations and motives for the immediate renewal of hostilities."[94] That summer Deputy Prime Minister Yigal Allon, who as a general had been a hero in the War of 1948, declared "Egypt had no military option at all."[95]

The circularity of all this reasoning was described by military analyst Trevor Dupuy: "[The failure of Israeli intelligence] was a classic failure, in which military intelligence was focused on hostile intentions, while hostile capabilities were ignored because they were discounted; and this very discounting of Arab capabilities led to false assumptions about intentions."[96] Doctrinally distorted assessments of capability were used to justify conclusions about intentions that lacked any independent basis (consistent with the Assessing Intent Prediction).

### IGNORING FINAL INTELLIGENCE

In the final days before war broke out, Israel continued to explain away key intelligence. King Hussein of Jordan sent an explicit warning to Israel, which was taken seriously by Israeli intelligence analysts who specialized in Jordan.[97] Israeli military intelligence was thus aware of the "large scale movement of Egyptian troops" and extra ammunition supplies.[98] A key human intelligence source for Mossad, Israel's civilian intelligence agency, was the son-in-law of the late Egyptian president Nasser; a trusted source, he gave Israel very specific information in the days before war that was essentially accurate in warning of a looming attack.[99]

---

[93] Stein, *Heroic Diplomacy*, 69.
[94] Quoted in Dupuy, *Elusive Victory*, 406.
[95] Ritchie Ovendale, *The Origins of the Arab-Israeli Wars*, 3rd ed. (New York: Longman, 1999), 191.
[96] Dupuy, *Elusive Victory*, 585. For a similar point, see Stein, *Heroic Diplomacy*, 69.
[97] Rabinovich, *Yom Kippur War*, 51.
[98] Ibid., 55 and 61.
[99] Bar-Joseph, *Watchman Fell Asleep*, 47 and 103.

Yet all of these signals were ignored. Intelligence techniques that could be used only once would have provided unassailable evidence but were never activated.[100] Israel also failed to take intelligence pictures of the Egyptian front by airborne assets in the crucial period two weeks prior to the war.[101] When pictures were finally taken and reviewed on October 5, just one day before the war started, they showed an "Egyptian buildup all along the canal" including a 50 percent increase in artillery pieces.[102] Even in the face of such evidence, AMAN continued to be very reluctant to change its prior beliefs. That same day, the head of the Egyptian desk of AMAN issued a statement that typified the contradictions imposed by the doctrinal blinders: "Although the emergency deployment along the canal appears to show clear evidence of aggressive intent, our best assessment is that there has been no change in Egypt's evaluation of its relative strength vis-à-vis the IDF."[103] As late as the very day that war broke out, AMAN continued to downplay the prospects of conflict in the mistaken belief that "the strategic level in Egypt and Syria is aware of the absence of any chances of success."[104]

These numerous red flags were each explained away because the key precondition that the Israelis presumed necessary for war—a viable Egyptian offensive air threat—was not evident. The "concept," grounded in a mirror imaging of Israeli doctrine, distorted Israel's interpretation of the intelligence data. Doctrinal-difference theory's Downplaying Prediction expects precisely this sort outcome.

## BUREAUCRATIC POLITICS

Doctrinal-difference theory is supported by evidence of varying levels of concern in AMAN over the signs of Egyptian moves. Among the least concerned was Eliyahu Zeira, the head of AMAN, a former brigade commander with substantial experience on the general staff.[105] Immersed as he was in Israel's military doctrine, it is not surprising that he viewed Egypt through the lens of the IDF's own approach to warfare: "Major-General Eliyahu Zeira,

---

[100] Ibid., 135 and 149; Rabinovich, *Yom Kippur War*, 73. The specific nature of these means remains shrouded in secrecy.
[101] Rabinovich, *Yom Kippur War*, 69.
[102] Ibid., 73.
[103] Quoted in ibid., 78.
[104] Quoted in ibid., 98.
[105] On Zeira's background, see Uri Bar-Joseph and Arie W Kruglanski, "Intelligence Failure and Need for Cognitive Closure: On the Psychology of the Yom Kippur Surprise," *Political Psychology* 24, no. 1 (2003): 82.

the Director of Military Intelligence, had only been at his post for one year before the war and had found established patterns of work. But he adopted 'the concept' whose rigidity destroyed the openness required in confronting inflowing information."[106]

In contrast, many regional political experts within Israel's intelligence bureaucracy viewed the Egyptian moves as dangerous.[107] This variation is precisely what the Depth of Immersion Prediction of doctrinal-difference theory would predict: those inculcated with Israeli military doctrine would have the hardest time thinking in other terms, while those who studied other countries as their primary occupation would be more open to viewing intelligence in terms that made sense in context of Egyptian rather than Israeli doctrine.

## THE OVERSTATED ROLE OF DECEPTION

Deception was certainly a central component of Egypt's strategy during the Yom Kippur War. Might it be the case that Egyptian efforts to deceive played a larger role than doctrinal difference in accounting for Israeli surprise? This argument could only account for Israeli surprise at the timing of the attack, not at the conduct of combat once war broke out, nor Israel's flawed assessments of the balance of power. However, even on the core issue of Israeli surprise at the outbreak of the war, this alternative argument is not as persuasive as doctrinal-difference theory.

Extensive warnings were received but simply did not find a receptive audience in the Israeli military hierarchy. This point is reiterated by most scholars of the period:

> The praise [for] the attempts to cover Arab war preparations and deceive Israel into believing that it was merely a regular exercise seem, in retrospect, exaggerated.... [In fact] Israel received excellent information about their war plans, the nature of their preparations, and their intention to launch war in the first week of October.[108]

Further, the Egyptian deception efforts were not particularly sophisticated: "When compared to... [other such operations] the Egyptian deception operation seems to be rather primitive.... They succeeded so well not because of

---

[106] Shlaim, *Iron Wall,* 353.
[107] Bar-Joseph, *Watchman Fell Asleep,* 239.
[108] Ibid., 236. See also Bar-Joseph and Kruglanski, "Intelligence Failure and Need for Cognitive Closure," 76–77.

the quality of their deception but because of grave deficiencies in the Israeli analysis of available war information."[109] Egyptian secrecy and active efforts at deception contributed to the tactical surprise in the opening days of the war, but enough information did arrive in Tel Aviv that the explanation for Israel's strategic surprise must lie elsewhere.[110]

The two adversaries' divergent doctrines led to flawed assessments of the signals inherent in statecraft and diplomacy and flawed measurement of the balance of power. The Israelis' underestimation of Egyptian military capabilities led them to misunderstand the balance of power and thus to act on an inappropriate diplomatic strategy. Further, evidence of this misperception is seen in Israel's behavior during the military conflict.

## SURPRISE AFTER THE OUTBREAK OF WAR

The outbreak of the Yom Kippur War is widely regarded as an archetypal successful surprise attack. I do not challenge that understanding, but focus specifically on the ways in which the development of conflict surprised Israel's military during the first days and weeks of the war. The Egyptian forces shocked the Israelis with specific weapons and tactics, and not simply with the timing of their attack. The initial Israeli counterattacks reflected Israel's continued difficulty in grasping the novelties in the Egyptian doctrine and altering its expectations about the development of the Egyptian offensive. The nature of Israel's surprise provides further evidence in support of doctrinal-difference theory and the Surprise Prediction in particular.

### SHOCK AT EGYPTIAN EFFECTIVENESS

The Israeli way of war failed spectacularly both on the ground and in the air.

*Ground Forces*
The key theme in the military history of the war is Egypt's "humbling of the tank" through revolutionary tactical adaptation.[111] Egyptian antitank infantry was stunningly effective, knocking out 180 of the 290 tanks that Israel had deployed in the Sinai region.[112] Over half of the Israeli soldiers killed in the

[109] Bar-Joseph, *Watchman Fell Asleep*, 31–32.
[110] Indeed, there would have been no need for the Agranat Commission if Israel's surprise had been due to effective Egyptian deception and operational security.
[111] The phrase "humbling of the tank" is from a chapter title from Rabinovich, *Yom Kippur War*, 112.
[112] Ibid., 125.

war were tankers.[113] The tactics used by the Egyptian forces drew on well-integrated combined-arms practices:

> The RPG-7 men, who had to hold their fire until the range was down to less than 200 meters, inflicted heavy losses on the Israelis, as did the Saggers.... Recoiling from the unexpectedly heavy and accurate fire, the surviving Israeli tankers regrouped a few thousand meters to the east, then moved back to repeat the attacks and to incur the same kind of casualties. By evening the [lead strategic reserve] brigade had lost almost all of its 100 tanks.[114]

The shock to the Israelis was manifested in many ways, most devastatingly in the rigidity with which the Israeli force clung to its own doctrine, preventing any flexibility in response.

> Neither the divisional nor the front commanders were coming to grips with the new reality. Instead they clung mechanically to Dovecote [the existing Israeli war plan] even after it should have been clear that a single division could not hold the waterline against a five-division crossing and that the air force was unable to take up the slack.[115]

This lack of flexibility had catastrophic effects on the units thrown into the teeth of the Egyptian advance. On the second day of the war, for example, entire armored units of battalion size were destroyed in reckless offensives:

> The Israeli tanks pressed on, however, and one battalion got close to the embankment, within range of the Egyptian's guns and missiles on the towers on the far banks, and got a taste of the same medicine which had wiped out half of [the lead brigade's] tanks the previous day. After losing more than 20 tanks in a few minutes—nearly half of his strength—[brigade commander Col. Gabi] Amir pulled back and reported the situation ....
> When Yaguri and his 190th Battalion pushed aggressively into the area previously chosen by the Egyptians to be killing ground, they

---

[113] Ibid., 501.
[114] Dupuy, *Elusive Victory*, 419.
[115] Rabinovich, *Yom Kippur War*, 119.

found themselves under devastating antitank fire from three directions. Within ten minutes the 190th Battalion was practically annihilated.[116]

Overconfidence pervaded the Israeli force. General Ariel Sharon, commanding an armored division, was particularly prone to this:

> His periodic assertions that the Egyptians were about to break were not supported by events. The IDF was able to deal handily with Egyptian tanks but it had not developed tactics for breaking through entrenched infantry armed with antitank weapons. Since the Egyptian defenses in Sinai were based on entrenched infantry, talk of imminent collapse was unwarranted.[117]

Twice on the second day of the war, Sharon argued for crossing the canal.[118] Given the destruction being wreaked on the IDF over the course of the first week, such an offensive would have been unsustainable.

Sharon was not the only Israeli leader to maintain an unjustified degree of false optimism. General Shmuel Gonen, the overall commander of the Sinai theater, was similarly unrealistic: "His optimism was untempered by the fact that the Egyptian army had less than forty-eight hours before put five divisions across the canal, destroying two-thirds of General Mendler's crack tank division, with no significant losses to itself."[119] Even individual soldiers clung to a belief in the invulnerability of tank forces:

> A twenty-one-year-old tank commander patted Levy [an infantry soldier separated from his unit] on the shoulder and said, "Soldier, you're saved. There is nothing that can stop this tank."...Shortly after the convoy started forward again, the half track and rear tank were hit by RPGs....The [lead] tank resumed movement but after four hundred yards it too was hit.[120]

One of the IDF's key operational failures in the early days of the war was the scarcity of artillery and a failure to use what it had properly. "The most

[116] Dupuy, *Elusive Victory*, 429.
[117] Rabinovich, *Yom Kippur War*, 407.
[118] Ibid., 222 and 225.
[119] Ibid., 223.
[120] Ibid., 226–27.

effective weapon for dealing with the advancing infantry was artillery but there was none."[121] This was not only a failing of Israel's prewar deployments but also a persistent neglect during the early days of the war:

> Nor did [General Shmuel Gonen, commander of the southern front] take into consideration his paucity of artillery, which was more essential than ever now because of the need to surprise the Egyptian infantry wielding antitank weapons. Artillery had lower priority than tanks on the roads into Sinai, and the bulk of the guns would not reach the front till late in the day.[122]

### Air Forces

Like the tank, the air force was held in high esteem. The losses the Egyptians and Syrians imposed on the IDF's air force were similar in scale to those inflicted on the armored forces. "One-eighth of the entire air forces—forty-nine planes—had been shot down in just four days."[123]

> The day's results were calamitous for the air force and for Israel's entire defense posture. Tagar [the air war plan against Egypt] had been aborted and Dougman [the air war plan against Syria] had failed miserably.... [IDF Air Force commander] Peled had warned his senior commanders two days before that they might have to "go into the fire" if the SAMs could not be destroyed. They had gone into the fire and were rapidly being consumed. In the first two days of war, thirty-five planes had been lost and there was little to show for it. The [adversaries'] air defense missiles remained intact.[124]

Israel was never able to even attempt to deliver a knock-out blow to its opponents' air forces. The situation continued to worsen even as its air force was forced by the dire situation on the ground to intervene. The Egyptian defense, however, forced the Israeli Air Force (IAF) to cut back rapidly on its close air support sorties.

> According to one source, 30 to 40 percent of the close air support sorties the IAF flew were lost to ground defenses in the first 72 hours

---

[121] Ibid., 250.
[122] Ibid., 233.
[123] Ibid., 261. See also Pollack, *Arabs at War*, 112.
[124] Rabinovich, *Yom Kippur War*, 179.

of combat....Eventually Major General Peled, the Israeli Air Force Commander, ordered Israeli planes to keep 15 miles away from the Suez Canal in order to keep losses at a manageable level.[125]

This would have pronounced costs for the Israeli counteroffensives, as offensive use of airpower against Arab ground forces had been central to the overall Israeli strategy.

Even Israel's attempts at tactical innovation during the war were flawed by the distortions of the doctrinal blinders imposed by prewar thinking. Rather than undertaking a comprehensive rethinking to adjust to the fundamentally new nature of the air threat, Israel attempted only minor tinkering at the margins, reflecting the hold of doctrinal thinking.[126]

Both Israel's difficulty in dealing with the original situation and the incomplete nature of its wartime response are telling.

FLAWED COUNTERATTACKS

Israel's initial response to the failures of its strategy was flawed and lacked creative thinking. Even its more carefully planned counterattacks later in the war were, as we will see, imbued with the original doctrinal thinking that pervaded the Israeli military.

Israel initiated its first major counterattack early on the third day of the war, October 8, but the lead probes of this attack were crushed:

Just five hundred yard to his front, [armored battalion commander] Adini could see the canal. That was as close as he got. An Egyptian soldier five yards in front of his tank hit the turret with an RPG before he was run down. Adini, wounded, ordered the battalion to pull back. Seven disabled tanks were left behind on the battlefield. Of the fourteen that returned, only seven were still fit for battle.[127]

Similar devastation resulted from battles the next day.[128]

In both cases, the Israelis threw armor, unsupported by infantry or artillery, into the teeth of dug-in, established infantry with capable antitank weapons. The idea that armored forces could not break through such a defense

---

[125] Cordesman and Wagner, *Lessons of Modern War*, 91.
[126] Dupuy, *Elusive Victory*, 472; Rabinovich, *Yom Kippur War*, 176.
[127] Rabinovich, *Yom Kippur War*, 244 (for a similar example of overoptimism, see 248).
[128] Ibid., 280.

to initiate an exploitation phase was apparently inconceivable to the Israelis, because they repeated the error over and over.

The Israelis' first counterattack, on October 8, was a total failure:

> The division had lost some fifty tanks. More grievous was the profound blow to self-confidence. In this first attack initiated by the IDF in Sinai, failure had been total, except for the desperate blocking action at sunset. At times during the battle Adan [division commander for the armored reserve in Golan] had wondered if he would still have a division when the day ended.[129]

General Shazly, the overall commander of the Egyptian forces, gloated about these attacks in his war diaries:

> The enemy has persisted in throwing away the lives of their tank crews. They have assaulted in "penny packet" groupings and their sole tactic remains the cavalry charge. In the latest manifestation, two brigades have driven against 16th Division. Once again, the attack has been stopped with heavy losses. In the past two days [that is, October 7–8] the enemy has lost another 260 tanks. Our strategy always has been to force the enemy to fight on our terms, but we never expected them to cooperate.[130]

The Israeli overconfidence persisted on the Syrian front in the north as well; brigade commanders, overriding their subordinates' concerns about "suicidal" attacks, counted on breaking the morale of the opposition.

Even a week later, as the tide began to turn in favor of the Israelis, their offensives continued to rely on throwing armor-centered formations against entrenched infantry. For example, a key point known as the "Chinese Farm" threatened to choke off the Israeli offensive across the canal and into Egypt proper:

> The Egyptians were still stubbornly clinging to the Chinese Farm. [The Israeli divisional commander] had lost 56 of his 97 tanks. The brigade would lose 128 dead and 62 wounded in the Chinese Farm—tank crewmen and foot soldiers—without causing a significant dent in the

---

[129] Ibid., 252.
[130] Shazly, *Crossing of the Suez,* 240.

Egyptian defenses. By objective standards, the attack was a failure, a bold enterprise that had come undone.[131]

For days, repeated attempts to take this Egyptian infantry stronghold continued to rely primarily on armor.[132] This provides support for both the Doctrinal Confidence Prediction and Depth of Immersion Prediction.

## ISRAELI EXPECTATIONS REGARDING THE DEVELOPMENT OF THE BATTLE

One final set of evidence is particularly telling regarding the degree to which doctrinal differences distorted the perceptions of the Israeli leadership. Over the course of the initial Egyptian offensive, General Gonen, Israel's overall commander of the Sinai theater, kept looking for specific Egyptian probes, main threat offensives, and breakthrough attempts. He could not believe that he was not facing that sort of offensive. Exasperated, he repeatedly insisted that his divisional commanders in the Sinai answer irrelevant questions: "Where are the concentrations [of enemy infantry]? You told me [about] two concentrations in front of the two infantry divisions. Where? Excuse me, you will decide on the two points where you assume that the crossing may take place and only there will you deploy."[133] Not recognizing that the offensive was in fact a dispersed attack across the entire front, Gonen misused his operational reserve by throwing it at a few points, to disastrous effect.[134]

## SUMMARY

The Egyptians had faced Israel with a sort of combat it had not expected. In the air and across the ground, the IDF found itself facing an adversary that found success using weapons and means that differed from its own. After the war, Israel undertook dramatic changes to respond to these failings: "Israel went from a tank and fighter force to a combined arms force."[135] But that was too late for 1973. Defense Minister Dayan summarized the failures:

> We thought our tanks could stop the Egyptians from putting up bridges but we didn't imagine the forest of antitank missiles. The air force had

---

[131] Rabinovich, *Yom Kippur War,* 381.
[132] Ibid., 426–27.
[133] Bar-Joseph, *Watchman Fell Asleep,* 207.
[134] Ibid., 206.
[135] Cordesman and Wagner, *Lessons of Modern War,* 110.

plans for eliminating the antiaircraft missiles but they didn't work. We have to learn life anew. The Arab world has gone to war. They have much power and we must understand that there is no magic formula.[136]

Doctrinal-difference theory makes a major contribution to explaining the outbreak of the Yom Kippur War. The Israeli assessment of the balance of power prior to the war was biased by Israel's own doctrine and its divergence from that of Egypt. The evidence links the doctrinal difference to the central intelligence construct that the consensus historiography puts at the core of Israel's failure to anticipate the Egyptian attack. It has also shown the degree to which the Israeli diplomatic strategy was shaped by that same assessment of the military balance, leading Tel Aviv's diplomats to take a much tougher position than if the assessment had been less biased.

In the pre-1973 period, the history presents more nuanced support for the theory. The basic causal processes that underlie doctrinal-difference theory can be seen: from 1956 through the early 1970s, when both Egypt and Israel approached warfare with rather similar doctrines, a clarity existed in understanding both the overall balance of power and the military signals each side sent. The major outbreak of conflict in this period—the Six Days' War—occurred despite acute pessimism on the Arab side, and was attributed to Soviet manipulation of Egyptian threat perceptions.

Thus, this chapter presents strong evidence for doctrinal-difference theory. Although the early period is mixed due to exogenous factors, the latter period shows precisely the sort of effects predicted by doctrinal-difference theory in many areas, including assessment of the balance of power, interpretation of the other side's bargaining positions, and expectations about the nature of conflict during the war. Doctrinal-difference theory thus enriches our understanding of this crucial conflict.

[136] Rabinovich, *Yom Kippur War*, 257.

# 8

# IMPLICATIONS FOR THEORY AND DANGERS IN THE TAIWAN STRAIT TODAY

THIS STUDY SHOWS how adversaries' doctrinal differences can cause misperception and the failure of attempts at coercion or deterrence, leading to conflict, escalation, and war. In case after case—China, Israel, Egypt, and the United States—we see a country looking at the world through its own military lens and failing to see how the differences between its own and its adversary's military doctrine could impede communication and accurate signaling. In three of the cases, this contributed to deterrence failure and escalation of conflict. In the two cases where the doctrinal differences were smaller, by contrast, communication was easier, misperceptions smaller, and conflict was less likely to escalate to war.

For effective international communication, both sides must share a language of diplomacy. When the language of diplomacy and signaling includes military threats, differences in theories of victory can lead to problems in translation and thus to avoidable conflict. A nation's policymakers in situations similar to those studied here—attempting to deter or compel an adversary with a different doctrine—would do better if they recognized the acute difficulties in such a project and adjust their policies and expectations accordingly.

This final chapter summarizes the results of the five cases, highlights the arguments supported most strongly by each, and acknowledges some shortcomings of the cases and evidence. It then turns to the implications of this research for both theorists and practitioners. Finally, application of doctrinal-difference theory to contemporary Sino-American relations in the Taiwan Strait suggests similar dangers and raises cautions for the future.

## THE RECORD SUPPORTS
## DOCTRINAL-DIFFERENCE THEORY

In three of the five cases examined in this book, deterrence failed and con-flict escalated where adversaries' theories of victory differed deeply. The causal role of doctrinal difference on escalation is clear-cut in the case of the U.S. crossing of the 38th parallel on the Korean Peninsula, and played a supportive role in China's willingness to cross the Yalu River and enter the war. In the third Sino-American case, the fact that the two sides' theories of victory were similar facilitated their mutual communication of intent and of capabilities over Taiwan. In the Middle East cases, during the period of doctrinal similarity before the 1970s, there was no sign of misperception and underestimation, although other factors nevertheless led to war. In contrast, doctrinal differences played a major role in the outbreak of the 1973 war.

The eleven predictions of the book's theory set forth in chapter 2 thus received wide support in all five cases. By contrast, the conventional wis-dom, framed here as the Weakness Hypothesis, received only mixed support: the strength or weakness of the signal did not correlate as closely to out-comes. Using both types of approaches together—Doctrinal-Difference and Weakness—would improve policy.

In all five cases, the outcomes correlate with predictions based on the characterization of the adversaries' theories of victory. This by itself would be thin evidence; much more convincing is the evidence that shows that the process by which the outcome was reached corresponds to the theory's de-tailed predictions. The strongest evidence presented in each of the cases is process-tracing data.

Evidence confirming specific predictions also pervades the historical re-cord. In all five cases, the signals sent reflected the sending nation's theory of victory; the military signals reflected the dominant doctrine on each side. Additionally, in the cases where a state's attempts at coercion failed, there is copious evidence that in each case, the United States, China, or Israel was surprised by the effectiveness of its adversary, as well as by the limitations of its own forces: each side had high expectations of quick victory against its adversary. Instead, what each got was a bloody stalemate that did little to advance its national interests. There was evidence of shock regarding specific tactical issues, the strategic success of the opponent, and that the opponent was even involved in the conflict.

All five cases thus support doctrinal-difference theory: significant differ-ences between adversaries' theories of victory did indeed lead to mispercep-tion, miscommunication, and miscalculation. In turn, these errors played important roles in key deterrence failures in the Korean War and the war of

1973, leading to a substantial worsening of these conflicts. Mistakes and escalation were avoided in the cases where the opposing sides' theories of victory were more similar. The conventional wisdom regarding deterrence failure, which focuses on the "objective" clarity or strength of the signal (reflected in the Weak Signals Hypothesis), did not explain the cases as well as doctrinal-difference theory. (See table 8.1 for a summary of the cases.)

Further research could advance understanding of the doctrinal-difference hypotheses. Learning between the same two adversaries might be illustrated by cases from the U.S.-Vietnamese War: the 1962 decision by China to support the North Vietnamese; the escalations following the 1964 Gulf of Tonkin incident; and Chinese attempts to deter the United States from widening the war in 1965 and 1966. Other cases might focus on crisis diplomacy between China and another country that was not as far ahead of China technologically and that had less divergent doctrine and theory of victory, such as the Sino-Vietnamese War of 1979 or the Sino-Indian War of 1962. Other promising cases might be found in the history of World War II, particularly (as discussed in chapter 2) the assessments of blitzkrieg by Germany's opponents in the interwar period. The Napoleonic period offers promising cases, given the range of conflict that occurred. So does the pair of U.S.-Yugoslavia/Serbia crises of the 1990s. Cases from the Crimean War, the Sino-Indian war of 1962, or the Austro-Prussian War might also be instructive. In many of these cases, doctrinal-difference theory is likely to enrich our understanding of the sources of these conflicts.

TABLE 8.1
Results of Cases

| Case | Doctrinal Differences | Outcome | Misperception Hypothesis | Escalation Hypothesis | Weakness Hypothesis |
|------|-----------|---------|--------------|------------|----------|
| U.S. crosses the 38th parallel | Large | Deterrence failure | Strongly supported | Strongly supported | Weakly supported |
| China crosses the Yalu | Large | Deterrence failure | Moderately supported | Moderately supported (other explanations) | Not supported |
| China postpones Taiwan invasion | Small | Deterrence success | Strongly supported | Moderately supported (thin evidence) | Weakly supported |
| Pre-1970s Middle East | Small | Mix of spirals and deterrence success | Moderately supported | Weakly supported (spirals explain exceptional 1967 war) | Not supported |
| 1973 Israeli-Egyptian War | Large | Deterrence failure | Strongly supported | Strongly supported | Not supported |

## IMPLICATIONS FOR THEORY

This study contributes to several different theoretical literatures in political science, most importantly the large one on deterrence. Deterrence is often more difficult than many analysts posit. Achieving successful deterrence by making credible threats requires understanding how the adversary will interpret those threats. Although the existing literature has paid substantial attention to the Weakness Hypothesis, which emphasizes the importance of being able to back up a deterrent threat (credibility), this study shows that understanding how an adversary perceives power and how it may communicate threats is also critical. Net assessments, weighing the balance within particular dyads, are insufficient.

Focusing on both sides' perceptions as influenced by their theories of victory can enhance the accuracy of analysis. This requires detailed knowledge of the adversary that a country is trying to influence, which requires strong language skills and deep understanding of other countries, their history, and their military culture. For someone who is already trained in these areas, information regarding national approaches to military strategy is accessible, because even relatively closed societies often publish their doctrinal debates in open sources.[1] Lack of language and cultural knowledge is harder to remedy; thus doctrinal-difference theory shows how the neglect of area studies in the United States threatens national security.[2]

This study also contributes to the formal literature on the causes of war that views war as a bargaining failure.[3] That literature identifies one of the primary sources of such failures as deliberately created informational asymmetry, due to leaders' incentives to keep secrets and make misrepresentations. Doctrinal-difference theory draws attention to a different informational problem: opacity and perceptual bias. There are times when the source of informational asymmetries is not each side's incentive to misrepresent, but each side's perceptual bias, which hampers its ability to see information in the same way as its opponent does. This is the case even when one side is sending signals of its capabilities and its intent in an attempt to communicate clearly. Such informational asymmetries may be almost unavoidable and

[1]  See the discussion of this point in Eliot A. Cohen, "Toward Better Net Assessment: Rethinking the European Conventional Balance," *International Security* 13, no. 1 (1988): 86.

[2]  Peter J. Katzenstein, "Area and Regional Studies in the United States," *PS: Political Science and Politics* 34, no. 4 (2001).

[3]  Bruce Bueno de Mesquita, "An Expected Utility Theory of International Conflict," *American Political Science Review* 74 (1980).

are deeply ingrained. This further undermines arguments in favor of the rationality of most decisions to go to war.[4] Rather, it emphasizes the pervasive dangers of false optimism.[5]

This project also contributes to the literature on the effects of military doctrine. One link between military doctrines and crisis outcomes is already well understood: scholars have identified how offensive military doctrines can worsen the security dilemma and increase the propensity for spirals.[6] However, this project points to another potential problem that traces its roots to a related independent variable, that of differing military doctrines.

Many scholars of strategic coercion preach general lessons that are similar to those of this study regarding the dangers of "mirror imaging" and the importance of understanding the adversary's distinct perspective.[7] Keith Payne argues that the solution to problems of post–Cold War deterrence is to "examine as closely as possible the particular opponent's thinking—its beliefs and thought filters—to better anticipate its likely behavior in response to U.S. deterrence policies, and structure those policies accordingly."[8]

The existing literature on "putting yourself in your adversary's shoes" generally focuses on considering the opponent's national interests, asking how important a specific piece of territory is, or whether a particular concession would be difficult to make. This alone, however, is not enough. As this study demonstrates, policymakers must understand how their adversary assesses power, both its own and that of others; this requires understanding its perspective on effective military doctrines, that is, its theory of victory.

This project highlights the importance of opening up the "black box" of the state. The dominant view in political science is that the most important insights into international relations come from studying the international

[4] James D. Fearon, "Rationalist Explanations for War," *International Organization* 49, no. 3 (1995); Bueno de Mesquita, "Expected Utility Theory."

[5] See footnote 2 in chapter 1.

[6] Jack L. Snyder, *The Ideology of the Offensive: Military Decision Making and the Disasters of 1914* (Ithaca: Cornell University Press, 1984); Stephen Van Evera, "The Cult of the Offensive and the Origins of the First World War," in *Military Strategy and the Origins of the First World War: An International Security Reader,* ed. Steven E. Miller (Princeton: Princeton University Press, 1985); Barry R. Posen, *Inadvertent Escalation: Conventional War and Nuclear Risks* (Ithaca: Cornell University Press, 1991); Robert Jervis, *The Illogic of American Nuclear Strategy* (Ithaca: Cornell University Press, 1984).

[7] Alexander L. George, *Presidential Decisionmaking in Foreign Policy: The Effective Use of Information and Advice* (Boulder, Colo.: Westview Press, 1980), 66–67; Hans Morgenthau and Kenneth Thompson, *Politics among Nations: The Struggle for Power and Peace,* 6th ed. (New York: McGraw-Hill, 1985), chapter 32.

[8] Keith B. Payne, *The Fallacies of Cold War Deterrence and a New Direction* (Lexington: University Press of Kentucky, 2001), xi.

system and the relations among its units, that is, states.[9] This project suggests, however, that not all of the elements important to explaining the outbreak of war come from state-level variables; substate variables must also be considered. Specifically, the nature of thinking about how to win wars generally comes from within a state's military. Ignoring such factors sacrifices too much at the altar of parsimony.

## IMPLICATIONS FOR POLICY

Attempts at coercion of one sort or another are frequent in international politics. The United States has done this in more than half a dozen major cases just since the end of the Cold War: Iraq in 1991 and 2003, Somalia in 1992, Haiti in 1994, Yugoslavia in 1995, Serbia in 1999, and Afghanistan in 2001. It is remarkable how often such attempts fail, even when the nation attempting coercion is, like the United States, dramatically and visibly more powerful than the target nation. This book helps to explain such failures.

This book also lays out a path for states to avoid such dangers. Deterrence theory has long emphasized the importance of assessing what an adversary values in order to enhance coercive threats. However, that may often be insufficient. For deterrence or compellence to succeed, states must also understand how the target understands military power. In order to send an effective deterrent or compellent signal, states must understand the perceptual lens through which that signal will be evaluated. This requires understanding the adversary's theory of victory.

Perhaps the most important policy implication of this study is the reminder that coercion is very, very difficult. State leaders who understand this fact will restrain their expectations about their ability to shape other countries' behavior, and instead recognize that target states with differing doctrinal lenses will tend to misunderstand threats. Compellence and deterrence seem to promise victory on the cheap: rather than using brute force to achieve one's goals, a state may hope that threats backed up by limited uses of force might suffice. However, this study shows how compellence and deterrence will often fail, leaving the threatening state in a position where brute force will have to be used to achieve its goals. For many goals, this more costly policy will not be worthwhile.

This book's conclusions are particularly relevant today for two reasons. First, the expensive, high-technology developments of the "revolution in military

[9] Kenneth N. Waltz, *Theory of International Politics* (New York: McGraw-Hill, 1979); John J. Mearsheimer, *The Tragedy of Great Power Politics* (New York: W.W. Norton and Company, 2001).

affairs" (RMA) mean that U.S. military views of warfare will increasingly diverge from those of adversaries.[10] The U.S. theory of victory will increasingly emphasize technologies such as precision-guided munitions, space-based intelligence gathering, electronic warfare, information warfare, stealth, heavy strategic bombers, standoff weaponry, "total battlespace awareness," and systems integration. In every single one of those areas, the United States has and is likely to maintain a substantial lead on the rest of the world.

When, therefore, the United States sends deterrent or compellent signals relying on the threat or actual use of this sort of military power, it cannot assume that its adversaries will view U.S. forces as Washington does. For instance, Saddam Hussein is said to have believed that "the United States relies on the Air Force, [but] the Air Force has never been the decisive factor in the history of war."[11] This may well have led Iraq into misperceptions and miscalculations before the 1991 Gulf War.[12]

Such problems are likely to become even more pronounced as the United States continues to invest heavily in high-technology weapons programs and systems integration. Over time, the gap between the American theory of victory and that of nearly all of its potential adversaries is likely to widen. The risks due to differing theories of victory will rise accordingly, and must be guarded against.

The dangers that this book highlights are severe and can lead to unnecessary conflict, but they are not inevitable. It is true that the independent variable of this study is not directly manipulable by policymakers: it is not easy for a nation to change its own theory of victory, let alone that of another nation. Theories of victory are deeply rooted in systemic pressures, technological opportunities, bureaucratic procedures, and historical experience. However, several specific steps could help ameliorate the problems identified by this book.

First, a state can strive to tailor its signals to its adversary's perceptual framework—that is, to its theory of victory. Policymakers' signals would then be easier for the other side to interpret correctly. Although one side's military is not usually optimized to implement the other's doctrine, most would

---

[10] For descriptions of the RMA, see Donald Rumsfeld, "Transforming the Military," *Foreign Affairs* 81, no. 3 (2002); Vice Admiral Arthur K. Cebrowski, retired, *Planning a Revolution: Mapping the Pentagon's Transformation*, WebMemo #292 (Washington, D.C.: Heritage Foundation, June 12, 2003).

[11] Merrill A. McPeak, "Leave the Flying to Us," *Washington Post,* June 5, 2003, 33.

[12] A similar dynamic seems at work in the lesson's Hussein took from the Al-Khafji battle regarding his forces ability to maneuver despite U.S. technical prowess; see Kevin M. Woods, *The Mother of All Battles: Saddam Hussein's Strategic Plan for the Persian Gulf War* (Annapolis, Md.: Naval Institute Press, 2008), 18–27. A similar case could be made regarding Saddam Hussein's expectations for Iraq's various guerrilla strategies prior to the Iraq war launched in 2003.

include some types of forces that are parallel to those of the other; using these types of forces could enhance the clarity of the signal. Thus, for example, if the United States in 1950 had left a substantial ground presence in Korea, this would have sent a clearer signal to China than airpower deployments. The result might have been a different conversation between Kim and Mao in May 1950. If China had deployed troops to North Korea earlier—in August, before the U.S. landings in Inchon—this might have deterred the United States from crossing the 38th parallel in October. At times, material conditions will not allow a state to send precisely the signal it would prefer, but even the cost of very expensive signals must be weighed against the cost of inadvertent war.

Second, leaders could also "red-team" their own net assessments of the adversary's forces. This does not simply mean instructing intelligence analysts to make worst-case assumptions.[13] Rather, analysts and scholars who are experts on the country being studied should be asked what they understand the adversary to believe regarding its own forces. The aim of such red-teaming is not to help a state assess the overall balance of power better, but rather to understand better what its adversary thinks the balance of power is, and thus to provide insight into how the adversary views the world. This will facilitate communication and thus make strategic coercion more likely to succeed.

Third, developing military-to-military ties can help each side understand the other's theory of victory, improving the prospects for accurate communication to avoid unnecessary escalation. Doctrines come alive during exercises in ways that could not be predicted on the basis of written documentation (which may, in any case, not even be available to outsiders). A deeper engagement with an adversary's military and intelligence structures (who often conduct such military analysis) can address this.

## PRESENT DANGERS: DOCTRINAL DIFFERENCES IN THE TAIWAN STRAIT

Doctrinal differences pose dangers in Sino-American relations today. This section begins by developing brief sketches of current American and Chinese military doctrines, noting their substantial differences. Thereafter, it speculates about the sorts of misperceptions that might arise, given the difficulties

---

[13]  On the dangers of simple-minded "worst-casing," see Jane Kellett-Cramer, "National Security Panics: Overestimating Threats to National Security" (PhD diss., Massachusetts Institute of Technology, 2002); Seymour M. Hersh, "Selective Intelligence (Annals of National Security)," *New Yorker,* May 12, 2003.

each side has already displayed in accurately assessing the balance of power and the challenges the two sides will face in sending and interpreting signals in a crisis.

The Sino-American relationship poses the greatest risk of great-power war in the world today. Although there are sources of stability in the bilateral relationship—extensive trade flows, regular diplomatic contact, and cooperation on some regional issues[14]—the issue of Taiwan presents acute challenges for policymakers in both countries.

At the broadest level, realist factors suggest that this region is likely to be vigorously contested by both great powers. Additionally, nationalism—one of the most powerful forces in international affairs—increasingly separates Taiwan and China. Despite the lowering of bilateral tensions following the 2008 elections in Taiwan,[15] the increasing plurality of Taiwan's population is shifting their sense of identity away from being "Chinese" toward being "Taiwanese."[16] Doctrinal-difference theory suggests that overlaying those two problems is another set of concerns that heighten the dangers of conducting crisis diplomacy.

Although conflict has been avoided in recent years despite significant tension, this should not lead to complacency. The Cuban Missile Crisis was also navigated without escalation to global thermonuclear war. No one would counsel repeating that crisis a dozen times. So much of any international crisis depends on inherently unpredictable events that cannot be anticipated or controlled. When situations possess particular potential for destructive inadvertent escalation, policymakers should be particularly cautious. The risks in the Taiwan Strait are extremely high, and doctrinal differences only exacerbate them.

CHINESE AND AMERICAN DOCTRINE TODAY

Through its involvement in a number of intense military conflicts since the end of the Cold War, the U.S. military has honed a robust set of doctrinal practices. At the broadest level, in the event of conflict the U.S. intention is

[14] See Christopher P. Twomey, "Explaining Chinese Foreign Policy toward North Korea: Navigating between the Scylla and Charybdis of Proliferation and Instability," *Journal of Contemporary China* 17, no. 55 (2008).

[15] On the long-term outlook, see Robert S. Ross, "Taiwan's Fading Independence Movement," *Foreign Affairs* 85, no. 2 (2006).

[16] David D. Yang, "Classing Ethnicity: Class, Ethnicity, and the Mass Politics of Taiwan's Democratic Transition," *World Politics* 59, no. 4 (2007); Melissa J. Brown, *Is Taiwan Chinese? The Impact of Culture, Power, and Migration on Changing Identities* (Berkeley: University of California Press, 2004); Suisheng Zhao, *A Nation-State by Construction: Dynamics of Modern Chinese Nationalism* (Palo Alto: Stanford University Press, 2004).

to go on the offensive with overwhelming force aimed at the adversary's key centers of gravity.[17] These include command and control assets and the most potent elements of the enemy's combat power. The United States would expect to attack these within days, even hours, of the start of a conflict. Elements of the military infrastructure are likely to be targeted as well. Models for such a campaign include the opening days of the 2003 Iraq War with the "Shock and Awe" air campaign and the associated "Thunder Run" to Bagdad by fast-moving armored units;[18] the air campaign against Serbia to compel Belgrade to desist from oppressing Kosovo;[19] and the 1991 Gulf War.[20] Central to the Pentagon's conception of military power is reliance on advanced technology, and specifically airpower, precision-guided munitions, and command, control, communications, and intelligence (C[3]I) systems. Similarly, as American strategic doctrine continues to evolve along the lines implied in the 2001 Nuclear Posture Review, it is likely that nuclear forces will become more integrated with conventional forces.[21]

Chinese doctrine presents a sharp contrast in many areas. The primary aim of Chinese strategic development is the creation of options for coercing Taiwan while deterring U.S. involvement. China's nuclear doctrine also has a role to play in this arena.

China is engaged in an effort to develop asymmetric strategies that might be used in a coercive manner to counter current American conventional dominance.[22] That is, it seeks to develop options specifically for use to pressure

[17] In the wake of the failures in the Iraq War, the Pentagon undertook major doctrinal reform. Nevertheless, it is unlikely that the current (relative) emphasis on stabilization operations is likely to be accepted as a core element of the Army's doctrine, nor that of the other services, in the long term. For a discussion of the doctrinal debate, see Michael R. Gordon, "After Hard-Won Lessons, Army Doctrine Revised," *New York Times*, February 2, 2008.

[18] Michael R. Gordon and Bernard E. Trainor, *Cobra II: The Inside Story of the Invasion and Occupation of Iraq* (New York: Pantheon Books, 2006).

[19] Benjamin S. Lambeth, *NATO's Air War for Kosovo: A Strategic and Operational Assessment*, MR-1365-AF (Santa Monica, Calif.: RAND, 2001); Barry R. Posen, "The War for Kosovo: Serbia's Political-Military Strategy," *International Security* 24, no. 4 (2000).

[20] Michael R. Gordon and Bernard E. Trainor, *The Generals' War: The Onside Story of the Conflict in the Gulf* (Boston: Little, Brown, 1995).

[21] Walter Pincus, "Pentagon May Have Doubts on Preemptive Nuclear Moves," *Washington Post*, September 19, 2005, 5; American Association for the Advancement of Science Nuclear Weapons Complex Assessment Committee, *The United States Nuclear Weapons Program: The Role of the Reliable Replacement Warhead* (Washington D.C.: American Association for the Advancement of Science, April 2007).

[22] Thomas J. Christensen, "Posing Problems without Catching Up: China's Rise and Challenges for U.S. Security Policy," *International Security* 25, no. 4 (2001); Office of the Secretary of Defense, *The Military Power of the People's Republic of China: Annual Report to Congress* (Washington, D.C.: Department of Defense, 2005); David L. Shambaugh, *Modernizing China's Military: Progress,*

the United States.[23] The extensive discussions within China of so-called assassin's mace (*shashou jian*) strategies and weapons are evidence.[24] These strategies explicitly target American vulnerabilities with innovative concepts of operations and newly developed weapons.

Weapons do not determine doctrine, but they do signify priorities in Chinese doctrinal thinking. China has imported capable heavy-missile destroyers and deployed scores of advanced diesel submarines that are all designed to penetrate the defenses provided to U.S. carrier battle groups by the Aegis missile defense platforms.[25] Indeed, the Chinese submarine threat far transcends threats to U.S. carriers alone, and poses a wide range of strategic problems for the United States and its partners in the region.[26] Similarly, China has obtained SU-30 long-range strike fighters designed to counter American carrier-based air assets, and engaged in very substantial modernization (including accuracy improvements) of its growing ballistic missile arsenal.[27] There are signs that China is developing an operational maneuvering ballistic missile capability that could be used against U.S. carriers.[28] China is integrating many of these capabilities into a set of "anti-access" tactics. These could be used to deny the United States the ability to utilize any area within a few hundred miles of China for military purposes.

All of these Chinese strategic systems could be used in a tactically offensive manner, attacking what Beijing perceives as key centers of gravity for America or for Taiwan. In most cases, the utility of such systems would be coercive: their mere existence gives them some utility for deterring U.S. involvement.[29]

---

*Problems, and Prospects* (Berkeley: University of California Press, 2002), chapter 3: "Doctrine and Training"; Dennis J. Blasko, *The Chinese Army Today: Tradition and Transformation for the 21st Century* (New York: Routledge, 2006).

[23] In this sense, the parallels with the Egyptian doctrinal development in 1973 explicitly focused on a single adversary, Israel, may prove particularly instructive.

[24] These discussions are reported in Office of the Secretary of Defense, *Military Power of the PRC.*

[25] Eric A. McVadon, rear admiral (U.S. Navy, retired), *Recent Trends in China's Military Modernization* (Washington, D.C.: U.S.-China Economic and Security Review Commission, September 15, 2005).

[26] Lyle Goldstein and Williamson Murray, "Undersea Dragons: China's Maturing Submarine Force," *International Security* 28, no. 4 (2004). For a more sanguine view, see Michael Glosny, "Strangulation from the Sea? A PRC Submarine Blockade of Taiwan," *International Security* 28, no. 4 (2004).

[27] China has nearly fifteen hundred M-9 and M-11 short-range missiles with which it could threaten Taiwan.

[28] Office of the Secretary of Defense, *Military Power of the People's Republic of China: Annual Report to Congress* (Washington, D.C.: Department of Defense, May 5, 2008).

[29] This is precisely what comes through in the discussions on many of these tactics reported by Christensen, "Posing Problems."

This might be contrasted with a strategy aimed at more completely defeating a potential adversary, which the PLA recognizes would be beyond its means.

Several of China's new strategic capabilities have potential applications beyond a conventional battle in the Taiwan Strait. Although nuclear weapons have been an element in Chinese military capabilities since 1964, antisatellite weapons and offensive cyberwarfare are more recent capabilities. Since at least 2007 the Chinese have engaged in several tests of a kinetic antisatellite missile.[30] They have also apparently used a ground-based laser to dazzle an American satellite.[31] Such capabilities could threaten satellite communications and intelligence gathering capabilities that are critical force multipliers for the U.S. military.

China also has been identified as the source of a large number of cyber attacks on government computers in the United States and elsewhere.[32] Although the Chinese government denies that these are deliberate government or government-sanctioned attacks, several sources from outside the PRC insist that the attacks emanate from within China. While most such attacks have been unsophisticated, in a few cases more significant penetrations have been reported. This is yet another asymmetric tactic designed specifically to target American vulnerabilities.

The United States has not deployed similar capabilities. The U.S. tested antisatellite systems in the 1980s, but this is not an important element of U.S. military strategy today. Although the scope of U.S. cyberwar capabilities is not publicly discussed, little publicly available information suggests development of a large offensive capability.

China is substantially modernizing its nuclear missiles and nuclear warheads.[33] It is deploying road-mobile, solid-fueled ICBMs far less vulnerable to a "bolt from the blue" first strike than China's previously fielded systems. It is also in the process of deploying a small fleet of more reliable ballistic missile submarines and its force will eventually include long-range sea-launched ballistic missiles (SLBMs). Nevertheless, the core doctrine underlying China's

---

[30] General James E. Cartwright, "Testimony at Armed Services Subcommittee on Strategic Forces," *U.S. Senate,* March 28, 2007. Also see Geoffrey Forden, "How China Loses the Coming Space War (3 Part Series)," *Wired News,* January 2008.

[31] Cartwright, "Testimony."

[32] Bryan Krekel, George Bakos, and Christopher Barnett, *Capability of the People's Republic of China to Conduct Cyber Warfare and Computer Network Exploitation* (Washington, D.C.: Prepared for US-China Economic and Security Review Commission, October 9, 2009).

[33] Lyle J. Goldstein, with Andrew S. Erickson, ed., *China's Nuclear Force Modernization* (Newport, R.I.: Naval War College Press, 2005).

force posture—minimum deterrence—has remained fairly consistent.[34] Chinese official statements as well as the views of many analysts portray this as a retaliatory, no-first-use doctrine that aims solely to deter nuclear attack on China, and its size is thought to reflect China's belief that small numbers of deliverable warheads are sufficient for this task:

> Chinese strategists take the concept [of minimum deterrence] as a relative one, defined not only by pure numbers, but more importantly by such key criteria as invulnerability of nuclear forces, assurance of retaliation, and credibility of counter-attack. When a Chinese document says that China intends to possess nuclear weapons only at the minimum (or lowest) level for the needs of self-defense, that means to have the minimum but assured capabilities for a retaliatory second strike.[35]

Given an increased degree of confidence in the reliability of its second-strike capability, China would not be under pressure to dramatically increase the overall size of its arsenal, as it would if it relied on most war-fighting doctrines.

For a range of asymmetric "Assassin's Mace" strategies pursued by Beijing, the "asymmetry" is explicitly defined relative to U.S. strategy. Thus, by definition it is a doctrine or theory of victory very different from that of the United States. Washington deploys force and projects power by fielding well-rounded, balanced forces whose aim is to dominate a particular region for a sustained period; this requires different forces than getting off a few quick devastating strikes to deter an adversary from continuing a course of action and is a pronounced contrast to the Chinese view. Doctrinal-difference theory tells us that these vast differences are likely to pose problems.

## PROSPECTS FOR MISPERCEPTIONS
## DUE TO DIVERGENT DOCTRINAL CULTURES

What do the lessons of the earlier cases, applied to these facets of current Chinese and American doctrine, imply? Substantial differences between Chinese and U.S. doctrines in both the conventional and nuclear arenas will

---

[34] Alastair Iain Johnston, "China's New 'Old Thinking': The Concept of Limited Deterrence," *International Security* 20, no. 3 (1995–96).

[35] Senior Colonel Yunzhu Yao, "Chinese Nuclear Policy and the Future of Minimum Deterrence," in *Perspectives on Sino-American Strategic Nuclear Issues,* ed. Christopher P. Twomey (New York: Palgrave Macmillan, 2008).

pose challenges for both sides in evaluating signals as well as assessing the overall balance of power consistently in any crisis.

*Assessing the Balance of Power*

One of the dangers of doctrinal difference is that states will tend to overestimate the favorability of the balance of power. In this particular case, there has been no empirical test of the actual balance. Instead, one can only look at each side's perceptions about that balance, and tentatively evaluate them. If the two sides have fundamentally contradictory perceptions, then at least one side must be mistaken about who is likely to win in the event of actual combat.

One way to tease out this issue is to pose the question whether either side feels the need to bolster its conventional military position over Taiwan through recourse to nuclear threats or bluster? For example, if the United States felt itself to be in a position of conventional inferiority, it might seek to compensate by enhancing the credibility of its nuclear position, by means of declaratory policy and perhaps by means of forward deployment of nuclear weapons or by other readiness moves. What we see, however, is that, rather than rattling nuclear sabers, both sides appear to believe that the most acute pressures to engage in nuclear escalation will fall on the other side.[36] This indicates that each side is confident of its own conventional position. However, such confidence may be unwarranted or false optimism.

There are other examples of apparent overconfidence, on both sides. U.S. Navy carriers are increasingly vulnerable to various Chinese tactics. Although this is gradually being recognized among some in the civilian leadership in the Pentagon, there has been no innovative thinking about the need to diminish reliance on such easily observed platforms;[37] for example, the "arsenal ship" alternative proposed during the 1990s was panned by so-called naval traditionalists who have emphasized traditional capital ships. Nor has the U.S. Navy shifted toward increased reliance on submarines; procurement rates for such boats remain unchanged from the previous decade.[38] (Indeed,

---

[36] See, e.g., Christopher P. Twomey and Kali Shelor, *U.S.-China Strategic Dialogue, 3rd Annual Meeting, Conference Report* (March 2008), reporting on "track II" meetings bringing together Chinese and American nuclear weapons strategists, analysts, and policymakers in an unofficial and informal setting over three years, at which the perspective outlined in this paragraph has been displayed consistently.

[37] For an exception, see Wayne Hughes, captain (U.S. Navy, retired), "A Bimodal Force for the National Maritme Strategy," *Naval War College Review* 60, no. 2 (2007).

[38] Although at least here, there are calls to address that. *Quadrennial Defense Review Report,* (Washington, D.C.: Department of Defense, February 6, 2006). As yet, they are unfunded, however.

even the degree of antisubmarine warfare competence today is minimal in comparison with its Cold War–era level.[39]) Today, the U.S. Navy remains centered on carriers. Increasingly, this looks dangerously narrow.

In other areas too, the United States has not responded to evident Chinese threats. Regional land bases such as Guam or Okinawa can now be threatened gravely even by conventional Chinese missiles, which have rapidly improved their accuracy in recent years.[40] Simple U.S. moves to enhance concealment, deception, and survivability have not been made. U.S. Air Force officers routinely seem to expect that the United States will be flying combat air patrol (CAP) missions over Chinese airspace on the opening days of any military conflict.[41] This seems unlikely given China's unprecedentedly sophisticated surface-to-air missile systems (developed by Russia). In neither the Iraq wars nor the various Yugoslavia conflicts did the United States face Soviet or Russian first-line systems like those China now uses.

In some of these areas, the beginning of a reaction is apparent in the United States. But doctrinal innovation is challenging for any organization, particularly for one as large as the U.S. Department of Defense. Signs of shifts will not come from a line in a policy statement or a study by an official think tank.[42] Rather doctrinal revision, shifts in training plans, and new procurement patterns are required. This has not happened.

In China too there are signs of unwarranted optimism. China has never faced attack with precision-guided munitions. Although a diffuse "People's War" approach to warfare might not depend on a limited and therefore vulnerable number of command and control nodes, or on specific pieces of military hardware, the People's War approach no longer characterizes the elements of the PLA that would be used against the United States. Today, China would depend on a small number of *Sovremenny* destroyers to attack American carriers. It has several squadrons of SU-30 long-range strike fighters that might be used against U.S. assets, but these would face hundreds of

---

[39] Dozens of conversations with U.S. naval officers across a range of ranks and specialties bear this out.

[40] This threat has long been an emphasis of the Office of Net Assessment's forward-looking studies. Thomas J. Welch, "Warning Indicators for China's Military Transformation," *International Journal of Intelligence and CounterIntelligence* 18, no. 1 (2004). See also David A. Shlapak et al., *A Question of Balance: Political Context and Military Aspects of the China-Taiwan Dispute*, MG-888 (Santa Monica, Calif.: RAND, 2009), 2.

[41] The author has spoken with a half dozen pilots who express this view, as do a smaller number of senior officials.

[42] Indeed, the Depth of Immersion Prediction predicts precisely this pattern: a doctrinal lens will blur the vision of intelligence analysts and think tank scholars less since they are outside its routine implementation.

more advanced U.S. and allied aircraft. It has many short-range missile systems, such as the M-9 and M-11, that are useful against Taiwan, but it would
need the longer range but much scarcer DF-21 missile to attack U.S. bases
or carriers at sea. Both the DF-21 and its C³ISR (command, control, communication, intelligence, surveillance, and reconnaissance) support are highly
vulnerable to U.S. attack. Some U.S. observers have argued that "China is a
cruise missile sponge." However, this is only the case for infrastructure targets
vulnerable to any American coercive campaign; the military target set pertinent to such an attack is considerably smaller.

Even without a sophisticated net assessment, it appears clear that neither
side has realized the extent of its own dependence on capabilities that can be
put at risk by an opponent that may well might attack in a radically different
way than either has previously faced. Each such instance of overoptimism occurs in an area where the two sides have radically different doctrines. Each
has worrying implications for crisis stability.

*How Does Each Side Send Military Signals in Crises?*
The second concern highlighted by doctrinal-difference theory is that two
sides whose doctrines are different may have difficulty in signaling each
other clearly during a crisis. Although there have been remarkably few
militarized crises between the United States and China in the past decade,
there have been a few low level-incidents that show how each side chooses
to send military signals of its commitment and intentions. However, as predicted by doctrinal-difference theory, these signals are shaped by the military logic of the doctrines of their respective militaries. This does not bode
well for communication between the two powers in an intense crisis in the
future.

In the past decade, there have been a number of instances when China
appeared to be trying to use a display of force to emphasize its national security interests or send other signals. Most prominently, in late 1995 and
early 1996, Beijing launched several short-range ballistic missiles at desig-
nated target zones near Taiwan to protest the latter's moves toward independence.[43] More recently, a number of incidents have involved submarines:
in November 2004, during a period of relative tension between Japan and
China involving heightened nationalism in both countries, a *Han*-class
Chinese nuclear attack submarine apparently circumnavigated the islands

---

[43] See Robert S. Ross, "The 1995–96 Taiwan Strait Confrontation: Coercion, Credibility, and
the Use of Force," *International Security* 25, no. 2 (2000).

of Okinawa and Guam.[44] Chinese diesel submarines have surfaced near or shadowed American carriers on several occasions in the past few years.[45] In September 2005 China deployed a five-ship flotilla into the Chunxiao region of the East China Sea, which both China and Japan claim. The flagship of this group was an advanced *Sovremenny*-class destroyer.[46] On January 11, 2007, the PRC destroyed an aging weather satellite in a test of an antisatellite missile.[47] Each of these steps has a especially large resonance in the context of Chinese doctrine.

On the nuclear side, the record is, of course, more sparse. In 1969, during the Sino-Soviet border clash, China pushed two nuclear tests to completion in unprecedentedly rapid succession and rushed missiles to its Second Artillery, which had been placed was on alert.[48] Since then, however, there have only been statements from various senior Chinese officers. In 1995 Lieutenant General Xiong Guangkai is said to have made a deterrent threat, asserting to Chas Freeman, then a Pentagon official, that the United States would be unwilling to trade Los Angeles for Taipei. More recently, in remarks in an informal press conference, a lower-ranking officer, Major General Zhu Chenghu, said "if the Americans draw their missiles and [precision]-guided ammunition onto the target zone on China's territory, I think we will have to respond with nuclear weapons."[49] These are all fairly general signals, suggesting that China is considering some form of retaliation that emphasizes countervalue targeting.

Although an American military audience might understand some of these signals accurately, the Pentagon would likely choose a different approach to

[44] James C. Bussert, "Oil May Be Focal Point of Sino-Japanese Dispute," *SIGNAL Magazine,* November 2006.

[45] A *Song*-class submarine surfaced near the USS *Kitty Hawk* operating near Japan in October of 2006. In late November 2007 there was a similar incident. "Report: Chinese Ships Confronted Kitty Hawk," *Kyodo News Service,* January 1, 2008.

[46] Bussert, "Oil May Be Focal Point of Sino-Japanese Dispute." Immediately thereafter, Beijing announced it was establishing a "naval reserve squadron" to patrol this region. "Foreign Ministry Spokesman Qin Gang's Press Conference on 29 September 2005," available at http://wcm.fmprc.gov.cn/ce/cein/eng/fyrth/fyrth/t214751.htm.

[47] Forden, "How China Loses the Coming Space War (3 Part Series)." Arguing that the test was not intended to signal anything, but rather was a product of Chinese bureaucratic and scientific processes, see Jeffrey Lewis, *A Different View of China's ASAT Test* (Washington, D.C.: Carnegie Endowment for International Peace, November 13, 2007).

[48] The tests were mere days apart; more typically a year or so would have separated such events. John Wilson Lewis and Litai Xue, *Imagined Enemies: China Prepares for Uncertain War* (Palo Alto: Stanford University Press, 2006), 59–70.

[49] Quotation from Office of the Secretary of Defense, *Military Power of the People's Republic of China: Annual Report to Congress* (Washington, D.C.: Department of Defense, May 23, 2006), 28.

signaling itself. At the center of any American military signaling to China would be deployment of aircraft carriers. This was the primary means of signaling in the 1995–96 Taiwan Crisis,[50] and it is used routinely. For instance, the March 2008 Taiwanese presidential elections were accompanied by the noisy deployment of the *Nimitz* to the region.[51] Another U.S. signal frequently used is the deployment of nuclear-attack submarines toward Chinese waters.[52] Heavy bombers (B-2s) and advanced fighters have also been deployed to Northeast Asia as well.[53]

Washington engages in rather less nuclear signaling today than it did at the height of the Cold War. During that period, quite specific steps were frequently used, such as bomber patrols and heightened alert levels for strategic forces. The nuclear rhetoric emanating from U.S. military sources emphasized American counterforce capabilities. In recent crises, however, the United States has sharply limited its use of nuclear bluster. Instead, vague statements are made about "keeping all options on the table," typically in a context of addressing deeply buried targets, which emphasizes a counterforce role for nuclear weapons.

Thus, there is a substantial difference in the way the two sides chose to send military signals, particularly on the conventional side.

*How Does Each Side Interpret the Signals?*
The record of sending military signals between China and the United States is thin, and it is difficult for outsiders to assess how each side has interpreted those signals. States tend to keep this sort of assessment and deliberation extremely closely held (because of this, previous chapters of this book focused on decades-old examples). Thus, the persuasiveness of the doctrinal-difference argument must rely on the evidence and arguments presented elsewhere in the book. However, a few points may be made.

---

[50] Ashton B. Carter and William J. Perry, *Preventive Defense: A New Security Strategy for America* (Washington, D.C.: Brookings Institution Press, 1999), chapter 3, "Dealing with a Rising China," esp. 92–99.

[51] Sui-lan Lo, "The Deployment of US Aircraft Carrier USS Nimitz in Japan May Have Something to Do with Taiwan's Presidential Election," *Asia Times Online WWW-Text,* February 2, 2008, OSC Translated Text #CPP20080219436001.

[52] Three such submarines have been shifted to Guam. See Christopher P. Twomey, "Grasping Tactical Success, Missing Strategic Opportunity in US China Policy since 9/11," *Asian Survey* 47, no. 4 (2007). Additional submarines are routinely deployed to Northeast Asia in times of tension. See, for instance, "U.S. Nuclear Submarine Arrives in Busan for Drill," *Korea Times,* February 2, 2008.

[53] B-2s have rotated through Guam during times of tension (especially on the Korean Peninsula); the first overseas deployment of the F-22 occurred in Japan in 2007.

The one recent case of intense signaling provides only ambiguous evidence. Some argue that the Chinese viewed the U.S. deployment of carrier battle groups to the Taiwan Strait region in 1995–96 as a strong signal.[54] However, the evidence is not entirely clear; Beijing's view of the crisis overall has been described by many observers as "successful" from its own perspective by showing China is willing to engage the United States militarily.[55] Interviews in Beijing in June 2005 with half a dozen strategic analysts from a range of think tanks supported that view. This would suggest that Beijing did not correctly understand the signal that the United States was trying to send.

Shifting perspectives to consider American interpretation of Chinese signaling, strategists in the United States have debated the implications of the 2007 Chinese ASAT test extensively. However, rather than reinvigorating a recourse to diplomacy or forcing a reconsideration of U.S. support for Taiwan as China presumably wished, the American response seems to have been to increase its own space capabilities. The subsequent U.S. downing of its own defunct satellite has little technical rationale; an attempt to "send a signal" to the Chinese seems to be the best remaining explanation.[56] Thus, rather than deterring an American challenge, the effect of China's signal may have been to provoke a spiral with the United States.

Instances of vague nuclear threats from senior PLA officers, described above, did not change the American calculus of the strategic relationship either. Since the United States is focused on the war-fighting elements of nuclear strategy, assertions of China's countervalue capacity did not lead to any fundamental rethinking in Washington or Omaha.

In other areas, the discussion must be entirely speculative. Were China to surge its heavy attack destroyers, for example, it seems unlikely that the United States would recognize the depth of concern the Chinese might intend to convey, since this is a force the U.S. Navy feels comfortable addressing. A surge of Chinese submarines might receive more U.S. attention, but here, too, for reasons discussed in the balance of power section above, the U.S. military has recently tended to underappreciate this threat. China is likely to undervalue or misperceive U.S. signals that centered on precision-guided

---

[54] Pointing to several pieces of evidence on this point is Ross, "The 1995–96 Taiwan Strait Confrontation," 118–21.

[55] Suisheng Zhao, ed., *Across the Taiwan Strait: Mainland China, Taiwan, and the 1995–1996 Crisis* (New York: Routledge, 1999). In particular, see You Ji, "Changing Leadership Consensus: The Domestic Context of War Games," in ibid.

[56] Yousaf Butt, "Technical Comments on the U.S. Satellite Shootdown," *Bulletin of the Atomic Scientists*, Web edition (August 21, 2008).

munition delivery systems (heavy bombers in particular).[57] Similarly, given the Chinese doctrinal view on the limited operational utility of nuclear weapons, here too Beijing is not likely to understand the enhancements to capability that such weapons might provide for U.S. military forces under the recent evolution of nuclear thinking. (Indeed, Chinese analysts seem blissfully dismissive of Russian work on "fourth generation" warheads that would be primarily of tactical or operational, rather than strategic, utility.)

One important mitigating factor in this arena is that the development of Chinese asymmetric strategies focuses explicitly on their utility against American forces. This might reduce the challenges posed by such large doctrinal differences because it is explicitly based on China's close study of U.S. doctrine. Similarly, the specifics of Chinese doctrine are receiving added analytic attention in the United States. Even so, doctrinal cultures tend to emerge and harden over time, which could lead the PLA to excessive confidence in the strategies it practices and employs. Similarly, the attention Chinese doctrine has received in analytic and political spheres in Washington has only imperfectly permeated through to operational commanders. Both these would make the conduct of military statecraft more challenging. The danger is that Washington and Beijing might misperceive the overall balance of power and the degree of intent communicated by military signals when the other side's doctrinal culture or theory of victory is different from its own.

## IMPLICATIONS

The interaction between Chinese and American doctrines in the Taiwan Strait is dangerous for many reasons. Taiwan is geostrategically important, is characterized by an emergent nationalism, and exists in a military situation characterized by first mover advantages, worsening the security dilemma.[58] Doctrinal differences exacerbate these concerns.

This book shows that the lens of military doctrine can contribute to our understanding of important events in international politics even beyond what an analysis of military capabilities alone can explain. In historic cases in the Far East and Middle East, doctrinal differences have complicated the

---

[57] Both sides, however, seem to share a common view regarding the utility of tactical aircraft today; thus, deployments of Chinese SU-30 or U.S. F-22 fighters would be more likely to send a clear message to the other side.

[58] On the empirical points, see Christensen, "Posing Problems." On the dangers this poses, see Stephen Van Evera, *Causes of War: Power and the Roots of Conflict* (Ithaca: Cornell University Press, 1999).

assessment of the balance of power and the interpretation of signals during crises. The description of contemporary Chinese and American doctrines suggests that we should be concerned about similar misperceptions today. Both Washington and Beijing must carefully tailor their signaling to avoid these pitfalls.

The U.S. military believes it has strategic options to address Chinese military tactics; indeed, Washington often seems complacent about the military balance.[59] U.S. strategies themselves would, however, often require rapid escalation. For instance, the best solution to the threat posed by the *Sovremenny* destroyers is to sink them long before they are in a position to attack American carriers. The United States ought to plan, similarly, to bomb Chinese submarine ports from the air before any surge occurs, because the best place to catch deploying quiet diesel subs is as they exit their ports; antisubmarine warfare against quiet diesels in the deep sea is far more challenging. Maneuvering ballistic missiles may be too fast for terminal intercept by missile defense systems; the incentive exists, therefore, to destroy the adversary's ground-based surveillance assets such as over-the-horizon radars so as to render the missile impotent. Thus China should expect an early U.S. strike, as required by all of these tactics. The United States seems willing to contemplate the early-strike option, but it is not at all clear that China understands this American confidence, stemming as it does from a set of rapid attacks that China has not faced before.

Any military signals either side might send in such a circumstance might themselves be dangerous. However, they may also raise additional dangers of inadvertent escalation, since neither side will understand how the other side will interpret its signals, and both sides will be overly optimistic. Signaling that appears clear to the sender may be less comprehensible to the receiver and the intended message may get lost in the background noise of international diplomacy. Thus, doctrinal-difference theory counsels caution for policymakers.

The arguments of doctrinal-difference theory also have specific implications for Washington as it faces China in the rest of the twenty-first century. It will be critical to consider how its signals appear to Beijing. When evaluating Chinese military moves for any messages they might contain, intelligence analysts will need to consider the perspective of Chinese doctrinal guidance. When Washington or the U.S. Pacific Command wants to send a message

---

[59] "Do I lose sleep over the fact that the PLAN may in five, 10, 15, 20 years be able to project power? I'm not worried about it." Admiral Timothy J. Keating, "Asia-Pacific Trends: A U.S. Pacom Perspective," *Issues and Insights* 7, no. 14 (2007): 16–17.

to Beijing, it will have to tailor its message to the doctrinal predilections of the PLA. Thus, rather than deploying a carrier as a signal, the United States might do better to deploy a half-dozen nuclear-attack submarines. Rather than surging bombers, an emphasis on tactical fighter aircraft is likely to be more persuasive. This book thus provides justification for U.S. development of conventional variants of the Trident ballistic missile that could be launched against China (although this weapons system is not without its own issues for crisis stability and for distinguishability from nuclear attack).[60] On the other hand, if the United States chooses to make nuclear threats—having weighed the costs—it ought to emphasize countervalue targeting first and foremost.

To take these steps, the United States does not have to forgo other military preparations that enhance its readiness and military posture. However, it does need to recognize that for such mobilizations to have communicative benefits in signaling American intentions toward the Chinese, they must be in a military language that Beijing understands.

Strategic coercion is a high-stakes foreign policy under the best of circumstances. When nations see the world through different military lenses, the risk of misperception and miscommunication in the conduct of their diplomacy and statecraft is even higher. Mitigating these dangers in the Taiwan Strait and beyond would help advance the cause of peace and stability.

---

[60] Despite the zeroing of the budget for the Trident missile program by Congress, support for it remains alive and well within the Navy.

# INDEX

Note: Italic page numbers refer to figures and tables.

Acheson, Dean, 104, 112, 127, 151, 188
Almond, Edward, 78, 119
amphibious operations: and China, 173,
    174–79, 181–85, 193, 195, 196; and U.S.,
    173–74, 177, 179, 181, 182, 184–85, 196
Arab-Israeli conflicts of 1956 to 1970s: and bal-
    ance of power assessments, 216, 218, 222,
    230; and doctrinal similarities, 9, 206–7,
    230, 232; and Egyptian air force, 201; and
    false optimism, 201, 214, 215–16, 218,
    225; militarized incidents of, 203, *204;* and
    peace talks, 218–19; and Sinai Peninsula,
    200, 202, 206, 209, 210, 214–15; summary
    of, *233;* and surprise, 200, 202, 216, 218,
    222–30, 223n110; and War of Attrition, 200,
    202, 204, 208, 212–13
Arab-Israeli War of 1967, 9, 14, 15, 199, 201,
    203, 205–8, 230
Arab-Israeli War of 1973: balance of power
    assessment in, 3, 9, 216, 218, 222, 223,
    230; deterrence failure in, 232–33; and
    doctrinal-difference theory, 9, 14–15, 199,
    200, 211–12, 232; and Egypt's changes in
    doctrine, 208–12, 214, 217, 223–24, 227,
    229, 230; and ground forces, 223–26; and
    Israel's flawed counterattacks, 227–29; and
    Israel's reliance on tanks, 207–8, 209; sum-
    mary of, *233*

Arquilla, John, 20, 28, 28n46, 29n47, 38
Assessing Intent Prediction, 41, *44,* 132, 192,
    219, 220
asymmetries: and bargaining failure, 4, 6,
    234–35; China's use of, 240–41, 242, 243,
    250; and strategic coercion, 19
atomic weapons: and China's policy changes,
    165–66, 240, 242–44, 244n36, 245, 246–47,
    247n48, 249, 250; and China's theory of
    victory on land, 64–66, 64n709, 65n74,
    66n82, 76, 82–83, 141, 144, 146–49;
    Mao Zedong on, 64, 65–66, 82, 135, 146,
    147–48, 149, 166; U.S. arsenal of, 54–55,
    54n16, 54–55n17, 56n25; and U.S. theory
    of victory on land, 53–56, 56n27, 60, 76,
    82–83, 130, 145, 148, 148n49, 166, 240,
    243–44, 244n36, 248, 249, 250

balance of power assessments: accuracy of,
    6–7, 10; and Arab-Israeli conflicts, 216, 218,
    222, 230; and China crossing Yalu River,
    161; and China postponing invasion of
    Taiwan, 169, 195–96, 232; and doctrinal
    differences, 3, 4, 5, 6, 10, 11, 235, 238,
    244–46, 249, 250–51; and predictions of
    doctrinal-difference theory, 40–41, *43;* and
    U.S. crossing 38th parallel, 113, 132
bargaining failure, 4, 6, 234–35

false optimism: and Arab-Israeli conflicts, 201, 214, 215–16, 218, 225; and balance of power assessments, 4; and China crossing Yalu River, 144, 156, 167, 193; and China's deterrence of U.S. in Taiwan Straits, 245–46; dangers of, 235, 251; definition of, 4n2; and misperception, 7; source of, 39; and underestimation of adversary, 12–13, 35; and U.s. crossing 38th parallel, 121

First Campaign of PLA, 87, 103n74, *117,* 120, 120n130, 121n139, 134, 159

Gonen, Shmuel, 225, 226, 229
Gromyko, Andrei, 65–66
Guam, 141, 245, 247, 248n53
Guderian, Heinz, 36–37
Gulf War of 1991, 21, 237, 240

Hainan Island region, 175, 179, *180,* 181–82
Hussein, Saddam, 237, 237n12

India, 97–99, 98n47, 233
information asymmetries, 4, 6, 234–35
innovation, 23, 26–27, 28, 32n60
intentions, 41, 42, *43–44,* 149–53, 220. *See also* Surprise Regarding Intentions Prediction
Iraq, 236, 237, 240, 240n17, 245
Ismail, Ahmad, 210, 219
Israel: adversaries of, 199; "concept" of Egypt's military doctrine, 216–18, 220, 221, 222; and doctrinal differences, 7, 9, 15; founding of, 200. *See also* Arab-Israeli conflicts of 1956 to 1970s; Arab-Israeli War of 1967; Arab-Israeli War of 1973
Israel's theory of victory on land: and airpower, 208, 209, 210, 211, 226–27; and blitzkrieg strategy, 199, 201–3, 207–8, 209, 210, 223–25, 227–28; and combined-arms practices, 229; and first-strike attacks, 206, 208; and peace talks, 218–19

Japan, 60, 62, 68, 80, 150n59, 246, 247, 247n46
Jervis, Robert, 11, 12, 14n27, 35, 37–38, 39, 39n94
Jinmen Island, 177–78, 179, 182
Joffe, Ellis, 61, 162
Jordan, 203, 220

Kennan, George, 138, 138n15
Khrushchev, Nikita, 65, 84–85, 150

Kim Il Sung, 89, 167, 238
Kissinger, Henry, 213, 214, 215, 219
Korean War: as cause of Cold War, 14n27, 15–16; and China's theory of victory on land, 62, 66, 70–71, 83; and Chinese goals in Taiwan, 172; deterrence failures in, 232; and doctrinal differences, 15; effects of military signals on, 3, 5, 48; escalation of, 13–14; Soviet role in, 89, 90, 91, 97, 108–9, 133, 136; and U.S. defense budget, 139, 139n18; and U.S. grand strategy, 138–39; U.S. theory of victory on land, 54, 56–57, 59–60. *See also* China crossing Yalu River; U.S. crossing 38th parallel
Kuomintang (KMT): and civil war, 62, 63, 72, 74, 75, 81; and Hainan, 179, 181–82; and PLAN, 175, 175n19, 176–77, 184; and Taiwan, 169–70, 183

Lajiwei Island, 184
Lewis, John Wilson, 64, 164
Lin Biao, 102, 136, 154–55, 154n76, 154n78
Liu Shaoqi, 61, 150n60, 164, 182

MacArthur, Douglas: and amphibious warfare, 184, 185; and armor component, 58n36; and atomic weapons, 56; and China crossing Yalu River, 134, 136; interpretation of China's doctrine, 107; interpretation of Chinese signaling, 96–97, 97n41, 100, 103, 103n73, 104, 105; strategic appraisal of Korea, 142; in Taipei, 186, 186n77; and Taiwan Straits, 172n9, 188, 189; and U.S. crossing 38th parallel, 8, 89, 90–91, 119–23, 121n139, 125–29, 130; and World War II, 174
Manchuria, 99–105, 104n77, 126
Mao Zedong: on air force, 81–82, 165, 184n72; on atomic weapons, 64, 65–66, 82, 135, 146, 147–48, 149, 166; and China crossing Yalu River, 51, 136, 137, 150, 153, 156, 184n72; on Chinese military superiority, 144, 145; and dissent in China, 154; ideology of, 60–64, 61n49, 164, 176; and intervention timing, 110; and Kim Il Sung's attack on 38th parallel, 89, 238; lack of critiques on, 84; and limited war, 109; military signals of, 95–96, 104n77; optimism of, 135; on People's War concept, 67–71, 75, 161, 164; and Taiwan, 169–70, 183, 193; and U.S. crossing 38th parallel, 94, 95; on U.S. doctrine, 79, 81, 84, 107;